MORE PRAISE FOR *Undue*

"Author Jonathan D. Moreno presents convincing evid
biological, and chemical experiments have long been ]
subjects, and that the experimentation continues to th......... ιnιs is an
extraordinary and important chronicle."                    −Fatbrain.com

"Moreno served on a Clinton-appointed advisory committee that blew the lid
off the government's secret radiation experiments from WWII through the
mid-1970s. . . . A chilling, meticulously documented casebook."
                                                         −*Publishers Weekly*

"*Undue Risk* is a powerful and humane call for moral vigilance as we face
complex issues of medical research in the present and the future."
                                                         −Allan M. Brandt,
                                              Kass Professor of the History
                                          of Medicine, Harvard University

"*Undue Risk* should be mandatory reading for all those concerned with not
only the protection of human subjects but the appropriate moral
underpinnings of government action in a liberal democracy."
                                    −Harold T. Shapiro, President, Princeton University,
                                      Chairman, National Bioethics Advisory Commission

"Important documentation of what the 'good guys' have done and are doing."
                                                         −Booklist

In *Undue Risk,* Jonathan Moreno presents the first comprehensive history of the use of human subjects in atomic, biological and chemical
warfare experiments from World War II to the twenty-first century.
From the courtrooms of Nuremberg to the battlefields of the Gulf War,
*Undue Risk* explores a variety of government policies and specific cases.
It is also the first book to go behind the scenes and reveal the government's struggle with the ethics of human experimentation and the evolution of agonizing policy choices on unfamiliar moral terrain. A new
afterword by the author covers recent objections by U.S. military personnel to required anthrax vaccinations and new developments in government policies on experiments involving vulnerable human subjects.

**Jonathan D. Moreno,** a former senior staff member of President Clinton's
Advisory Committee on Human Radiation Experiments, is Kornfeld Professor
of Biomedical Ethics and Director of the Center for Biomedical Ethics at the
University of Virginia. He has been a columnist for ABCNews.com, and is a
frequent television and radio commentator on current bioethical issues.
Moreno is the author of *Deciding Together: Bioethics and Moral Consensus.* He
lives in Charlottesville, Virginia and Washington, D.C.

# UNDUE
# RISK

## Secret State

## Experiments

## on Humans

## JONATHAN D. MORENO

Routledge
New York and London

Routledge edition published in 2001
Routledge
29 West 35th Street
New York, NY 10001
www.routledge-ny.com

This edition published by arrangement with W. H. Freeman and Company.

*Routledge is an imprint of the Taylor & Francis Group.*

Text Design: Victoria Tomaselli

Library of Congress Cataloging-in-Publication Data

Moreno, Jonathan D.
    Undue risk: secret state experiments on humans / Jonathan D. Moreno.
        p.     cm.
    Previously published by W.H. Freeman in 1999
    Includes bibliographical references and index.
    ISBN 0-415-92835-4
    1. Human experimentation in medicine—United States.   2. Weapons of mass destruction—United States—Testing.   3. Informed consent (Medical Law)—United States.   I. Title.

R853.H8M66  2000
174'.28–dc21                                                          00-059140

10 9 8 7 6 5 4 3 2 1

## For Jillian Alea Moreno

The innermost nature of the Reality is congenial to the powers that you possess. . . .

*William James*

# CONTENTS

# PREFACE

One day in March 1994 I was leaving a meeting with my medical school's provost when his secretary handed me a pink telephone message slip. The message read, "Has a proposition for you." The call was from my friend and colleague Ruth Faden, a professor at Johns Hopkins University in Baltimore. Ruth had recently been named by President Clinton to chair a special commission that was to investigate allegations of government-sponsored radiation research on unknowing citizens during the cold war. Triggering the investigation was a series of newspaper articles by Eileen Welsome in *The Albuquerque Tribune*. Welsome had put names and faces to long-standing rumors that American citizens had been injected with plutonium during World War II.

I was intrigued by the group's mission, which included not only figuring out whether anything wrong was done to American citizens by military-medical research but also exactly what happened. A *New York Times* piece on the newly appointed presidential Advisory Committee on Human Radiation Experiments reported that an important part of its job would be to plough through old archives to reconstruct events and policies, including many still-classified documents. A history buff, I was more than a little jealous of the opportunity to work through primary records of secret experiments from the 1940s to the 1970s.

Several days later I walked into rented offices in downtown Washington, already bustling with activity and strewn with office supplies, government-issue furniture, and the core of a hastily assembled staff, of which I was to be a senior member. Eventually the group included philosophers, lawyers, radiologists, historians, archivists, epidemiologists, and physicists. The committee itself was composed of experts in all those fields and a private citizen. Under Ruth Faden's leadership the committee members and their staff worked together closely. It was surely one of the more eclectic groups that have been called into government service.

The task ahead seemed daunting. Many stories had floated around the country about a dizzying array of government-sponsored radiation experiments, with all sorts of nefarious purposes theorized. People who felt aggrieved represented as wide a range as the American public itself: veterans of the armed forces, former convicts, mothers, people who had been treated or institutionalized for emotional disorders, Native Americans, Alaska natives, people who had been hospitalized, cancer patients who had been subjected to radiation treatment, people who lived "downwind" of atomic tests, people who lived near nuclear plants.

The diversity of people who felt they had been harmed or their civil rights violated by government-sponsored radiation experiments gave numerous regional newspapers specific reasons to follow the story closely, depending on the local controversy. In Cincinnati, for example, family members of deceased cancer patients brought suit against a distinguished radiologist for alleged experiments on their loved ones. In Nevada and Washington State residents worried about their increased cancer risk because of above-ground detonations or field experiments with fission material. In Tennessee women charged that they and their fetuses had been guinea pigs in radiation experiments.

With so many aggrieved parties there were plenty of journalists around, and under the law governing federal advisory committees virtually all the committee's business was considered public. Once when a small group of committee members and staff sat down to a working lunch, a reporter seated herself at the end of the table, notebook at the ready. For scholars unused to working in the glare of so much publicity, the process was disconcerting, to say the very least.

Worse, there was precious little hard information about the events themselves. President Clinton ordered the creation of the advisory committee at the urging of Hazel O'Leary, then Secretary of Energy, whose agency had inherited much of the portfolio of the Atomic Energy Commission (AEC). Previous presidential administrations under Ronald Reagan and George Bush had resisted opening investigations of the radiation experiments, in spite of a 1986 report on "America's Nuclear Guinea Pigs" by the staff of

Massachusetts Congressman Ed Markey. Apparently unaware of the Markey report, O'Leary learned of the allegations about radiation experiments in 1993 from Eileen Welsome's Pulitzer Prize-winning newspaper series and saw that clearing the air fit into the president's agenda for openness in government.

Unfortunately, in the beginning the Department of Energy knew little more about what the AEC had done nearly forty years ago than anyone else. Other federal agencies that probably had something to do with the experiments, such as the Department of Defense, had lost their institutional memory of sensitive matters from decades before. Surely there were documents, somewhere, that might tell the story. But, as an archivist patiently explained to me at an early meeting when I asked one of many naive questions about government records, "You have to understand. There is no box somewhere in the Pentagon basement labeled 'Human Radiation Experiments.'"

So this presidential advisory committee was to be unique. It was charged not only with resolving questions of medical ethics but also with determining who was harmed and recommending just compensation. Before those tasks could even be addressed, a heretofore-secret history had to be reconstructed. To help the committee do its work, the president ordered a massive declassification process that involved scores of government workers in half a dozen agencies. For the first six or seven months I mostly dug through archival boxes that were daily rolled into the committee offices, amounting to tens of thousands of separate items. Never did historians have such ready access to so much primary material that, only days before, had been considered as possibly sensitive information. Together, the committee members and staff were able to tell a remarkable story that led to a final report in October 1995, released at a White House ceremony. One reviewer likened the thousand-page document to *Ulysses* in its scope as well as its size.

One of the obstacles we faced in piecing together the radiation experiments story from 1944 to the 1970s was the need to declassify the relevant information as quickly as possible, within the short eighteen-month life of the committee. Several staff members were asked to apply for "top secret" security clearances so that we could examine documents in secured archives and determine which ones should be put on a "fast track" toward declassification. Owing to the nature of my assignment, to reconstruct the evolution of U.S. policy on human experiments for national security purposes, I went through an exhaustive background check. My neighbors were both amused and discomfited by the "suits" who crawled around our street for a day.

But poring over classified material is less glamorous than it might sound. Well over 99 percent of what I read was irrelevant and quite uninteresting. If decades-old documents are still classified, it is usually because there is no impetus to go to the trouble of looking at them after all these years; even at the time many memoranda and reports were marked "classified," "secret," or "top secret" for wholly arbitrary reasons, such as containing words like *atomic* or *nuclear*. A later presidential commission, compiling records on the Kennedy assassination, found that much classified information consisted of duplicate documents, and much of the rest comprised innocuous items such as old newspaper and magazine clippings. The romance of working through boxes full of "secret" documents like this can wear thin.

The potential for embarrassment and even scandal that concerned an earlier generation of government officials was not lost on members of the armed forces who were ordered to help the advisory committee find old materials so it could tell the radiation experiments story. They were conflicted. On one hand, no one was more eager to get the truth out than the uniformed officers who were our contacts in the Pentagon. They were as outraged as anyone else at the thought that soldiers, sailors, or airmen might have been abused in government experiments—perhaps more, given their sense of comradeship with previous generations of armed forces personnel. At the same time, they were concerned that the image of the armed forces, largely recovered from the tarnish of the Vietnam era, might again be damaged by simplified accounts that could appear in the press. During a coffee break at a Defense Department briefing, one naval officer confronted me about a story that day in *The Washington Post* in which I had been quoted.

The article described some documents the committee had released that suggested that the military might have experimented with its own people in the early 1950s. "The fathers and mothers of America trust us with their sons and daughters," he said with emotion, "and stories like that undermine their trust."

Still, the overriding concern of the government officials with whom I worked, both uniformed and civilian, was to get the truth out. After another Pentagon briefing I chatted with a senior Army physician, a conversation that helped put me on the road to writing this book. At one point he leaned back in his chair, put his hands in his pockets and said, "If you ask me, you won't stop here." What do you mean?, I asked. "I think you go on to biological and chemical (weapons). That's where the real action is."

Only as the months went by did I grasp his point. The use of radioisotopes was relatively well scrutinized from the inception of the AEC in the late 1940s, but the handling of biological and chemical agents was not. It appears that controls on these agents were not nearly as tightly drawn during the cold war. They lacked the drama of association with a history-changing event like Hiroshima, so they were mostly off the radar screen of the public imagination. Also, while psychoactive drugs could be manufactured in a garage (one of my high school friends did exactly that), usable radioactive material required a considerably more complicated production process.

I also came to understand, as the Army physician implied, that the recent history and ethics of human experiments with radiation sources could not be separated from bacterial and chemical warfare research. By the early 1950s Pentagon advisors were treating all three as part of their tactical concerns, and the ethical problems of testing "ABC" (atomic, biological, and chemical) weapons were of a piece. Unfortunately, though logic might have dictated that we continue our work, politics did not. The chemical warfare scandal had its day in the sun years before in the mid-1970s, due to revelations of the Central Intelligence Agency's MKULTRA project, and the Iraqi biological warfare threat seemed to fizzle until the weapons inspection crisis in the later 1990s. In the absence of a sudden onrush of publicity, as was the case with rumors about the radiation experiments, there was not enough political momentum at the grass-roots level to continue the inquiry and expand the radiation advisory committee's mandate.

Had the investigation been extended to the history and ethics of biological and chemical experiments, there would have been a great deal of experience on which to draw. Studies of chemical and biological agents in the military context had a much lengthier history than radiation research. The studies did not always involve weapons but often had to do with promoting the performance of soldiers in battle. In 1883 Bavarian soldiers on maneuvers were given cocaine without their knowledge, to see if the drug would help them overcome fatigue. Another psychoactive agent, lysergic acid diethylamide (LSD), was tested on American soldiers seventy years later. At the turn of the century British soldiers fighting in the South African Boer War were offered typhoid vaccine, but very few volunteered to take it, though thousands of soldiers died of the disease. In the 1991 Gulf War, American soldiers were offered an agent that could protect against nerve gas, though few soldiers accepted the offer.

As to biological warfare, its history is ancient. "Experiments" with the possibility that organisms, microorganisms, or derived toxins could be used to military ends began long before these mechanisms were understood. The Persians, Greeks, and Romans used animal cadavers to pollute enemy drinking water, a technique that was copied several times in the medieval period and during the American Civil War. In 400 B.C. Scythian archers "weaponized" biological agents by dipping their arrows into decomposing cadavers or blood mixed with manure. In the fourteenth century the French launched dead horses into an enemy castle prior to storming the gates. A few years later a Mongol chief catapulted bodies of those who had died from bubonic plague into a Crimean city defended by Genoan forces, perhaps contributing to the subsequent European pandemic. Eighteenth-century Russians also cast plague cadavers over walls in Estonia, hoping to infect Swedish defenders. In the twentieth century, the "germ theory" developed in university laboratories gave impetus to controlled studies of biological agents as weapons of war, as well as to their defense.

Atomic, biological, and chemical warfare are often lumped together under the heading "weapons of mass destruction," but placing all three in this category is misleading. Chemical weapons have much more limited disruptive potential than the other two. When "weaponized" in hydrogen bombs, nuclear radiation has enormous initial destructive capacity and a lengthy half-life. Biological agents lodge themselves in mobile hosts and some are able to reproduce. On the other hand, the unpredictable nature of atomic and biological weapons gives them limited utility for aggressors, who may themselves become victims by virtue of a "return" effect.

In spite of my disappointment in not being able to continue the work, when the Advisory Committee on Human Radiation Experiments closed its doors late in 1995 it had clearly accomplished more than was specified by the president's mandate. The committee's findings made it possible to perceive a singular ethical drama, often played out in secret meetings from the end of World War II to the present day, as government officials struggled over the quandary of human experiments with new and terrible weapons. This drama went far beyond concerns about medical ethics to the core paradox of a modern democracy: the need for it to defend itself in a world Thomas Jefferson and James Madison could not have imagined, sometimes using undemocratic means to do so.

In this book I tell the story of the human experiment debates through both specific cases and government policies. My account has been shaped over a five-year period by conversations with dozens of people, including government officials, scholars, and medical researchers. My sources have included primary materials, previous government investigations, newspaper clippings, interviews with experts on various elements of the topic, and earlier studies of various aspects of biological and chemical warfare research.

I am persuaded (though others may not be) that the main outlines of the human radiation experiments are now publicly available following the work of the radiation advisory committee. I am not as sanguine about the history of biological and chemical weapons development, though even in that area much more is known in the late 1990s than was true even ten years ago. One realization has impressed itself upon me time and again since I began this work: Government secrecy is corrosive to democracy, constitutes a true threat to our way of life, and—although it cannot be eliminated in our dangerous modern world—it must be minimized.

Over the past twenty-five years scandals about national security-related experiments have periodically surfaced and then receded from public consciousness. Because different elements of the story have been treated separately, it has been hard to tell that the separate incidents are really part of a larger narrative. More important, there has been genuine progress in both the theory and practice of the ethical conduct of human experiments in the national security context. However, this progress is not obvious unless it is set against the evolution of government policies, along with the sometimes shocking abuses that finally gave birth— though often in painful and halting steps—to the protections in place today. At the end of this road lies a program of human experimentation that is a moral model for all others, civilian and military. In Chapter 9 I will describe this paradigm of ethical human testing, sure to amaze some, located at the very heart of America's biological defense program.

Today, as in decades past, there is a basic and striking moral difference between those who willingly and knowledgeably accept the risks of potentially dangerous substances and those who are manipulated or coerced. The former are often heroes, the latter truly "human guinea pigs" undergoing undue risks. No decent society can tolerate the exploitation of its vulnerable members. When this exploitation is conducted in the name of national defense there is something rotten at the core of that society's political culture.

In the twenty-first century, medical research will continue to play an important role in national security, developing the means to protect civilians as well as combatants from enemy weapons. As I noted, theorizing about effective defenses and studying animal and computer models can only go so far. As long as the nation's security is threatened by novel weapons of war, there will be scientific questions that can only be answered if human beings are subjects of medical experiments. And there will be moral questions about how some individuals can be allowed to accept the risks associated with that kind of research. If this book succeeds, it will have helped the citizens of history's most powerful republic, and its most medically sophisticated society, to face that uncomfortable and complex reality.

# ACKNOWLEDGMENTS

A developing manuscript has a way of becoming a familiar companion. Like the end of a relationship, the loss can be a shock. Fortunately, the process tends to spawn human companions, as well, lending truth to the maxim that all books are social products. Considering the range and complexity of this topic, I have been fortunate indeed to have many wonderful companions, people who have helped me develop my ideas and gather and interpret information in several fields.

Prominent among these collaborators were my colleagues on the staff of the President's Advisory Committee on Human Radiation Experiments, in particular its chair, Ruth Faden, and its executive director, Dan Guttman. Ruth gave me the professional opportunity of a lifetime, and Dan taught me how to "get into the boxes." Former fellow Committee staffers Jon Harkness, Trad Hughes, Valerie Hurt, and Gil Whittemore helped me locate sources and materials. During my work for the Committee and in the years since I profited from the insights of many Committee members and staff, including Alan Buchanan, Jim David, Patrick Fitzgerald, Eli Glatstein, Gregg Herken, Jeff Kahn, Jay Katz, Pat King, Ruth Macklin, Anna Mastroianni, Ron Neumann, Henry Royal, and Jeremy Sugarman.

Over the years I have also enjoyed the assistance of a number of very capable researchers who were undergraduates at the time, particularly Carlton Haywood, David Pantalone, Preya Bala Sharma, and Sasha Yamschikov, as well as law student Rob Tanner. Art Anderson, Wally Cummins, Ben Garrett, and Joan Porter were among those who permitted me to conduct interviews and provided me with many valuable insights and leads. I am grateful to all of them.

I benefited from conversations with colleagues at the University of Pennsylvania's Center for Bioethics while a faculty associate there from 1995 to 1997. I also profited from discussions with members of the Department of Clinical Bioethics at the Clinical Center of the National Institutes of Health as a visitor in the spring of 1998. Special thanks to Evan DeRenzo who read and critiqued the manuscript.

Archivists at the United States Holocaust Memorial Museum and at the University of Pennsylvania were most cordial and cooperative, and I thank them and their institutions for enabling me to conduct my research using their materials.

While writing this book I was fortunate to be offered a chair in the medical school at the University of Virginia, where I now direct the Center for Biomedical Ethics. The expertise of my colleague Paul Lombardo has aided my thinking, as has that of others at this wonderful institution I am now privileged to call my home.

Betsy Amster and Angela Miller helped me refine my proposal for the book, and the enthusiasm of Jonathan Cobb brought it to W. H. Freeman and Company. I am grateful to Erika Goldman and John Michel for picking up the project with such alacrity and interest.

Throughout this book I rely upon the path-breaking work of numerous writers, especially historians and journalists, who have illuminated aspects of this story over many years. I can only hope that I have done justice to their labors.

Justice, and gratitude as well, are owed to those who were both knowing and unknowing subjects of the experiments described, and also to those medical scientists, military leaders, and public officials who have elevated our medical and moral practices.

Finally, endless thanks to my family, the center of my life.

# THE LONG ROAD TO SALMAN PAK

There is incomprehension of why Iraq is persisting so strongly with both refusing to make the facts known about its biological weapons program and why it is so insistent on blocking the Commission's own effort to reach those facts.

*United Nations report, October 6, 1997*

## MURDER AND MEDICINE

About 30 miles south of Baghdad, nestled in a bend of the Tigris River, sits the military town Salman Pak, long considered the heart of Iraq's biological warfare establishment. In August 1991 a team of United Nations (U.N.) experts arrived in Salman Pak to inspect the remains of the facilities, which had been bombed during the Gulf War. They found little but scorched earth. Just two weeks before, the Iraqis had razed what was left of the laboratory structures and burned any documents that survived the Allied bombardment.

One tantalizing item remained, however, that gave a clue about some of the activity at Salman Pak: a chamber that could be used to expose subjects to bacteria, of the right size to hold "large primates, including the human primate," as one of the U.N. inspectors delicately explained.

Over the next several years Iraqi officials continued to defy the conditions of the peace agreement by placing countless obstacles in the way of inspectors charged with assessing Iraq's past and current biological and chemical warfare capacity. Gradually, though, the U.N. officials' dogged labors paid off, and by late 1997 they had accumulated indisputable evidence of field trials of biological weapons, including some involving human beings.

Human experiments were one aspect of their war preparation about which the Iraqis were particularly sensitive. Not only would they show that the Iraqis had illegally continued their weapons programs, they would undermine Iraq's moral high ground among the countries that sympathized with the country's suffering under U.N. sanctions. In early 1998 the inspectors surprised the Iraqis by pursuing the human experiments issue. Few now recall that it was this issue that provoked the first Iraqi shutdown of United Nations Special Commission (UNSCOM) operations. "The speculation," said a former U.N. inspector at the time, "is that it probably has to do with unsavory activities—unethical experimentation."

The UNSCOM team was led by American Scott Ritter, whose service in the Marines years before fueled Iraqi suspicions of spying.

Saddam Hussein's subsequent challenges to the U.N. operation precipitated a series of international crises during which UNSCOM's activities were partly suspended, each giving the Iraqis time to clean up surviving evidence. Ritter, who later resigned from UNSCOM in protest of U.S. weakness toward Iraq, himself recalled the circumstances in a December 1998 article in *The New Republic*:

> In January of this year, we embarked on an effort to expose Iraq's use of biological and chemical agents on live human test subjects.... We had received evidence that 95 political prisoners had been transferred from the Abu Gharib Prison to a site in western Iraq, where they had been subjected to lethal testing under the supervision of a special unit from the Military Industrial Commission, under Saddam's personal authority. But, just as we began moving in on facilities housing documents that would support our contention (for instance, transfer records of prisoners), Iraq woke up to the danger and ceased all cooperation with us.

Prior to the U.N. team's aborted efforts to obtain the prison records, the facts that they learned about Iraqi field tests were grisly. Prisoners were tied to stakes, bombarded with deadly bacteria and gases from bombs a few feet away or dropped from an aircraft, and died in agony. At other times they were locked in chambers while anthrax was sprayed from jets mounted in the ceiling. Death came from internal hemorrhaging. In one experiment Iranian war prisoners were the "test subjects"; in another, Iraqi criminals and Kurds were used. The Kurdish leader Massoud Barzani claims to have evidence that 2,000 Kurdish men who were abducted in 1982 were used to test Iraq's first generation of chemical weapons.

The continuing Iraqi weapons inspections crisis is part of a new chapter in national security policy following the cold war. American defense planners have realized that, in the hands of rogue states or terrorists, weapons that they had largely ignored for decades pose a substantial threat to the United States in the postcold war era. Bacteria like the ones that cause anthrax and botulism, and chemicals like nerve gas, are hard to control and deliver effectively but relatively inexpensive to produce and transport. And they could wreak havoc among civilians, especially in heavily populated areas. Government officials are now trying to make up for years of neglect and develop defenses against the danger of biological and chemical weapons. U.S. intelligence officials have estimated that seventeen countries were probably doing research on germ weapons in 1998, as compared to only three in 1979.

What the general public usually doesn't realize, however, is that human testing in connection with these agents, both to identify protections against biological and chemical weapons and to develop the weapons themselves, has a long and international history. In this the Iraqis are not unique. Nor are the Iraqis unique in proceeding with the use of human beings as "guinea pigs" (a term that true research volunteers hate), while at the same time worrying about public opinion at home and abroad if the facts were to become widely known.

With feelings around this issue always at a fever-pitch, tales of illicit human experiments are rampant and incendiary. Throughout the preparation of this book, and especially when I was working on long-rumored historic incidents and on more recent events in troubled parts of the world, I encountered various claims and counter-claims. They must be treated with caution. Unlike radiation research, the history of biological and chemical warfare experiments, including clinical tests and field trials, has never been subjected to nearly as careful or comprehensive an analysis. Nonetheless, enough evidence is now available to render in some detail the policy debates about human experiments in America since World War II.

In spite of the unhappy history I will describe in this book, the United States has never descended into the depravity of some countries. Nevertheless, although American military-medical experiments have generally been conducted for defensive purposes, especially since World War II, the line between offensive and defensive military experiments—and the knowledge needed to conduct them—is not always easy to draw. As a result, for more than fifty years American officials have struggled with the knowledge that their practices could easily be lumped into some very bad company. Undeniably, in some cases these practices were so reckless that the association was deserved.

As I will show, the potential for national disgrace in human testing of "unconventional weapons" or "weapons of mass destruction" has been a constant source of tension in American defense planning since the end of World War II. Though human experiments for military purposes were conducted during the war, and though they were sometimes done in secret, they were not generally regarded as a potential source of embarrassment. It was, after all, a time of national crisis when all were expected to do their part. It was also before the world learned how far Hitler's doctors had gone in service of the Nazi war effort. As the first several chapters explain, the revelations of the Nazi doctors' crimes put American defense planners in a tough position as they prepared for a possible World War III.

Today and ever since the end of the World War II, the universal sensitivity about human experiments is coupled with the fact that they are probably unavoidable in the real world of national security. Textbook theories, laboratory experiments, and computer and animal models can only go so far. At some point, when information is needed about how human beings will react to new forms of weaponry, human experiments will have to be done. Odds are that the United States will have to continue in this business. In a dangerous world one might well argue that it would be irresponsible for us not to do so. The painful problem before contemporary Americans, as for previous generations, is how this work can be done without contradicting the values of democracy and human rights that we profess to uphold.

## APARTHEID'S SECRET WEAPONS

Iraq was not the only nation-state engaged in the development of chemical and biological weapons during the 1980s. A report commissioned by the South African Truth and Reconciliation Commission (TRC), chaired by Nobel Peace Prize winner Bishop Desmond Tutu, uncovered the former Apartheid regime's secret medical research program during its investigations that concluded in 1998. As usual, human experiments were an important part of the development effort.

The TRC was formed to uncover the unscrupulous means used by both apartheid and anti-apartheid forces prior to the creation of the current government. At the TRC's request, an investigation of South Africa's former biological and chemical weapons was filed by the Netherlands Institute for Southern Africa (NIZA), funded by the Dutch government. Among the incidents reviewed in the report was one that occurred on January 16, 1982, when 300 to 400 Mozambican troops were attacking Renamo rebels in their stronghold in southern Mozambique near the South African border. The rebels were supported by the white South African government. According to the NIZA report:

> As they approached the camp on foot in box formation one company forming each side of the box a white jeeptype vehicle was seen in the vicinity of the camp. At about this time, also an unidentified light aircraft was seen flying above the area. The troops passed into the recently deserted Renamo base. They left the base again and a few kilometres away they came under limited small arms fire, not more than 15 shots. They took cover and then an explosion occurred overhead within the outline of the box between 150 and 250 feet above their heads, releasing a dense cloud of black smoke which then dissipated. The wind was blowing towards the rear of the formation.
>
> After 15 minutes the first complaints occurred: "It became very hot. Some of us were going crazy," told Second Lieutenant Joaquim Jonassa. He said they felt severe chest pains, were tired and thirsty, and when they drank water the

next morning some of them vomited. Others said they had difficulty seeing. (Guardian 28/1/92) [an internal reference in this passage]. As a consequence a considerable disorganization of the troops occurred.

The troops' "disorganization" resulted in four deaths and two injuries during the uncontrolled shooting. Despite the remote chance that the incident was caused by dehydration from severe heat, the report concludes that "there remains a fair possibility that the above incident was, however, an example of the testing of chemical weapons in a combat situation against foreign soldiers as part of South Africa's chemical and biological weapons programme." In its final report the TRC stated that it found the dehydration theory "unlikely."

A mere field test with nerve gas does not give the full measure of the innovative quality of the South African weapons program. In some ways it provides a preview of future biological weapons, including an attempt to target a specific racial group with a biological agent in order to cause mass sterility. The program, sponsored by the former Apartheid government, was among the targets of the commission. Besides various chemical and biological weapons developed in the program to harass or kill individuals opposed to apartheid, the commission has also investigated "claims of research on infertility drugs that targeted the Black population." The Dutch researchers for the commission concluded that "further study of these chemical and biological weapons related facts will show that human rights' violations were committed under this programme."

For military reasons the white South Africans and the Iraqis would have wanted to keep their biological and chemical weapons programs secret. But for political reasons, they had even more reason to keep secret the human experiments aspect of those programs, so as not to alienate their few allies. For while weapons programs might be defensible as part of national security, the bad odor associated with human testing is virtually universal. Echoes of the Nazi doctors can be heard in the TRC's final report: "The image of white-coated scientists, professors, doctors, dentists, veterinarians, laboratories, universities and front companies, propping up apartheid with the support of an extensive international network, was a particularly cynical and chilling one."

Days after Bishop Tutu's commission report was released, the *London Times* carried an Associated Press report from South African sources that the Israeli government was attempting to develop an "ethno-bomb," a biological weapon that could target Arabs. In light of the genetic similarity between Arabs and Jews, who are both semitic peoples and must therefore share nearly all their genes, this would be a considerable technical achievement. An unnamed Israeli scientist at Nes Tziyona, Israel's military biological institute, is quoted as saying that, despite the challenges, "they have, however, succeeded in pinpointing a particular characteristic in the genetic profile of certain Arab communities, particularly the Iraqi people."

Responding to the report, a member of the Israeli parliament recalled the Jews' experience with racial medicine in the concentration camp experiments. "Morally, based on our history, and our tradition and our experience, such a weapon is monstrous and should be denied." The Israeli prime minister's spokesman dismissed the allegations out of hand. In fact, the timing of the report was suspicious: It appeared in mid-November 1998, just as the United States was preparing air strikes against Iraq for violating the terms of its UNSCOM agreement.

Whatever the truth behind these stories, they highlight the fact that any innovative military program, whether for offensive or defensive purposes, must at some point involve human experiments. Governments have never been eager to acknowledge this fact, because it raises ethical questions that can jeopardize an entire national security research program. Even many people who do not find biological or chemical weapons inherently more objectionable than conventional weapons have a hard time defending the experiments needed to develop them or to defend against them. The topic of medical-military human experiments will always lie within the shadow of the Nuremberg trials of the Nazi doctors.

## DUCK AND COVER

Many Americans over the age of 40 have felt a strange sense of déjà vu in the recent scare about biological and chemical weapons. We can recall being marched to school basements for "duck and cover" civil defense drills, and many of us had cellars at home where canned goods were stored against the possibility of a long siege following a nuclear war. In fact, in the fear it can engender and its power to disrupt civilian populations, atomic warfare has much in common with biological and chemical threats. And the history of the production and defense of these "unconventional" weapons since 1945 binds atomic, biological, and chemical war preparations closely together. All were part of defense planners' strategizing in the late 1940s and 1950s, and all created a perceived need for human experiments. These experiments were usually the dark and embarrassing side of what was thought to be military necessity.

In the United States, while fears about biological and chemical weapons were being faced in 1997 and 1998, headlines also appeared about the aftereffects of atomic testing. Although the U.S. government was reassuring civilians in the 1950s that atomic bomb testing posed no health problems, in 1997 the National Cancer Institute concluded that 10,000 to 75,000 extra thyroid cancers had been caused by the increased radiation in the atmosphere. To make matters worse, at the same time that health concerns were being dismissed, federal officials were warning film manufacturers that atomic fallout could damage their products. In the words of Iowa Senator Tom Harkin, "It is really odd that the Government warned Kodak about its film but wouldn't warn the general public about the milk it was drinking."

The thyroid damage from nuclear weapons was not caused by a medical experiment, but by a military exercise. Yet radium was used from the 1940s though the 1960s in many doctors' offices for the treatment of ear infections, especially in the armed forces. Between 8,000 and 20,000 service members, as well as many of their dependents, received the treatment, which involved placing small rods in the nostrils to relieve inflammation. One 1982 Johns Hopkins University study suggested that the treatment, by then out of favor because of radiation risks, might lead to higher rates of head and neck cancer.

These stories pointed to the great interest in the uses of nuclear radiation for both military and medical purposes. Early in April 1999 the University of Cincinnati announced that it had settled a lawsuit for $5 million with families of ninety cancer patients. It had long been charged that from 1960 to 1971 Dr. Eugene Saenger had engaged in harmful total-body and partial-body irradiation experiments with terminally ill patients. Dr. Saenger is a distinguished radiologist whose work was partly supported by the Pentagon.

Also making headlines in the late 1990s was the fact that atomic energy was also used in activities that combined military purposes and medical projects. In 1997, on New Year's Eve, the Quaker Oats cereal company joined with the Massachusetts Institute of Technology (MIT) to settle a lawsuit brought by a group of unwitting test subjects from the 1950s. The victims were then young boys at the Fernald School in Waltham, Massachusetts, where they were fed cereal containing trace amounts of radiation to identify the pathway of nutrients in the human digestive system. Their parents had given permission for them to be in a special club at the state school for children who were supposed to be "mentally retarded," but no mention was made of the radiation. Although unharmed by the very low doses to which they were exposed, an MIT spokesman agreed in 1998 that their civil rights—the right to give informed consent to being in an experiment—had been violated. The $1.85 million settlement covered about thirty of the alumni of Fernald's "Science Club."

The studies at Fernald and another school called Wrentham point up another problem: the scope of the term *national security experiments*. If the term is taken narrowly, then only human experiments that provide direct and foreseeable information relevant to the national defense will be included. An example is the development of vaccines against a biological weapon. But I believe that the term must be taken in a broader sense, to include any study supported partly because it *might* yield results that can be applied to military purposes, however remote from the security context the study seems to be. Especially with regard to the early radiation studies, the latter interpretation more closely matches the facts, and that understanding of the scope of national security experiment will be used in this book.

The radioactive material for the Fernald project came from another sponsor, the Atomic Energy Commission (AEC). The AEC was a civilian agency responsible for the nation's nuclear resources. For reasons of national security and public health, how the human body absorbed and eliminated radiation were critical questions in the early 1950s, only a few years after the Soviets developed their own atomic bomb. Was this a justifiable experiment at the time? Or was it an unacceptable violation of the boys' civil rights? How far can a nation-state based on democratic principles of individual rights go to defend itself in the modern world of weapons of mass destruction? May it use medicine, the craft dedicated to healing, as a party to its self-defense? Is it appropriate for physicians to involve themselves in such work? Have the rules changed over the decades, and how are these matters handled today? These questions reveal the way moral intricacies are unavoidably woven into scientific and technical problems in the use of human beings in military medical research.

C
H
A
P
T
E
R

## TWO

# THE HOME FRONT: OUR SCIENCE, OUR BOYS

The problem was never that of finding volunteers; rather it was the difficult one of selecting among the large number who wanted to become subjects.

*Nathan Leopold, federal prisoner*

The government has lied to us for 50 years over and over again. If I would have been shot on the front lines at least I would (have) had it on my record and would have received medical treatment.

*John William Allen, U.S. Navy veteran*

One day in the spring of 1941, Vannevar Bush, a former MIT dean, who had become President Franklin Roosevelt's science advisor, strode into the Lincoln Room in the White House for breakfast with the president's aide and close friend Harry Hopkins. Bush had been assigned the job of coordinating the nation's scientific research for a war in Europe that most people in government now expected would soon involve America.

Roosevelt's science advisor was also a remarkably accomplished electrical engineer. He invented an analog computer and is today celebrated by computer scientists as perhaps the first person to anticipate the information age. Near the end of the war Bush published a seminal article in the *Atlantic Monthly* called "As We May Think," which described a machine he called the Memex, the first account of a device that linked files to one another through words and concepts in what is now called hypertext.

That day in 1941 Bush's "bird dogs," as he called his White House informants, had told him that Roosevelt was about to appoint an Executive Office panel to coordinate America's medical research needs in the event that the United States was drawn into the European war. Not wishing to offend the powerful and intensely self-protective medical profession, President Roosevelt planned to put the new Committee on Medical Research (CMR) into the hands of some influential members of the American Medical Association (AMA). "Like many of my friends," Bush later recalled, "I had a deep-seated distrust of that organization," and so he informed Hopkins that "the Great White Father was about to put his foot in it." The crusty Yankee told Hopkins that three of the men he was about to appoint were "under criminal indictment in the District of Columbia."

Though Bush's assertion was technically correct, the reality was not quite as felonious as it sounded. The AMA leaders were boycotting Washington, D.C., hospitals in an attempt to stop a new movement in favor of group practices, early versions of what we know today as health maintenance organizations. The senior doctors were charged with violating antitrust laws. Having done his homework on this case, Bush got control over the new enterprise that he seems to have wanted. Bush records that FDR became so "weary of hearing about medical research"—and, it seems, dealing with obstreperous "medical men"—that "he sent a message to the Bureau of the Budget, which drew up executive orders, saying that he wanted this medical show put under Bush, and that he did not want to hear a damned thing more about it."

As director of the Office of Scientific Research and Development (OSRD), Bush was already leading the country's efforts in the physical sciences, including the nascent atomic bomb project. With a June 28, 1941, presidential order, his portfolio was expanded to cover both the OSRD and a new CMR, under a newly created National Research Council (NRC) with Bush at the helm. Now he was also in complete charge of staffing and setting priorities for the most ambitious national medical research effort in the nation's history, one that, by war's end, had sponsored 638 scientific studies in contracts with 135 institutions, and spent the then-astronomical sum of $25 million. Among the projects the CMR sponsored were dozens involving human subjects, including the development of the miracle drug penicillin and a prison malaria experiment that would prove to be a key issue in the war crimes trial of Nazi doctors in Nuremberg after the war.

Many civilian and military officials earnestly struggled with the issue of whom to use in human experiments, but they also generally accepted that some human use was necessary for the war effort. Authorities had very little time to sort out these issues and precious little guidance from existing codes or conventions. They were also operating in a national and international emergency. As the social historian David Rothman has noted, "because it was wartime, the [Committee on Medical Research] underwrote protocols that in a later day (and an earlier one as well) would have produced considerable protest." Under these conditions, it is not surprising that U.S. policies and practices in medical experimentation during the war were wildly inconsistent. The defense attorneys at the Nazi doctors' trial exploited these inconsistencies to the full advantage of their clients, but they were not the whole story.

Sometimes the national security establishment was highly protective of military personnel. At other times it used them as what may rightly be called "guinea pigs." Sometimes care was taken to establish strict rules for patriotic volunteers. At other times people in a poor position to decline, such as prisoners and the mentally disabled, were used in dangerous experiments.

Still, this was an era in which patriotism ran high, and the vast majority of Americans were genuinely enthusiastic about the war effort, including those experimental subjects who were capable of consenting. Though American human research never approached the gross inhumanity of the Nazis, wartime dictates its own morality. The desperate push for victory in the midst of the bloody mess that was World War II eased the way for expedience to run roughshod over high-toned principle. Under these conditions, what is perhaps most remarkable is that any principles were intoned at all.

## VOLUNTEERS FOR AMERICA

Walter Reed's turn-of-the-century yellow-fever research was often cited before and during World War II as a precedent that justified military-medical human experiments. In 1900 the Army scientist was assigned to Cuba, where yellow fever had killed thousands more American soldiers than had the Spanish army in the recent war. Death came to most of those who caught the disease, and it was an awful way to die: yellowing skin as the first sign followed by violent hiccuping and uncontrollable, incessant retching and black vomit. Nothing seemed to stem the tide. By the time Reed arrived, a third of the army's general staff had already died, as had untold hundreds of natives of the big island every day.

Captain Reed and his colleagues on the Yellow Fever Commission were aware of Giuseppe Sanarelli, an Italian bacteriologist at Louis Pasteur's Paris institute. Sanarelli claimed to have reproduced yellow fever in five human beings by injecting them with a microbe called *bacillus icteroides*. Unfortunately, his results were clouded by ethical protests because his subjects had not given permission for the experiment and three had died. Reed and his colleagues also noticed the disease's odd epidemiology, that the illness claimed some but not all family members, and that it would skip a house or even whole blocks to attack another home, often people who had nothing to do with one another. It occurred to them that the pattern was indeed consistent with a culprit traveling on the wind.

The story of the Yellow Fever Commission was charmingly—and somewhat inaccurately—told in *Microbe Hunters*, a 1926 best seller that introduced generations of lay readers to the wonders of public health microbiology. In prose that was itself fevered Paul de Kruif reconstructed the decision to do a test.

That was perfectly easy to say, but how to go on with it? Everybody knew perfectly well that you cannot give yellow fever to any animal—not even to a monkey or an ape. To make any kind of experiment to prove mosquitoes carry yellow fever you *must* have experimental animals, and that meant nothing more nor less than human animals. But give human beings yellow fever! In some epidemics—there were records of them!—eighty five men out of a hundred died of it, in some fifty out of every hundred—almost never less than twenty out of every hundred. It would be murder!

Here, wrote de Kruif, Reed's "strong moral nature" took hold. "Here was a blameless man, a Christian man, and a man—though he was mild—who was mad to help his fellow men. And if you could *prove* that yellow fever was carried *only* by mosquitoes . . ." Somehow it was suggested that the members of the Commission subject themselves to the mosquito's bite first. Then, somehow, seven more volunteers were obtained. It had to be done secretly. "It was a breach of discipline in its way," wrote de Kruif, "for Walter Reed then had no permission from the high military authorities to start it."

On de Kruif's account, of nine bitten by mosquitoes engorged with the blood of dying men, seven remained, at the time of writing, in perfect health. Then Yellow Fever Commissioner Jesse Lazear, a microbiologist trained in Europe, became ill from the bite of a bug that had feasted on four cases of yellow fever. Lazear came from a wealthy family and enjoyed a highly successful career, culminating in his appointment as the first chief of clinical laboratories at Johns Hopkins Medical School. A few days after Lazear became ill, he died, at the age of 34, leaving behind a widow and two children. According to de Kruif, Reed then reported the event to his commanding general and asked permission to use himself and other men as subjects, which was granted. "Now it is my turn to take the bite!" Reed supposedly declared, as he and the other physicians on the Yellow Fever Commission agreed to subject themselves to the experiment.

Well, not exactly. The accurate version of the Reed story, recently retold by journalist Lawrence Altman, has the physicians, including Lazear, pledging themselves to become subjects on the evening of August 3, 1900. But the next day, for reasons that are not entirely clear, while his colleagues took the bite, Reed himself left Cuba, perhaps having been ordered to report to his commanders. Lazear and the other eight survived the initial bites, but Lazear then was bitten a second time, perhaps by accident, and he died on the following September 25, a true hero of medical science.

Another unsung hero, or heroine, of the yellow-fever experiments was a nurse, Clara Maass, of East Orange, New Jersey. Maass was working as a contract nurse in Cuba when the Havana Sanitary Officer put out a call for volunteers for Reed's experiment. She agreed to be bitten in dune 1901, contracted a mild case, and agreed to be bitten again on August 14.

She died two weeks later, only 25 years old, and was buried in Newark. Clara Maass has the distinction of having both Cuba and the United States issue stamps in her honor.

Though Reed deserves credit for managing the entire operation, it is unlikely he would have achieved such heroic proportions in military medical folklore had it not been for the myth, and had Reed himself not died only two years later due to a colleague's medical error. It was the courageous actions of Lazear and his colleagues that proved beyond a reasonable doubt that the mosquito was responsible for the epidemic. Two decades later there was barely any of the virus left in the world. If there were justice in history, the famous military hospital in Washington should be named the Jesse Lazear Army Medical Center.

Yet it is interesting that Reed apparently had to proceed in secret at first, and that he asked for permission to continue with himself and others as volunteer subjects, indicating that there was a policy (albeit perhaps an informal one) prohibiting such experimentation in the army. This is not surprising, considering that the assignment of soldiers to new duty, and especially that which places them at risk, must be a matter for command decision and responsibility. Medical experiments are no more disqualified from the requirements of military discipline and regulation than any other activity in which one might participate while in the armed forces. But perhaps Reed's resolve was strengthened by the suspicion that as a physician intending to benefit his unit under desperate circumstances he was unlikely to be seen as insubordinate.

More men were needed to confirm the mosquito theory, and they could be obtained from among the soldiers stationed in Cuba. Upon recruiting these soldiers, Reed presented them with an innovative contract of his own devising. Those who agreed to be in his research were to sign it. The contract warned them that they might die in the experiment, though they might also die outside of it.

The contracts also mentioned an important financial inducement for being part of the study, an offer made by Reed himself, through the generosity of the general in command of Cuba's American forces. As de Kruif laconically put it: "A handsome amount of money they would get—two hundred, maybe three hundred dollars, if the silver-striped she-mosquitoes did things to them that would give them one chance out of five not to spend the money." There is some disagreement about the exact terms of the offer. A recent medical historian claims the men were offered one hundred dollars in gold to sign up and an additional one hundred dollars if they contracted the disease.

One point on which all accounts agree is that some Spanish immigrant workers received the money for volunteering, but not the soldiers. De Kruif claims that the Americans declined the offer out of patriotism. Though it is also possible that the story is more complex, and that the military command viewed paying the soldiers to take the mosquito's bite as a bad practice and a bad precedent, patriotic motives are an important element in the story of medical research.

Though *Microbe Hunters* doesn't mention them, copies of the contracts have survived. Where did Reed get the idea for this early permission form? It is likely that he knew of the furor then taking place in Prussia about human experimentation. In 1892 a medical school professor had given blood serum from people with syphilis to four children and three young prostitutes. Professor Dr. Albert Neisser of Breslau was searching for a syphilis vaccine. Apparently, he did not ask the permission of those he infected, or their legal guardians, and several contracted the disease. Newspapers carried banner headlines about details of the scandal, stoking public outrage. The Prussian government responded in 1900 by directing that medical research must have the human subject's consent, right around that time Reed was conducting his yellow-fever research. But how did Reed learn about the incident? An answer can only be speculative, but recall the unfortunate young commissioner Jesse Lazear: He was fresh from his German training when he reported to Walter Reed for work in Cuba.

Medical historian Susan Lederer attributes the written contract idea to Reed's boss, Surgeon General George Miller Sternberg. As a young medical experimenter in San Francisco, Sternberg had tried to induce gonorrhea in several young male volunteers, then tried it on himself, without success. In 1897 the great Johns Hopkins professor of internal medicine, William Osler, denounced the yellow-fever experiments of Giuseppe Sanarelli, who had used patients in his studies, as "criminal." When Reed arrived in Cuba, relations with the Spanish workers were sensitive, giving Sternberg and Reed more reason to be cautious about the human volunteer issue. Throughout his subsequent career, Sternberg was careful to emphasize the voluntary nature of the yellow-fever studies.

Even if Reed were inspired, not by the Prussian example, but by his boss's experience, law and morality in the United States at the beginning of the century did have most of the same concepts that we have today. One of these concepts was that people should not in general be forced to do things against their will. Doctors were often exempt from this moral principle, whether formally or informally, on the assumption that they intended to do good for their patients and knew what was best for them. When it came to experiments, however, it was often harder to justify that exception. While some experiments are meant to help a patient because all else has failed, many are conducted in order to gather new knowledge, with benefit to the patient highly unlikely or even deliberately sacrificed in favor of gaining some information. The differences between these kinds of experiments can be subtle, and for a very long time the courts and public opinion went back and forth on the amount of discretion the medical profession should be given in doing human experiments.

In the military there was still another complication. Because sacrifice is part of what it means to be in the armed forces, it stands to reason that, if anyone is to be exposed to danger for the nation's good, these men and women would be prime candidates. Especially in a shooting war, when the risks of a medical experiment pale before battlefield dangers, military personnel can seem an obvious and justifiable source of experimental subjects.

On the other hand, those responsible for the young men and women in military service usually feel this responsibility deeply. It is one thing to lead them to death or injury while in combat for their country, quite another to "waste" them in something like a medical experiment, especially when noncombat personnel would do just as well. This is a sensibility that has been widely shared among military officials. The Nazi official Heinrich Himmler railed against sacrificing sturdy young Luftwaffe pilots when non-Aryan prisoners were available for lethal research. There are also public relations reasons for authorities to prefer nonsoldiers as subjects. Military establishments do not generally want to be perceived as experimental laboratories by those they are trying to recruit, nor by their mothers and fathers who may be willing to send their children to be heroes but not "guinea pigs."

These opposing attitudes about soldiers as experimental subjects among military officials—sometimes as the most suitable

candidates but at other times as resources to be carefully managed—also help explain some of the paradoxes in U.S. policies and
practices. For while there were many rules prohibiting the use of
soldiers and sailors as experimental subjects, from World War II
on those rules were often violated.

Long before civilian medicine, the American military had rules
on record that only "volunteers" are to be used in research. The
U.S. Army had such a rule at least by 1925, as part of a regulation
on "The Prevention of Communicable Diseases in Man—
General." In the early 1930s the Navy was obliged to draw up a
policy because sailors were working on a new submarine escape
device at the Navy Yard in Washington, D.C. In 1932 the secretary of the Navy was given a protocol for the planned experiments.
"SecNav approved the request for the work," according to an
internal Navy history, "with the understanding that all subjects
should be informed volunteers; that the detailed protocol be
approved in advance, and that every precaution be taken to prevent accidents." Even at the height of World War II, when victory for the Allies was far from assured, the Navy secretary sent a
memo "to all ships and stations" requiring that all human experiments involving service personnel receive his approval before they
begin.

Historian Sydney Halpern has discovered that, as early as 1945,
the Armed Forces Epidemiology Board (AFEB) kept track of the
way the press characterized its research subjects. When a
Philadelphia newspaper asked for permission to publish a story on
AFEB-sponsored jaundice research at the University of
Pennsylvania, Colonel Stanhope Bayne-Jones granted the request
but urged that the article adopt a "moderate tone, and that exag-
geration of the facts will be avoided." Bayne-Jones continued:
"May I suggest that the term 'guinea pigs' for those volunteers is
undignified, hackneyed, threadbare and hardly appropriate. I hope
you can find a more fitting term for these men." As historian
Halpern notes, the newspaper was hardly in a position to decline
this advice if it wanted to use the story.

Besides public relations, a reason for the policies that required
experimental subjects be volunteers was that military personnel

who were injured as the result of an experiment could in theory sue the government for damages. Legal barriers to lawsuits against the U.S. government for non-combat-related injuries sustained due to negligence while in the armed forces were not as well established in those days. But the primary reason for caution in the use of soldiers and sailors for medical research was the same as it is today: that the nation's heroes must not be used indiscriminately as guinea pigs. Though secret research with military personnel was always an option, others had the honor of serving the nation's need for medical breakthroughs in public.

## THE COMMITTEE ON MEDICAL RESEARCH (CMR)

One of the many amazing features of the American war effort was how quickly it made up lost ground in scientific knowledge, as compared with the integration of science and strategic goals in Germany and Japan during the 1930s. Just as the U.S. Army became little more than a gentleman's club as a result of massive disarmament following World War I, and research and development in ordnance basically ground to a halt, so also America's armed forces in general were woefully ill-prepared for the medical aspects of modern warfare. The United States did have a considerable civilian medical science establishment, however. The challenge that faced the Roosevelt administration was how to organize it into the public service as rapidly as possible, to answer some of the many questions presented by more powerful armaments, aircraft that could fly higher and faster, and operational environments riven with infectious disease.

The job of crafting a systematic response to military medical problems fell mainly on the shoulders of two hugely talented men. One was Vannevar Bush, the other a University of Pennsylvania medical school professor named A. Newton Richards, whom Bush identified for his distinction and his wisdom, "trusted by all who knew him." "Of all the men of science I have known," Bush wrote, "he was the most fully respected, yes, and the most beloved by his colleagues and by everyone who knew him." Coming from a hard-nosed engineering genius who had known just about every important scientist of his time, or every American scientist of note anyway, this was high praise indeed. Though the record shows that Richards was indeed beloved by his colleagues, there might have been another reason for Bush's choice.

Richards was a Ph.D. scientist, not an M.D. However, since his professional stature was beyond question and his personal character widely admired, the organized medical fraternity of which Bush and Roosevelt were so suspicious could hardly object to his leadership. In fact, Richards had wanted to attend medical school but after receiving his undergraduate degree at Yale in 1897 his parents were unable to afford the tuition. Instead, Richards received a scholarship from Columbia for a doctorate in physiological chemistry. After a period on the Northwestern faculty Richards was called to the University of Pennsylvania, where he was vice president in charge of the medical school when appointed to head the CMR. The boy who couldn't afford medical school was now in charge of dispensing grants from the largest federally funded medical research program in U.S. history, with the professional futures of the nation's greatest medical scientists in his hands.

As the president had transferred medical research issues to Bush, so now Bush was eager to do the same with Richards, and for the same reason: the fierce insistence by medical investigators that they retain their professional autonomy. Bush made certain never to interfere with "professional judgments." "Nothing gets in the hair of medical men more thoroughly than that," he said. It was a revealing statement, because it meant that, though the lions of the AMA might not be in control, nonetheless the medical scientists were left to govern themselves in this great national project. For who was to determine exactly what counted as within the purview of "professional judgments?" This question-begging division of labor did not necessarily serve the public interest. Still, rampant confidence in physicians' ability to guide their own conduct was typical of this era, when doctors became indignant at the mere suggestion of outside review, even by the president of the United States, and certainly by an electrical engineer. Though organized medicine might not control the CMR, once the committee granted an award, the conduct of the work was left up to the researchers themselves.

Under Richards the CMR—which was composed of presidential appointees and representatives of the Army, Navy, and Public Health Service—sponsored a stunning array of research in very short time. The key was a unified and coordinated effort from various parties that had rather little systematic contact with one another before the war. Not only college and university departments but also, Bush related, "research laboratories, agricultural experiment stations, pharmaceutical manufacturers" and, importantly, "inmates of penitentiaries who volunteered their help—all pulled together. Some fifteen thousand new chemical compounds were synthesized in this endeavor and tested in animals and some of them in men." The crown jewel of the chemical research was penicillin. The completion of its development and its early allocation fell to the wisdom of the CMR. "When at last success was accomplished, the precious small supply had to be rationed—the medication used to treat the first case had cost about $50,000—and rationing was managed with consummate skill by Dr. [Chester] Keefer," the CMR's medical administrator.

After the war the CMR's work was summarized in a two-volume report called *Advances in Military Medicine*. Among the dozens of research areas discussed in the included papers, the report's editors emphasized the further development of penicillin, antimalarial drugs, and insecticides as especially noteworthy achievements. The published record of the CMR's work contains only a few hints of attitudes concerning the use of human subjects, still less of rules or policies. Without question, patriotism was a far more dominant element in the atmosphere of 1940s America than it is today, perhaps even beyond our ability to appreciate it, and the researchers did not need to dwell on the recruitment of their "volunteers."

A measure of this patriotism, the sense that all Americans were "in it together," is the fact that *Advances* is full of tributes to the experiment volunteers, far more than one sees in almost any scientific paper today. In a chapter on "Problems in Nutrition," it was explained that much of the needed information could only be

obtained with controlled experiments on humans, a familiar justification that nevertheless seemed to bear repeating: "The latter
often involved hard work, much physical discomfort, tedious days
of living in close quarters under prescribed conditions in extremely
hot or cold, humid or dry environments, and acceptance at the
same time of limited diets, which in many instances were continued at starvation or semistarvation levels for long periods of time."

Students, soldiers, and hospital patients served thus in some of
the projects, but in most cases the subjects were conscientious
objectors who volunteered their services and were assigned to the
respective projects from Civilian Public Service Camps. In a project at the University of Minnesota, for example, "65 of these men
were resident subjects in the laboratory for a period of one year."

Protecting against the effects of mustard gas, which had been
used by both sides in World War I with devastating consequences
for the victims, also required human experiments.

> While tests on goats, guinea pigs, rabbits, and other laboratory
> animals might give a rough idea of effectiveness, the reactions
> of the skin vary so greatly from species to species that it was
> soon found that the only constantly reliable test object was
> man. Eventually all promising preparations were tested on a
> series of volunteers.

In spite of expressions of patriotic camaraderie with the subjects, no account of how they were recruited was given. According
to a chapter on treatment and protection of the skin, the most
important consideration was that the human subjects must be
"volunteers." No further information was provided about populations from which test subjects were drawn, let alone about the
conditions under which it was thought appropriate to use them. In
those days, little content seems to have been given to the idea of
volunteering, except that physical coercion was unacceptable.
Anyway, it was widely assumed that prisoners and conscientious
objectors had a debt to pay.

However impressive the scientific accomplishments it detailed,
·*Advances in Military Medicine* was still an official history. It gave

hardly a clue about the extremes to which the CMR went in evaluating some human studies, or the high rhetorical bar it set on subject protection, while approving other dangerous experiments, nor did it fully report how many subjects were involved, or who they were.

One group of gravely ill human subjects whose identities are unknown can be credited with extraordinary service in the fight against cancer. They were part of a radical series of CMR-sponsored experiments with a poison called nitrogen mustard that led to modern cancer chemotherapy. These studies, begun in 1942, are perhaps the best single example of the way that a national security experiment can have terribly important "spin-offs" into civilian medicine.

The nitrogen mustards (there are three kinds) were discovered by accident in 1935 by Czech scientists. Both American and German chemical warfare scientists went to work on the military applications of the new agent, and both sides produced and stockpiled it during World War II. The United States kept the work classified in order to make the Germans think they had discovered a new and better "mustard gas," hoping that Third Reich scientists would squander resources trying to come up with a similar improvement. The ruse failed because the Germans never learned the "secret."

Using some of their stockpiled supply, American authorities also supported related nitrogen mustard research in the medical sphere. In the radical experiment, a patient dying of lymphosarcoma at Yale-New Haven Hospital was injected with nitrogen mustard, which was known to be poisonous to cells. His tumors receded, and another five patients were started on this first clinical chemotherapy trial. But the bone marrow that the nitrogen mustard had killed to reverse the generation of cancer cells started regrowing, and all of the patients got sick again and died.

Still, this was the beginning of modern cancer treatments, which have grown increasingly refined. By the end of the war, hundreds of people had been treated experimentally at several institutions by means of this paradoxical approach: a poison that could heal. However, scientific research conducted under the auspices of

war making suffers from severe limitations. In the case of chemotherapy and, as we shall see, also in the early radiation experiments,
the results of the early chemotherapy trials had to remain under
wraps until the end of the war. The substances being experimented
with were, after all, highly classified agents that could be used in
chemical warfare. The medical research was in effect "piggy-back-
ing" on the primary motivation for experiments with nitrogen
mustard, which made the funding available to the medical
researchers. For reasons of national security, the dying cancer
patients and their families could not have been told much, if anything, about the first bold chemotherapy experiments.

## THE QUIET WAR ON "VD"

Studies to combat sexually transmissable diseases—then commonly
known as venereal diseases, or VD—were among the most carefully considered human research projects sponsored by the CMR.
Notwithstanding rules against fraternization with the local population and taboos about homosexuality, sexually transmitted diseases were a significant concern of the American army in the early
1940s, as they have been for military leaders throughout history.
John J. Pershing, commander-in-chief of the American Expeditionary
Force in World War I, called the battle against venereal disease
among American troops one of great military and moral significance. It was in the context of the World War II that the first reliable medication for syphilis—penicillin—was developed.

One of the young doctors who participated in the struggle
against VD under Pershing who later helped develop penicillin
was Joseph Earle Moore, probably the greatest venereologist of
his generation. Moore spent virtually his entire professional career
at Johns Hopkins, where he was very popular with both his
patients and colleagues. He had the distinction of being the first
practicing physician to be named a full professor of medicine at
Hopkins. Moore authored the chapter on venereal diseases in
*Advances in Military Medicine*, pronouncing it an "urgent problem"
for the armed forces, as indeed it was. Reliable estimates were that

as many as 7 million man-days per year were lost to gonorrhea. In 1946 Moore received the Medal of Merit for his part in the conquest of this ancient scourge, one of the great victories of American wartime medicine.

In his chapter for *Advances*, Moore only mentioned human testing with an expression of frustration about "the insuperable difficulty of producing gonococcal infection in experimental animals within the period of the war and in time for this to be of value to the armed forces." With Moore as its consultant, the U.S. Public Health Service contacted the Federal Bureau of Prisons and arranged for the use of "two hundred volunteers" at the Terre Haute penitentiary. Moore reported that "efforts were made to produce experimental gonorrhea in these subjects by almost every conceivable expedient except the intraurethral inoculation of pus taken directly from the cervix or urethra of infected females or the natural method of infection—sexual intercourse." Moore explained that pus injections were avoided due to the risk of also transmitting syphilis; that infection of prisoners by sexual intercourse was disqualified seemingly required no further explanation.

What Moore did not report about exposing human volunteers to gonorrhea in *Advances* is at least as interesting as what he did report. Due to Vannevar Bush's considerable discomfort, the CMR went to great lengths to consider the wisdom of this project. The behind-the-scenes story began in 1942 when Moore, in his capacity as chairman of the National Research Council Committee on Venereal Diseases, forwarded a query from Charles M. Carpenter, a scientist at the University of Rochester. Carpenter was trying to "work out a human experiment on the chemical prophylaxis of gonorrhea," and asked "for an opinion that such human experimentation is desirable." Moore then asked the CMR how it could be done. A few weeks later the full committee provided a formal response to Moore's inquiry. It is the single most authoritative and detailed expression of the American position on human experimentation that survives from the war.

Human experimentation is not only desirable, but necessary in the study of many of the problems of war medicine which confront us. When any risks are involved, volunteers only should be utilized as subjects, and these only after the risks have been fully explained, and after signed statements have been obtained which shall prove that the volunteer offered his services with full knowledge and that claims for damage will be waived. An accurate record should be kept of the terms in which the risks involved were described.

Brief as it was, Richards' reply to Moore was a firm statement that, under certain conditions, the CMR (and therefore the Roosevelt administration itself) not only condoned but also encouraged the advance of medical science through research with human subjects. More experiments with humans were viewed as necessary for the war effort, so long as only informed "volunteers" who signed waivers were used.

But Vannevar Bush wasn't so sure. He raised several concerns with Richards: "first, the legality of the proceedings; second, the social hazards involved; i.e., the political expediency; and third, that desired results could not be obtained by any other means." Why was Bush being so cautious? Historian Jon Harkness theorizes that he might have been shaken by the recent death of an inmate at Norfolk Prison Colony in Massachusetts, who had been a subject in a bovine albumin study. Then there was the sensitivity associated with giving people a disease that is normally transmitted through sexual contact, which might have offended many Americans in the early 1940s. Bush wanted the scientists to find another way to study the problem, but after considering various options and subject populations, Moore forcefully concluded that only prisoner volunteers would satisfy the experimental requirements.

In an effort to canvass as much scientific opinion as possible under the delicate circumstances, the CMR convened a sort of prototype of a scientific and ethical consensus conference, on December 29, 1942, with participation by military officials, state health department officers, and scientists. Warned about the potential legal liability of the gonorrhea research by the AMA's president, the conferees reviewed a fairly thorough experimental protocol. It included criteria for ruling out certain prisoners as

subjects, such as those who were chronically ill or allergic to sul-
fonamides, and a "Statement of Explanation of the Experiment
and Its Risks to Tentative Volunteers" that the prisoners were to
read and sign. The conference participants and other outside eval-
uators largely gave the CMR the green light, especially in terms of
the use of prisoners as the only feasible option, and Walter Reed's
famous experiments with yellow fever were cited as part of the history that justified the use of human volunteers.

Mollified about the legality of the matter, Bush still harbored
reservations about the public relations involved. He set out to get
as many high officials on board as he could, perhaps to help provide him with political "cover" if needed later on. Bush solicited
the opinions of the surgeons general of the Army, Navy, and
Public Health Service, of the president of the National Academy
of Sciences, and of the chairman of the National Research
Council. Bush also sent Richards to meet with the director of the
federal Bureau of Prisons to discuss practical arrangements. The
director recommended the men be offered a $100 payment and
medical insurance in return for participation. The payment was
acceptable, but the government was unwilling to give open-ended
insurance. With these conditions in place and a site chosen (the
U.S. penitentiary in Terre Haute), Bush finally approved the study
on March 6, 1943. In spite of all their preparations, the scientists
abandoned the experiment shortly after it began, apparently
because, as with test animals, they could not produce the disease
with enough reliability or frequency to test experimental preventive measures.

The review process and the policy that emerged from it could
have been a model for other human subjects research, and it could
have helped sensitize the public and the scientific community to
issues such as the importance of being a true volunteer. But, as
Vannevar Bush apparently calculated that research on this kind of
disease was best not widely broadcast, it was conducted away from
public view, limiting the lessons the whole experience could have
provided. Bush required that federal doctors from the Public
Health Service conduct the gonorrhea experiments, an arrangement that helped ensure the security of the study.

This was not the case with another highly successful assault on disease using prisoners, one about which the CMR was anything but publicity shy. In an odd historical nexus, one of the CMR's most important studies linked the unimpeachable characters of Vannevar Bush and A. N. Richards with a man who was then the most famous inhabitant of the American prison system, and perhaps its most brilliant ever, a man who had been convicted of the "crime of the century."

## A MODEL PRISONER FOR A MODEL EXPERIMENT

In 1924, Nathan Leopold was a 19-year-old prodigy who had entered the law school at the University of Chicago. Heir to a Chicago family fortune, he was already fluent in French, Spanish, German, Italian, Latin, and Greek. Leopold had a shining future by any measure, but it was not enough to sate his boredom. Jaded by wealth, he embodied the dark side of the Roaring Twenties, a decade whose bankruptcy was soon to be revealed in more senses than one. Seeking to relieve their ennui, Leopold fantasized with his lover Richard Loeb about "the perfect crime."

Leopold and Loeb hit upon a plan to kidnap a 14-year-old boy who lived in the neighborhood. For further sport they demanded $10,000 in ransom. When the ransom was not forthcoming, they made good on their threat and killed the boy. But the Chicago police cracked the case, found the boy's body, and won the case against the conspirators. The cold and calculated nature of the crime, inspired only by a lust for adventure, shocked the nation, newspapers declaring it the "crime of the century." Leopold and Loeb were sentenced to life plus ninety-nine years.

Leopold's brilliance could not be confined by the walls of the Stateville Prison in Joliet, Illinois. While there he established the first high school for prisoners, studied statistics, authored a scholarly article for a criminology journal, published his autobiography, and learned another twenty languages. But by his own account, the most "exciting" event of his years in prison was his part in a CMR experiment on the treatment of malaria, the same study that would attract the attention of the defense lawyers for the Nazi doctors at Nuremberg.

Malaria posed a significant threat to American plans for the final phases of the war against Japan, which appeared prepared to fight to the last. Worldwide, malaria attacked 300 million people a year and killed 3 million. It was especially severe in the climate typical of the Pacific theater of operations. Numerous tropical islands would have to be invaded and secured in the course of a march toward the enemy's homeland. Containing malaria became a significant goal of the U.S. armed forces in readying themselves for the final push.

By the early 1940s the antimalarial drug Atabrine had been tested successfully in human subjects. As a result of this encouraging experience, arrangements were made to test new malaria medication on volunteers who were deliberately infected with the disease. As the editors of *Advances in Military Medicine* wrote, "these volunteers were found among conscientious objectors relieved of military service, among patients in civilian hospitals, and among inmates of federal, state, and military prisons." The inmates seem to have been thought suitable for some of the most dangerous and unpleasant tasks. "The patriotic zeal with which the last-named group submitted themselves to infection with *vivax* malaria, with its distressing periodic recurrences, is particularly laudable."

Recalling his wartime service in his 1958 autobiography, *Life Plus 99 Years*, Leopold identified patriotic fervor as one of his motives. He "wanted very badly to do my bit" in the war and "being a malaria volunteer represented by far my best opportunity.... Here was a chance to get in a payment on my debt, an opportunity much more favorable and important than most to expiate some part of my guilt." Of course, as Leopold also acknowledged, his motives and those of his fellow prisoners were mixed.

A number of men had relatives or friends in the armed services; they were more than glad to do what they could if it would help the soldiers. Many took part because they hoped that their sentences would be reduced; some few actually took malaria to earn the hundred dollars [incentive payment]. And there were some who, I am convinced, went into the thing on an idealistic basis. They didn't want the money—indeed, they protested strongly against accepting it—and they had little hope of having their sentences reduced. But they saw a chance to do something decent and worth while [*sic*] for a change.

According to Leopold, the physicians handled the men with great sensitivity. "The young docs . . . leaned over backward in handling the matter of volunteering in a scrupulously ethical manner" and they "explained in great detail to each and every volunteer before he was used just what it was planned to do. We were told there was danger, that we might be sick, that we might die. No man was coerced or even persuaded." All the prison subjects signed a contract (though the rather technical language downplayed the risks), which would today be called a consent form. Indeed, even if Leopold could be charged with somewhat exaggerating the physicians' stellar conduct in the blush of memory about his own "good war." the fact is that there was an oversupply of eager recruits for the malaria experiments. Apparently no coercion or persuasion was needed.

Such was the pride taken in the malaria experiments that the investigators actually sought out public attention. Their best stroke of publicity was a June 1945 photo spread in *Life* magazine. So desirable was this publicity that the study was delayed several days so that photographers could be on hand when jars containing malaria-carrying mosquitoes were placed on the stomachs of prisoners, biting them through gauze-covered openings. The researchers could not have known that, only two years later, the publicity that they welcomed would be used to indict the ethics of American medicine in a war crimes trial.

Two months after *Life's* dramatic photo essay, Captain Paul W. Tibbets led a B-29 squad that released an atomic bomb over Hiroshima, followed three days later by another A-bomb that leveled Nagasaki. Thanks to grave anxiety in the War Department about the implications of a protracted Pacific war, advances were made in the battle against malaria, but they were no longer needed against a thoroughly broken enemy.

## THE CMR'S NAGGING PROBLEM

It is a truism that the life of an individual makes more sense in retrospect than it did at the time. Such is also the case in organizations. The contributors to Advances in Military Medicine were able to tie up the use of human subjects in a fairly neat package in retrospect, but the reality was not so neat. CMR Chairman Richards' personal papers on deposit at the University of Pennsylvania show that, almost as soon as it got started, the CMR received many inquiries about human volunteers and lots of advice about the issue. At an August 1941 meeting the CMR "agreed that clinical tests should be used in civilian hospitals" concerning sulfanylimide for the treatment of infectious diseases. At the same meeting a member asserted that eventually there would be a need for "human experimentation" to draw conclusions about new research in antimalarials. At the next meeting a month later it was mentioned that troops were being used in tests on the effect of nutrients on fatigue. In February 1942 the members agreed that human albumin could be tested, on a limited basis, in military hospitals (one of these studies led to the Norfolk inmate's death), and in May the committee learned that malaria experiments were being performed in men. Since early in the war conscientious objectors were being used in antilice drug studies for one of the traditional scourges of a soldier's life. Later in 1942 the CMR also considered, but apparently did not fund, a "large-scale test (of antilice medication) of civilian populations" in Latin America.

While obviously not high on its list of concerns in the midst of the national emergency, the human experiments issue continued to be an annoyance to committee members throughout the war. It was also a potentially serious enough public relations problem to require monitoring, even though no consistent public relations policy emerged. For instance, in 1943 the members strongly opposed releasing information to the general public about the use of conscientious objectors in medical experiments, but in 1944 they approved publicity about the prison antimalarial project that finally ended up in the *Life* magazine story. Did the difference in attitude about publicizing human experiments have to do with the kinds of people involved? Were sensitivities about the use of conscientious objectors greater than with regard to prisoners? Or had some other circumstances changed?

Even after the correspondence between Richards and Moore, the Johns Hopkins venereologist, in the fall of 1942, the apparently careful policies that were set out did not seem to be implemented when other cases came up for consideration. Research on dysentery involved subjects who could not be considered volunteers by any stretch of the imagination: adolescents at the Ohio Soldiers and Sailors Orphanage (where conditions were so filthy that they approximated battlefield hygiene) and mentally retarded residents. Also liable to be research subjects in diseases associated with inadequate public health systems were the poor. One published report about sulfonamide research described a "twenty-month-old colored female" with dysentery at Charity Hospital in Shreveport, Louisiana. After initial improvement following administration of the experimental drug, the child died. Though there was already reason at the time to believe patients did better with the drug than without it, there is no evidence that relatives knew or consented to the research.

This pattern would play itself out through the next two decades in national security medical experiments. Probably the most astonishing example of the inconsistency in applying sound policy took place in the largest set of medical studies for which Bush and Richards were largely responsible: experiments with mustard gas that involved thousands of sailors throughout the war. The real story of the mustard gas research, and who its subjects were and their number, did not find its way into the celebratory *Advances in Military Medicine*.


## DEADLY CHEMICALS

In 1944 a 17-year-old sailor named Nathan Schnurman was offered a three-day pass in exchange for his participation in a test of Navy summer clothing. He accepted the deal and was locked in a gas chamber that was filled with mustard gas. Named for its mustardlike odor, the substance dichlorethyl sulfide first causes sneezing, then vomiting, then reddening and blistering of the skin and eyelids, causing temporary blindness. When he started to become nauseated Schnurman asked to be released from the chamber, but his request was denied. He asked several times before passing out.

Another young recruit, John William Allen, also entered the Navy at the age of 17. In 1945 he, too, volunteered to test summer clothing so he could visit home before shipping out. Wearing pants, undershorts, a gas mask, and a shirt doused with toxic chemicals, Allen entered the chamber. And like Schnurman he was not released until he passed out, but not before suffering severe blistering injuries.

Both Schnurman and Allen seem to have been participants in "man-break" tests, experiments with toxic gases designed to determine at what point the agents can "break a man." These were not isolated incidents. In a 1993 report the National Academy of Sciences (NAS) estimated that during World War II over 60,000 servicemen were used in chemical research, 4,000 with mustard gas or lewisite, its chemical relative. This was a far larger number than had been suspected before the NAS study. Remarkably, virtually all of the subjects kept their promise of silence for decades, partly out of patriotism and partly out of fear of reprisals. Only in the 1980s did their stories come out, when they sought compensation for long-term medical problems they attributed to their gas exposures. Schnurman and Allen were among those who told their stories to a Senate committee in 1994.

The Germans had introduced gas against the British at the Battle of Ypres in 1917, during World War I. Fourteen thousand men were exposed during the three-week battle. Loaded in artillery shells, often with its telltale mustardlike smell disguised, the gas was quite effective in causing chaos in the ranks, especially since there was no adequate protection against it, as it disintegrated leather and rubber. Mustard gas was only one such poison developed during the World War I. Many gases were devised by both sides but, along with tear gas, mustard was the most successful, and the most feared. By the time the war ended the gas had caused nearly four hundred thousand casualties.

Recognizing the threat of toxic chemical weapons, the United
States established the Chemical Warfare Service (CWS) in 1918.
The director of the Bureau of Mines, Van H. Manning, was directed by the National Research Council "to carry on investigations
into noxious gases, generation, and antidote for same, for war purposes; also investigations into gas masks." In a classic example of
extending his agency's turf, Manning argued that his Bureau of
Mines had more experience than anyone else in dealing with mine
gases and in developing rescue apparatus.

Manning wasted no time in recruiting an elite group of chemical engineers, physiologists, toxicologists, pharmacologists,
pathologists, and others. Their first task was to design a gas mask
for the Army. Then they turned to studying the physiological
effect of toxic compounds, treatments for casualties from exposure
to chemical weapons, and "discovery of new toxic agents."
Universities throughout the country participated in the research,
including Yale, the University of Wisconsin, the University of
Michigan, Western Reserve University (now Case Western
Reserve), the University of Chicago, Massachusetts Institute of
Technology, and the University of Maryland. At about the same
time, the War Department began to develop a mobile laboratory
that could conduct research closer to the battlefront.

Manning's CWS approached its work vigorously, if not cautiously. The early days were filled with unfortunate accidents,
including several at its American University facility in northwest
Washington, D.C., called Camp A.U.

An electrical engineer for the Army, George Temple, was stationed at Camp American University while it was the center of the
Army's chemical warfare research program. Temple recalled his
experience nearly half a century later in an interview with the university's newspaper. Secrecy was all important, he said. "Personnel
of one laboratory were not permitted to enter any of the others."
After Temple had volunteered to participate in some research projects, he became "the guinea pig from then on," which resulted in
his receiving "gas doses for which he had not volunteered." Though
Temple survived his exposures at Camp A.U., others were not as
fortunate. Relates Temple: "One day, in the pitch black interior of

the smoke lab, three men were burned by a deadly dose of gas. The bodies were hauled away on a cart, the flesh 'jiggling off their bones.'"

Sometimes death was a slow process. Upon seeing one of his close friends and fellow workers for the first time in quite a while, Temple asked where he had been. "I got a bad dose of gas," the friend replied, "and I know I'm not going to get well."

Temple did not see his friend again. Sometime later he learned that the soldier had died. "More men were killed by gas on the experimental side," he believes, "than in actual use."

The burned men first referred to might have been victims of tests with poison or incendiary gas, the most likely latter agent being white phosphorous. Temple's friend could have been exposed to phosgene, which leaves one feeling fairly well for a brief period before the terminal process begins. Temple's account continued:

At the end of the day the camp personnel, their clothes impregnated by gas, would pile into trolleys. As the trolley cars neared the downtown area, civilians began boarding them. Soon they were all sneezing or crying, depending upon the type of gas the soldiers had been working with.

Neighbors were also affected, at least once, by accidental release of gas from Camp A.U. The residence of a former U.S. Senator from West Virginia, Nathan B. Scott, was located near the testing station. On August 3, 1918, lab apparatus at the camp exploded, releasing a cloud of gas that drifted to Scott's house. His wife reported to the press that she, the senator, and his sister had been "slightly gassed," but only Scott and his sister were treated by one of the camp's doctors. The district government, noting that the senator and his family had been "disagreeably affected" by the gas experiments, asked that the tests be moved elsewhere, apparently to no avail.

After the armistice, CWS operations were consolidated at Edgewood Arsenal in Maryland, where the service continued to conduct studies, making the most of the modest funding available between the wars. Over the next year and a half chemical warfare research grew rapidly, both in Manning's Bureau and in the Army. In spite of Manning's opposition, who saw his empire building about to end, President Wilson created a centralized chemical warfare command to coordinate the efforts of the several agencies. In 1918 the Chemical Warfare Service became a part of the Army.

There was no great sense of urgency in the CWS research effort during the 1920s and '30s, nor in the rest of America's drastically downsized military establishment. But in 1941 the CWS was quickly geared up and subsumed within the Committee on Medical Research (CMR). Taking a fresh look at the tactical possibilities of chemical weapons, by 1942 CWS researchers decided that animal experiments could not answer their renewed questions about how to prevent and treat human injuries. Apparently the CMR had reached the same conclusion. On April 7, 1942, Richards himself wrote to Secretary of War Stimson to inquire about the use of human subjects in gas testing. Stimson gave permission and three kinds of tests were done with tens of thousands of servicemen: patch tests of the outer surfaces of the body for burn prevention and treatment; chamber tests of the effectiveness of protective clothes; and field tests that contaminated areas of land.

Protective clothing was evaluated both in chamber tests and in field tests. The chamber tests consisted of outfitting soldiers in the clothing impregnated with chloramide or activated carbon, providing them with gas masks, and locking them in a sealed chamber, which would then be filled with a chemical agent such as lewisite or sulfur mustard. Soldiers would remain in these chambers anywhere from one hour to four hours. After being released from the gas-filled chambers, the soldiers would wear the protective clothing and their gas masks for up to twenty-four hours. "The men were required to repeat the procedure and enter the chambers either every day or every other day until they developed moderate to intense erythema."

The men did not necessarily link their later health problems to the mustard gas studies until many years had passed. Rudolph R. Mills told the Senate Committee in 1994,

I had on an experimental mask and the Navy was trying to determine if people wearing these masks could communicate with each other. I was enticed to sing over the intercom. . . . No one ever told me that the mask became less effective against the gas with each use. . . . We were sworn to secrecy. . . . At the age of 43 I underwent a long series of radiation treatments and later surgery to remove part of my voice box and larynx. . . . It didn't occur to me that my exposure to mustard gas was responsible for my physical problems until June 1991, when I read an article in my hometown newspaper.

Experiments with mustard gas were not limited to gas chambers. They also included field testing. Exercise Sandfly commenced in May 1944 on San José, an island off the coast of Panama. Under tropical conditions, 150 soldiers were marched into a

jungle area which had been heavily contaminated by means of mustard-filled bombs. Nothing was faked. Two flights of B-24 bombers had previously dropped over 200 bombs containing a total of five tons of mustard on the small target area. Chemical sampling revealed that the mustard concentration was sufficient to cause 100 per cent casualties from severe blistering and systemic poisoning among masked but otherwise unprotected troops. One hour after the planes had made their run, the fully protected troops moved into previously prepared positions in the area, established their lines of security, and prepared to stay. They had only to look about them to see the shining mustard on the foliage, to see the pools of mustard in the bomb craters around their position. Meanwhile an infantry combat patrol, also wearing complete protective equipment, set out to attack the position. A mile from its point of departure, the patrol ran into a tear gas concentration. Half a mile farther the patrol was exposed to phosgene when a 30-pound cylinder of the agent was fired statically as they approached.

The Report of Accomplishments indicates that the soldiers used in this experiment (or as the report calls it, "test") "had never experienced anything like it before and none of them were CWS-trained" And though they were "fully protected," some soldiers sustained injuries, comprising mostly burns to their faces, shoulders, and legs. Moreover, "there were moments when panic or mass hysteria seemed close to the surface among the occupying troops."

CWS field testing was conducted all over the world, and its purposes were to test protective clothing and produce data on exposure levels that produce injuries. In Sandfly these tests involved bombing areas with mustard gas and sending soldiers into the affected area "from 1 to 72 hours following the bombing." Some of the experiments involved sending soldiers into these areas without protective clothing or gas masks and sometimes requiring the soldiers to drop to the ground, causing them to be exposed to direct contact with the chemicals. Apparently some accidents were reported in these Army experiments, such as when, after a rainstorm, the soldiers in an infected area removed their gas masks, and "within two hours experienced ocular pain; three were hospitalized with acute conjunctivitis."

The Chemical Warfare Service was interested in testing the efficacy of "protective or decontamination ointments, treatments for [chemical] burns, effects of multiple exposures on sensitivity, and the effects of physical exercise on the severity of chemical burns." In conducting these tests the CWS used approximately sixty thousand human subjects. Development of new agents was part of its mission, but reevaluation of standard agents was deemed appropriate, too. One such agent ripe for reevaluation was lewisite.

This was the liquid agent made famous in the public prints after World War I by the assertion that "three drops of it on the tongue of a dog will kill a man." Demonstrations of lewisite in the laboratory and in gassing chambers proved that it was a very powerful agent. . . . New studies of lewisite made during the war, however, yielded definitive data not previously known. Despite the excellence of lewisite in the laboratory, in field tests in which volunteer human observers were subjected to its effects under simulated battle conditions, it was learned that unless a human being is defenseless or unconscious, the immediate irritation and pain caused by lewisite will make him leave the contaminated area at once.

And though research had produced guidelines for mitigating treatments for exposure, "nothing was available to prevent skin and lung damage. Even less was known about the long-term effects."

The National Academy of Sciences' (NAS) review of the early mustard gas experiments suggests that scientists in that era did not review what information was available from animal studies or historic exposures to determine whether the soldiers would be harmed. "It became apparent to the committee that the full body of knowledge available to the wartime scientists, especially information relevant to the long-term health outcomes of exposure to these agents, was not applied in the conduct of the human experimentation." Based on the NAS report, the Department of Veterans Affairs decided to compensate men like Mills who had suffered from disabilities due to in-service exposure to mustard gas and similar agents, or their survivors, fifty years later.

## BIOLOGICAL WEAPONS (BW) FIELD TESTS

The Army has asserted that it has been as open as possible about its biological warfare program. In 1994 an Army official stated that "throughout the biological warfare program, the Army has been as candid as possible without making classified material public." The qualifying phrase in this statement is, as usual, the critical one. At least one member of Congress (the body charged with the oversight of all executive agencies) has referred to the biological warfare program as cloaked with greater secrecy than the nuclear weapons programs. Another Congressman has said that although "the broad out-lines of the Army's biological testing program have been known for many years," revelations about open-air field testing in Minneapolis in the 1960s stunned his constituency. At the beginning of the biological warfare program the foundation for the secrecy was laid. The following is an example of the extent to which the Army would go to keep the public unaware:

> It was considered that accidents or illness of civilians which even remotely or presumptively might be connected with Camp Detrick [where testing of biological weapons was conducted] would be disastrous because of the resultant publicity. . . . Plans were made for the most extreme contingency that might occur, the disposition of the remains of civilian or military personnel in the event of death caused by a biological warfare agent. In March 1944, the Chief, Chemical Warfare Service, asked the Judge Advocate General of the Army for his opinion as the legal authority to make secret disposition of such remains. It was decreed that by establishing a restricted military area at Camp Detrick, deceased personnel might be placed in a hermetically sealed metal casket and interred by military personnel in the area, without disclosing by certificate, report or statement the nature or cause of death.

Though the CWS had for some time been interested in the application of bacteriological agents in warfare, it wasn't until 1941 that its Medical Division at the Edgewood Arsenal unit prepared for an expanded effort and planned a research program. Representatives from the Office of Scientific Research and Development (OSRD), The surgeon general, the CWS, the Department of Agriculture, the U.S. Public Health Service, and the NAS were convened to form the War Bureau Consultants, and in 1942 informed the secretary of war that biological warfare was indeed feasible. The consultants also recommended that a biological warfare program should be established. On this information President Roosevelt instructed that the War Research Service (WRS) should be created, within the Federal Security Agency, for the purpose of promoting public security and health. Roosevelt had announced a U.S. policy that biological weapons would be used only in retaliation. WRS had as its director George Merck, founder of the pharmaceutical company Merck, Inc. Through

CWS, the WRS contracted with private universities and private research foundations "to determine areas of investigation and special procedures necessary to maintain security, and to provide means of retaliation should the enemy resort to BW."

The War Department was reluctant to allow military agencies to participate in the universities' research, but eventually it became clear that field testing was necessary, and neither the universities nor the WRS was capable of carrying out such projects. Development of the biological warfare program thus came fully under CWS sponsorship. Although the CWS had conducted some biological weapons research at its Edgewood, Maryland, facility since 1941, by November 1943 the CWS had constructed its flagship biological warfare center in Frederick, Maryland, at what is now called Fort Detrick. Three other major facilities also were constructed to take up some aspect of the U.S. biological warfare program—the Vigo Plant, near Terre Haute, Indiana, used primarily for production of biological agents; a field-testing site on Horn Island near Pascagoula, Mississippi; and another site used primarily for field testing in Granite Peak, Utah.

At first the Army surgeon general had a key role in all aspects of biological weapons research, but at some point during the war it came to be seen as only secondarily a medical operation. Perhaps this change reflected the growing strategic importance attributed to biological weeapons. The CWS's official history blandly notes that the surgeon general "felt that it would not be proper or desirable for the Medical Department to accept responsibility for any phase of BW research" and was "thus relieved of responsibility for the technical program." The Special Projects Division of the CWS was created in the summer of 1944. This division took responsibility for coordinating the numerous biological weapons projects that were proceeding in various agencies throughout the country; it operated in "great secrecy, [and] expanded rapidly until its organization numbered almost 3,900."

It would appear that in 1945, testing biological agents for their virulence and affect on human beings was increasingly seen as unacceptable. The potentialities of biological warfare "remained potentialities only, for the agents and munitions that had been

developed could not be tested against human subjects and their
possible effectiveness as an instrument of war could not be confirmed." Nonetheless, the testing of the efficacy of gas masks and
other protective breathing devices was conducted using humans.
In one study a tent would be filled with atomized clouds of agents
three to ten minutes "prior to the entrance of the test subject into
the chamber. Every effort was made to keep the men in the tests
free from contamination prior to exposure to the test cloud." The
agents used were *Bacillus sterrimus*, *Bacillus niger*, *Bacillus globigii*,
and *Serratia marcescens*, common particles that were thought to be
inert and harmless to the men.

## TRAINING OR EXPERIMENTATION?

A conceptual puzzle permeates the history of military medical
research with human subjects, especially when military authorities
are mainly responsible for planning, funding, and executing their
own projects. The puzzle emanates from a seemingly simple question: What counts as a medical experiment in the armed forces?
Surely, any study conducted by or involving physician-researchers,
and motivated by a medical problem facing the military, is a medical experiment. The trouble is that a vast range of activities
undertaken by service personnel subject them to physical or psychological risk. This is, after all, a part of the raison d'être of an
armed force, to take risks that others do not need to take, from a
sense of duty and on pain of violating an order.

Many military endeavors are sufficiently innovative and hazardous to demand supervision by medical authorities; moreover,
they may also require systematic study of their human effects. But
not all of these activities are primarily medical experiments—or at
least are not categorized as such. Their fundamental motivation is
different, like field testing a new weapon or training soldiers to
operate in an unfamiliar battlefield environment. Nevertheless, the
activities clearly have medical implications, such as what is the best
treatment for the injuries that can be expected to arise in connection with new material or tactics. The resultant medical questions

may in turn lead to specific protocols to find answers to them. It is understandable as to why military tacticians not only would be interested in answering questions that arise in this way but also would be acting irresponsibly if they didn't try.

When medical questions are merely adjunct to such operations, the operations are not medical experiments. In that case, do the rules of medical ethics apply? Or do they apply only in part, and if so, how far do they go? And if medical ethics do not apply to certain military ventures, what rules limit the dangers to which military personnel may be exposed, and what is the source of these rules? The Uniform Code of Military Justice requires that combat soldiers accept any and all medical interventions that will get them back onto the field of battle. But does that include experimental drugs? How remote does the chance of benefit have to be for soldiers to be exempt from the treatment requirement?

These questions are among those that will surface repeatedly in this book. But whatever the rules or their source, the commitment to "voluntariness" that appears time and again in the U.S. armed forces from Walter Reed's research to World War II has more than a single meaning. Writing of the mustard gas experiments, the National Academy of Sciences observed that "although the human subjects were called 'volunteers,' it was clear from the official reports that recruitment of the WWII human subjects, as well as many of those in later experiments, was accomplished through lies and half-truths."

I have already observed that "guinea pig" is a term that has had remarkable staying power in popular understandings of medical research, and that, whatever it means, it is surely pejorative, and our young men and women in uniform have frequently been told it does not apply to them. In a Naval Research Laboratory report on the mustard gas chamber tests during World War II, the officers were careful to state: "It has been impressed on the men that they are not 'guinea pigs'. They are told that they are expected to use their heads as well as their bodies; and if they do not understand anything to ask questions, these questions being answered in a simple and non-technical language."

But two paragraphs later we learn that "occasionally there have been individuals or groups who did not cooperate fully. A short explanatory talk, and, if necessary, a slight verbal 'dressing down' has always proven successful. There has not been a single instance in which a man has refused to enter the gas chamber."

One thing is certain: If intellectual brilliance and good intentions were sufficient to prevent the needless human costs of the mustard gas experiments, then they would never have occurred. The nation simply had no better men to lead its medical research effort than Bush and Richards. As leaders, they bore responsibility for the prosecution of the medical research effort, and for its failures, moral as well as scientific. But, in fairness, their ability to assess the limits of wartime human research was itself constrained by a factor that is part and parcel of a war effort: secrecy. For just as openness is the lifeblood of a democracy, secrecy and deception are elements of successful warfare.

Nor did secrecy about human research end with World War II. Its leaders unwilling to be caught unaware again, the United States never fully gave up its martial posture to return to its pre-World War II level of preparedness. Even in 1993, nearly fifty years after the mustard gas experiments, the NAS panel went so far as to suggest that the Pentagon still withheld some of the facts about what took place in America's gas chambers with American GIs. Many of these men accepted the consequences of the undue risks they had been obliged to take with quiet dignity, and without expecting any rewards or recognition, for the rest of their lives.

## MEANWHILE, DOWN UNDER

The Navy's mustard gas experiments seem to have been an exception to the general American reluctance to use its own military personnel for medical studies, a limitation that was also adopted by the British during World War II. The quest for other sources of experimental subjects took many forms, including the U.S. prison malaria project. But at least one of the Allies hit upon an eminently available population for secret malaria experiments: Jewish refugees who sought asylum from German barbarity in Australia. There can hardly be a more sad and ironic story from the twentieth century than this one, which was broken by an Australian newspaper in April 1999 following a lengthy investigation.

Like the American and British forces in the Pacific, Australian troops were hard hit by malaria, aggravated by a shortage of quinine. The Medical Research Unit did its work at two sites, one in Cairns and one in Rocky Creek in Queensland. The human experiments continued even after the Australians and their American counterparts determined that Atabrine was effective, in 1944.

According to the *Sydney Morning Herald*'s investigation, more than 850 men, some recovering from war injuries and some permanently disabled, were engaged in Australian Army malaria studies. Among them were a number of Jewish refugees who arrived on the Dunera in 1940. Though the Jews and Australians enlisted in the Army, they were not allowed to volunteer for active duty "on account of certain physical disabilities," in the words of a secret Australian document. The Army report stated that "several men with one arm, one leg or one eye missing . . . were used."

Unfit for front-line duty, they were assigned to manual labor prior to their role in the experiments, then told that they were needed because Allied soldiers were "dying like flies" from the disease. In order to produce severe infections the doses were high, equivalent to the bites of 13,000 infected mosquitoes in some cases. Some of the men received multiple doses, 35 in one instance. High doses of experimental drug treatments were also tested for toxicity.

Reactions to the infections were often intense, with men shivering so hard their beds vibrated across the floor. They soaked their mattresses with perspiration in the next painful and fevered stage of the disease. Treatment was not always started right away, as the men "were allowed to have overt malaria with high temperatures for several days before therapy was commenced," according to research notes. To simulate blood loss from injuries, up to two pints of blood were also removed, and insulin injections were given to simulate starvation. Adrenaline was given to cause emotional levels similar to those that would be experienced in battle. A few men were chosen for decompression and hypothermia studies. Once again, the medical concerns of combat posed universal problems.

Following U.S. concerns that the project might be shut down, the Australian adjutant-general set quotas of human subjects that each command would have to fill. Subsequently, two drugs produced by American manufacturers, Sontoquine and Chloroquine, were also tested at Cairns. A similar process ensued when the British wanted to test their drug, Paludrine. Paludrine and Chloroquine were later marketed by British and American drug companies.

Did the Australian Army follow the elementary rules of consent that were at least sometimes honored in those days? Though considered volunteers, at least some of the refugees appear to have had difficulty communicating in English. "They never told us anything," said Frank Hogan, one of the surviving volunteers. Another, a Jewish author named Walter Kaufmann who now lives in Berlin, said, "At first I didn't realize it [the experiment] was dangerous. . . . I thought it would be an adventure and that is why I went." Though the mens' memories may have been clouded by the intervening decades, statements like these suggest that little information was provided.

Apart from the strict consent issues, it is chilling to imagine men who narrowly escaped from Nazi Germany being used in medical experiments by the enemies of Nazism. One of them, Fred Eden of Melbourne, recounted his 59-day journey on the crammed Dunera and his internment in a camp in New South Wales. Eden got out of the camp by volunteering for the Army but, as an interned alien, was denied active service and assigned to labor on Melbourne docks and railway yards. Seeking a way out, he signed up for an experiment in which he put his arms into cages full of mosquitoes and was then given Paludrine. "The type of malaria I got, you either lived or died," Eden told the Australian newspaper. "I recovered, but it took months."

Like many of the surviving malaria subjects, Eden has suffered from years of medical problems, but connecting later disease to participation in experiments is often difficult. The men or their surviving family members are now seeking redress from the Australian government. Some of them have filed for medical pensions and have been denied. Army medical records that might support a claim based on their role in the experiments appear to have been lost.

_____

**THREE**

# NUREMBERG'S SHADOW

There was war. In war efforts are all alike. Its sacrifices affect us
all. They were incumbent upon me.

*Karl Brandt, M.D.*

## THE TRIAL

In moral terms, light-years separate the Nazi concentration camp
experiments from America's medical-military research during
World War II. Unlike Hitler's Germany, in the United States
death was not an acceptable endpoint of an experiment, and no
ethnic or political groups were subjected to wholesale butchery in
the course of which some of them might be used in cruel

"research." Still, after the Nazi experience no one could view human experiments conducted by military or state security authorities in the same way. As in so many other respects, World War II caused a loss of innocence about military-medical research.

From late 1946 to the middle of 1947, twenty-three Nazi German officials, twenty of them physicians, were tried for complicity in medical experiments that led to the agonized deaths of thousands of men, women, and children. All military-medical human experiments, and even those that came before the cold war and the Holocaust itself, will forever look different once seen through the lens of the Nazi "doctors' trial."

Although the doctors' trial at Nuremberg was a shock for all medical science, it placed an especially great burden upon military-medical research. After Nuremberg those who would conduct human experiments in the name of national security, including those intending to uphold democratic values in the face of tyranny, were forced to reckon with the grotesqueries committed by the Nazi doctors. Even in America, defense planners wishing to use human subjects have themselves been perpetually on the defensive since Nuremberg.

Some of the Nazi experiments are now so familiar as to have become a part of popular culture. Many have been morbidly fascinated by the notorious Dr. Josef Mengele, who escaped Germany for Brazil, where he lived out his life in hiding. Characters based on Mengele have even appeared in several popular movies. His sadistic experiments, such as those he performed on helpless children, especially twins, were apparently motivated by a wish to achieve an honored place in the history of medical anthropology, in "racial science." But the nonsense of some of Mengele's more infamous efforts, like injecting dye in brown eyes to see if he could turn them blue, is a distraction from a major portion of the abuses of the human beings in the camps—Jews, Gypsies, Poles, Russians, political prisoners, and others. For the bulk of that research was part of a systematic program in support of the Nazi war effort.

The military purpose of many concentration camp experiments becomes clear through the transcripts of the trial itself.

Unfortunately, the forty-eight volumes of the trial record are only available on microfiche at the National Archives and the Holocaust Museum in Washington, D.C. In the spring of 1997 I spent nearly two weeks at the museum reading the trial transcripts. Time and again I had to sit back in my chair, amazed at what I had just read. It wasn't the grim details of the Nazi experiments or their inhumanity that surprised me; shocking and disgusting as they are, I expected them. What surprised me was the effectiveness of the Nazis' defense team in their attempt to turn the proceedings into a trial of the Allies' wartime medical research, as well as that of the Third Reich.

## THE ACCUSED

The doctors' trial was one of thirteen trials in Nuremberg, the first one being that of the major political and military figures of the Third Reich. Seven of the accused in "the Medical Case" were hanged for their crimes, eight were given lengthy prison terms, and the rest were acquitted. The stories of three of the accused serve both as an entry way to the story of Nazi experiments and a window into the drama of the trials.

One of those executed was Karl Brandt, M.D., Reich Commissioner for Health and Sanitation, Hitler's personal physician, and a major-general in the *Schutzstaffel*, the dreaded SS. An architect of the Nazi killing industry that began with the so-called euthanasia program of the disabled, Brandt was interested in racial theory and liked to discuss the finer points of Nazi biological policies. He enjoyed a wildly successful career, having the Führer's ear and considerable influence over the health system of all of Germany by the time he was in his mid-30s. Brandt's close ties to Hitler—who considered Brandt nearly an adopted son—combined with his chilly relationship with other Nazi leaders and his ambiguous relationship to war crimes made his case the most controversial of the Nazi doctors.

As Hitler's representative on medical affairs, Brandt was the primary administrator of the German health care system and

Hitler's main advisor on questions of medical science. Trained as a surgeon, Brandt frequently was confronted with Hitler's odd views about medicine, and more than once he had to disabuse the Führer from some form of quackery. Brandt was an architect of the early euthanasia, or T4, program, which started with the killing of the severely handicapped and led to the extermination of many mental patients and disabled children. In the distorted moral universe of the Nazi philosophy, Brandt was considered an idealist, because he favored the use of active euthanasia as an ethical intervention to end the lives of those "unworthy of life."

Another who was executed at Nuremberg was Karl Gebhardt, M.D., Heinrich Himmler's personal physician and boyhood friend, president of the German Red Cross, and chief surgeon and clinician of the SS. Gebhardt was an authority on sports and accident medicine and was the chief physician at the 1936 Berlin Olympics, intended to showcase Aryan athletic prowess. He had many prominent patients before the war, including the king of Belgium. A full professor in Berlin's medical school, Gebhardt conducted experiments on concentration camp inmates to test the new sulfa drugs. This required the creation of injuries that resembled those that might be acquired on the battlefield, and the instigation of infections like gangrene to test treatment with sulfanilamide.

Gebhardt took pride in his intellectual abilities. He had contempt for the leaders of the Nazi revolution, pointing out to his Nuremberg interrogator that Hitler, Hess, and Himmler had no profession. Their enthusiasm for medical science was mostly grounded in mysticism or in popular folklore about natural healing and alternative drugs. Yet Gebhardt and his well-connected colleagues were prepared to exploit their political superiors' great expectations for rapid experimental results using "research material" normally forbidden to scientists—otherwise healthy human beings.

A third defendant at Nuremberg was Siegfried Ruff, M.D., director of the Department of Aviation Medicine at the German Experimental Institute for Aviation. Ruff was an authority on what we would today call "human factors" research in airplane accidents. He had a key role in arranging a series of concentration camp experiments on low atmospheric pressure, but, for reasons I will examine later, was among those who was acquitted at Nuremberg. Legally exonerated, Ruff went on to a distinguished career in postwar Germany. Together, the cases of Brandt, Gebhardt, and Ruff exemplify the challenge that confronted the Nuremberg judges.

## NO MERE MURDER TRIAL

The prosecutors of the Nazi doctors were at pains to impress upon the court the special immorality of the crimes at issue in the case. The brief against the defendants was delivered on December 9, 1946, by chief prosecutor Telford Taylor. In his opening statement, Taylor declared that these men were on trial for "murders, tortures, and other atrocities committed in the name of medical science. . . . The defendants in the dock are charged with murder, but," Taylor stressed, "this is no mere murder trial." That these crimes were committed by doctors in what was supposed to be a medical context set them apart as especially heinous offenses.

Although the doctors directly involved in human experiments were those relative few with close connections to the Nazi hierarchy, their attitudes were not all that dissimilar to the German medical profession in general. The Nuremberg defendants represented hundreds of doctors who were involved in concentration camp experiments and hundreds more who were responsible for "selections" of those who were to be immediately exterminated, conscripted into forced labor, or exploited as human guinea pigs.

While the question of the "collective guilt" of the medical profession in Nazi Germany might be debatable, there is no question that the actual Nuremberg defendants were but a small portion of those who could have been tried. About three hundred fifty doctors were interrogated by the Nuremberg investigation team. Practical considerations limited the number of those whom the prosecutors chose to indict. One of these considerations was the

size of the defendants' dock, which was built to hold a maximum
of twenty-four chairs.

Even though "only" a few hundred doctors might have been
directly responsible for death and torture in Nazi Germany, they
were the products of a racist medical culture. Doctors had a central role in Nazi ideology, one that Hitler made clear in his mani-
festo, *Mein Kampf,* written years before he took power while
imprisoned for subversive activities. Doctors were considered in
Nazi philosophy to have a special place in improving the purity of
the *Volk*, the people. Much as bacteria cause disease in an individual, Jews, Gypsies, homosexuals, the mentally retarded, the physically disabled, and others were seen as corrupting the German
national body. Since Germany was said to be infected with crea-
tures that represented a public health menace, there was obviously
much work for the medical profession. For who else was qualified
to "diagnose" and "treat" disease?

Germany's doctors were hardly forced to comply with the role
Hitler envisioned for them. Instead, prominent physicians and
medical scientists were among the first to embrace his vision, and
they even helped to bring it about. Like popular biological theory
elsewhere in the world, especially the United States, eugenics was
a powerful force in German medical science. Eliminating the unfit
by discouraging their reproduction was virtually a social obligation to eugenicists; the Nazis' more aggressive approach to the
problem, applying "mercy killing" to the impaired, was welcomed
as a biologically sophisticated form of statecraft.

Not only theoretical but also commercial factors attracted
German physicians to the Nazis. In the early 1930s Jews were dis-
proportionately represented in medicine, both in academic chairs
and in private practices. Like most other Germans in the desperately depressed Weimar economy, doctors were underemployed.
The purging of Jews from medical schools and the medical profession meant higher incomes and prestigious positions for young
German doctors who came to owe their enhanced status to the
Third Reich. Appreciating the hand that fed them, nearly half of
German physicians joined the Nazi party, a higher proportion
than any other profession.

Those harboring ambitions to be pioneering scientists of "racial hygiene" might also, with the right connections and a strong stomach, have access to human experimental material beyond the wildest dreams of their colleagues in ordinary times. Those who could be made available for experiments by high authorities were slated to die anyway. And there was a war on; everyone had to make sacrifices, so why should criminals, like Jews who were said to have fornicated with German women, or Polish political prisoners, or members of other "inferior" races like Gypsies, be any different? As Reichsführer Himmler himself expressed it in a response to complaints that concentration camp experiments were being slowed by critics, "I regard these people as high national traitors who, still today, reject these experiments on humans and would instead let sturdy German soldiers die as a result of these cooling methods." By no means could the flower of German youth be guinea pigs, a duty that was reserved for others.

## THE INDICTMENTS

There were four indictments against the twenty-three Nazi doctors: conspiracy, war crimes, crimes against humanity, and membership in criminal organizations. The distinction between crimes against humanity and war crimes is important. Crimes against humanity were undertaken in the reckless pursuit of scientific knowledge or from sheer sadism, but war crimes were acts intended to aid the Nazi military. In this indictment we begin to see the close relationship between the Third Reich's military aims and concentration camp medical experiments.

One could recite a litany of medical experiments aimed at battlefield medical problems: typhus, phosphorous burns, bone and muscle grafts, the use of new drugs to treat infections, sterilization techniques, and others. In most of these no amnesty was granted those who survived their torments; usually they were summarily exterminated so that there would be no witnesses. Several of the experiments in the war crimes indictment were specifically aimed at providing medical breakthroughs that could benefit Luftwaffe pilots: high-altitude rescue experiments, experiments with sustained low temperatures (hypothermia), and experiments in making seawater potable. These experiments provide a good example of the military connection.

Survival at high altitude was a concern because British fighter planes were able to operate at higher ceilings than German aircraft. In addition, the Luftwaffe had taken heavy losses from British anti-aircraft guns, and often the Germans had little experience protecting men who had to bail out at high altitudes. The best way to rewarm victims of freezing (called *hypothermia* in medical science) was another concern. Many flyers who were downed subsequently froze to death in the North Sea. Those who survived to this point had only saltwater to drink until they could be rescued, raising the question whether there was some way of treating seawater to make it potable under combat conditions.

Among top Nazi leaders, Himmler was most energetic in pursuing the possible contributions of medicine to the Nazi war effort and especially to the Luftwaffe. He took a special interest in the work of a friend of his, Sigmund Rascher, a young doctor from a medical family. Rascher's connection to Himmler was Rascher's wife, Nini, some years his senior, who was a popular concert singer and may have been a former lover of Himmler. Nini Rascher seems to have had a penchant for handbags made from human skin, stretched and treated like leather. Frequently she was the one to correspond with Himmler and importuned him on her husband's behalf.

Himmler gave Rascher permission to use human guinea pigs at the Dachau concentration camp. The twin sources of Himmler's enthusiasm seem to have been the practical implications for the war effort of Rascher's researches, and his delight in pleasing Hitler with his own clever initiatives. Hitler was known to be dissatisfied with the performance of German medicine in reducing casualties at the front. According to Brandt, Hitler often said that "[the] criminals [referring to concentration camp inmates] are also here to serve their fatherland."

In fact, Rascher himself was a convenient front man for Erich Hippke, chief Luftwaffe surgeon. The American investigators of the Nazi medical atrocities later concluded that Hippke was the source of the idea for the experiments Rascher carried out, and he and those who reported to him kept careful track of the results. In the intensely politicized world of Nazi Germany, Hippke was quick to exploit Rascher's personal connections to Himmler.

Rascher started in 1942 by experimenting on conditions encountered at high altitude. In his original request to Himmler he suggested that "two or three professional criminals" might be made available, or perhaps feebleminded persons who would anyway be subject to euthanasia. Ultimately several categories of prisoner were victimized by Rascher's experiments, including political prisoners. As the doctors' trial prosecution showed, in spite of frequent reference to "criminals" to justify the experiments, true offenders in Nazi Germany were not incarcerated in concentration camps but in an independent prison system.

Through Hippke, Rascher obtained a decompression chamber from the Luftwaffe's Aviation Institute that itself caused deaths by air being pumped out of the sealed compartment, or that led to death after a session inside when the victims were dissected to study their lungs while still alive. Around one hundred people died this way. Again at Hippke's suggestion, Rascher then moved on to freezing studies that involved about three hundred prisoners. Experimenting with various rewarming techniques, Rascher engaged in a particularly perverse bit of sadism by surrounding some of his male victims with nude female inmates. Rascher took great interest in recording the fact that not only did some respond well to this maneuver but one actually began to copulate when he regained a measure of consciousness. Puritanical Nazi officials, including even Hippke, who originally proposed the "animal warmth" hypothesis, were shocked by Rascher's account of the incident. Rascher's enthusiasm for abusing human beings was hard to control, however, even by his own benefactor, and he was shot in 1944 by Himmler's men for having kidnapped babies.

Rascher was perhaps more colorful in his sadism than most of the Nazi experimenters but he was by no means unique. Oskar Schroder, M.D., chief of the Luftwaffe's Medical Service, was instrumental in the seawater experiments. In 1944 he asked

Himmler for permission to use "forty healthy persons full time for four weeks" chosen from among prisoners at Dachau, which "has the necessary laboratories." With Himmler's personal approval, forty to sixty Gypsies were starved and given only saltwater to drink. The resulting thirst was so intense, said witnesses, that many tried to drink the dirty water used in mopping the floors. Schroder was one of the defendants sentenced to life at Nuremberg, later commuted to fifteen years in prison.

It would be comforting to assume that the brutality of the experiments could only be tolerated by a handful of pathological personalities. In fact, though, extremists like Rascher were but convenient instruments for an extensive medical-military bureaucracy. For example, when the results of the freezing experiments seemed especially promising, a conference was held on October 26 and 27, 1942, in Nuremberg. Entitled "Medical Problems Arising from Distress at Sea and Winter Hardships," the meeting was attended by ninety-five physicians and biological scientists. The minutes of the conference emphasized that "it has now been possible to conduct a series of investigations of human beings who were rescued after having been in cold water for a long time." Care was taken not to mention the circumstances under which this new possibility arose.

One of the most active participants in the Nuremberg conference was Hubertus Strughold, M.D., friend and colleague of Siegfried Ruff in the Department of Aviation Medicine at the German Experimental Institute for Aviation in Berlin. Like Ruff, Strughold was also one of the world authorities on the effects of flight on the human body. After the war, while Ruff was successfully beating the indictment at the doctors' trial, Strughold was doing even better. As a pampered guest of the U.S. Army, Strughold became one of the first recruits in a top-secret project code-named Operation Paper Clip. Strughold's lucky star followed him throughout his long career under Army protection and into his key role in the manned space program. One of the more dispiriting episodes in America's cold war history, Operation Paper Clip, and Professor Strughold, will be revisited in a later chapter.

## BUILDING THE DEFENSE

Each of the Nazis was granted the right to retain his own lawyer. Karl Brandt's counsel was the distinguished jurist Robert Servatius of Cologne. Servatius had represented Fritz Sauckel in the major Nuremberg trial of Nazi political leaders a few months before the doctors' trial. Sauckel was responsible for the mass enslavement of foreign workers in the Nazi empire, mostly from Russia. Hundreds of thousands of these men and women died of starvation and disease. Servatius erred in Sauckel's defense by trying to portray him as misunderstood, in spite of Sauckel's obvious evasions on the witness stand. Sauckel was eventually executed. His first Nuremberg defense having been unsuccessful, Servatius had another chance with Karl Brandt. Servatius's defense of Brandt is emblematic of the themes that repeated themselves through all the defendants' arguments.

Servatius built his case on "natural law," which holds that legal reasoning and legal standards must be consistent with true descriptions of the world. Idealism is a fine thing, according to the pure natural lawyer, but it has no role in the law. In the vernacular, we would say that Servatius was a "realist." For instance, the idea that only "volunteers" should be used in experiments is admirable, but can anyone ever be said to be a fully informed volunteer? "On the contrary," wrote Servatius in his closing brief for Brandt,

> one can say that *all prisoners* are living *under* a certain compulsion. They expect from their participation in the experiment an improvement of their position or fear a worsening in case of refusal. Even though the regulations about the treatment of prisoners may be fixed, practically there remains in this particular world a very wide space for the punishment of prisoners with measures, which according to experience may hit the prisoner much more severely and more grievously than the sentence of the judge itself. [emphasis in the original]

In the final analysis, Servatius argued, "voluntariness is a fiction, the emergence of the State hard reality." As we will see, Servatius built his case for Brandt on precisely this formula.

## THE SEARCH FOR MEDICAL ETHICS

All of the defense lawyers tried to show that their clients were either not personally culpable for the experiments or in some cases were not even aware of them. Two more general themes also characterized their cases: there was no international consensus in the medical profession on the rules of human use, and in any case in war medical ethics could justifiably be suspended, as was allegedly true in the United States. Of course, even one of these two propositions would contribute greatly to excusing all the defendants' actions.

In response, the prosecution team tried to prove that the Nazi experiments were unacceptable by Germany's own standards, referring to a 1931 circular from the Ministry of the Interior. As so often happens, a scandal led to a 1931 attempt to reform medical ethics several years before the Nazis took power. In 1930, a Jewish doctor named Julius Moses reported that seventy-five children had died in Lübeck as a result of pediatricians' experimenting with tuberculosis vaccine. The German press was already highly critical of the powerful chemical manufacturers for using hospitals to test their new products. The scandal in Lübeck gave flesh to the accusations that people were being exploited for potential profits.

It happened that Moses was also a member of the German Parliament from the Social Democratic Party. In 1931 he played a key role in pressuring the Interior Ministry to respond to the Lübeck scandal. The resulting rules were far more comprehensive and sophisticated than anything introduced by any government until then. They included a requirement for consent from informed human subjects. Like so much progressive government in the ill-fated Weimar Republic, these regulations were trampled by Hitler's regime, and the defense lawyers at Nuremberg were able to call their legal status into question because they were not cited by international organizations monitoring health law in the 1930s.

Did the Nazi doctors cross a clear, sharp line that was well recognized in medicine throughout the civilized world, one that was universal and unequivocal? The prosecution was unable to rely on the 1931 rules or other documents that preceded the Third Reich; later it was shaken by the facts of America's own wartime research. The prosecution team thus came to rely heavily on its expert witnesses to make the case that clear research rules were broken by the Nazis, rules that were not violated by those who conquered them.

To help make its war crimes indictment stick, the prosecution wanted to prove that the concentration camp experiments were unjustifiable according to established rules of medical ethics. In response, the defense lawyers wanted to show that American experimentalists were doing much the same thing. Two prominent doctors, one American and one German, were called upon by the prosecution to provide expert testimony on the acceptable use of human subjects in experiments. The two were a study in contrasts.

Werner Leibbrand was a physician and historian of medicine who was persecuted by the Nazis during the war due to his racial background. He was the sort of idealist Servatius might have had on his mind when outlining his defense of Brandt. Leibbrand believed that ethical principles were absolute and reached down to the twentieth century from at least the time of Hippocrates, several centuries B.C., and that no political, scientific, or social conditions made any difference in ethical requirements.

The American expert on medical ethics was Andrew Ivy of the University of Illinois medical school, appointed by the American Medical Association as its representative. Though he agreed with Leibbrand that the Nazis had violated medical ethics, he claimed to base his conclusion on the reality of experimental ethics. Also unlike the German, Ivy was a very shrewd witness who was prepared to stretch the truth on the stand and manipulate public opinion at home.

Andrew Ivy was truly an American original. He grew up in Cape Girardeau, Missouri, where his father was a chemistry professor at the State Normal School and his mother a biology teacher. A superb musician and excellent debater, the young Ivy was also a fine athlete who excelled in every sport he tried and was offered a contract to play baseball by a St. Louis Cardinals farm team. Trained in medicine and physiology in Chicago, Ivy taught for many years at Northwestern University before accepting a vice presidency at the University of Illinois, where he was responsible for the schools of medicine, dentistry, and pharmacy. Not only was Ivy a tremendously productive scholar and a very busy teacher, by the end of the war he was probably also the most famous doctor in the country. Ivy was skilled at interpreting medical issues for the lay public. He was the prototype of today's media medical expert.

Ivy himself later experienced the collapse of his professional reputation because he supported a quack cancer cure called Krebiozen, a position he maintained despite being held up to public ridicule, until his death in 1978. In 1966 a *Life* magazine story asked "Whatever Happened to Dr. Ivy?," recounting the story of this once-famous doctor's strange obsession. But in 1947 Ivy was the right man in the right place to give the Nuremberg prosecution what it needed, someone willing to resort to extreme measures to convict the Nazis. He was also prepared to do what was needed to protect American medical research from a Nazi taint. As we shall see, because Leibbrand's idealism did not fit the facts, it fell to this brilliant but strange and complex man, Ivy, to make the case against the Nazi doctors.

## TROUBLE FOR THE PROSECUTION

In his cross-examination of Leibbrand and Ivy, Servatius focused on human research practices in the United States and elsewhere before, during, and even after the war. Among the most spectacular was the use of 800 prisoners in a malaria experiment, the one sponsored by the Committee on Medical Research, which had been the subject of a several page photo spread in *Life Magazine* for June 1945. The subjects were prisoners at the U.S. Penitentiary in Atlanta, the New Jersey State Reformatory, and the Illinois State Penitentiary. The defense's use of this case was to be of major concern to Andrew Ivy, who hailed from Illinois.

Another embarrassment for the prosecution came from the British side. Shortly before the trial the British occupational forces in the North Rhine region requested that a British researcher be informed of the birth of all infants with a meningomyelocele (a birth defect also known as spina bifida). Working for the British Medical Research Council, Professor R. A. McCance was said to have wished "to make some tests on these children, which will not in their experience do them any harm, but which they do not feel quite justified in carrying out on perfectly healthy children." Ten years before, in 1936, Professor McCance had published a study on human salt deficiency using human subjects with the observation that "in any case man is the best experimental animal to use in this type of research, so I decided to employ him."

Servatius also noted poison experiments conducted on eleven condemned prisoners in Manila, cholera and plague experiments on children, and other questionable research with human beings. But it was the CMR-sponsored malaria experiment recounted in *Life* magazine that gave Servatius an opening he could exploit in dealing with the prosecution's experts. In his January 1947 questioning of the idealistic Leibbrand, Servatius set a trap that created much work for the prosecution.

SERVATIUS: Witness, are you of the opinion that a prisoner who had over ten years' sentence to serve will give his approval to an experiment if he receives no advantages there from? Do you consider such approval voluntary?

LEIBBRAND: No. According to medical ethics this is not the case. The patient or inmate [is] basically brought into a forcible situation by being arrested. . . .

SERVATIUS: Are you of the opinion that eight hundred prisoners under arrest at various places who give their approval for an experiment at the same time do so voluntarily?

LEIBBRAND: No.

SERVATIUS: You do not distinguish as to whether the experiments involve permanent damage . . . or whether it is temporary?

LEIBBRAND: No . . .

SERVATIUS: If such prisoners are infected with malaria because they have declared themselves willing do you consider that . . . admissible?

LEIBBRAND: No, because I do not consider such a declaration of willingness right from a point of view of medical ethics. As prisoners they were already in a forced situation.

Servatius then read the entire *Life* magazine article into the record. He was ready to spring his trap.

SERVATIUS: Now will you please express your opinion on the admissibility of these experiments?

LEIBBRAND: On principle, I cannot deviate from my view mentioned before on a medical, ethical basis. I am of the opinion that even such experiments are excesses and outgrowths of biological thinking.

By "biological thinking," Leibbrand meant experiments in which doctors treat human beings as mere objects, their well being of no account. Servatius had succeeded in getting one of the prosecution's expert ethics witnesses to assert that what the American doctors had done in the malaria experiments was in the same category of unethical behavior as what the Nazi doctors had done. Leibbrand's uncompromising idealism did not allow him to consider mitigating factors of decisive importance, such as the fact that the American prisoners' situation was quite different from that of concentration camp inmates, who were doomed by their nationality or political or religious beliefs. For him, coercion was coercion.

Fortunately for the prosecution, they had another expert witness who was prepared to say whatever was needed to ensure that the actions of the Nazi experimenters would be viewed as isolated and not a reflection of medical science in general. Ivy's determination even led him to perjure himself on the witness stand, a perjury that proved crucial to a prosecution that was nearly bungled. Credit for piecing together the puzzle of Ivy's role goes to a young historian of medicine, Jon Harkness. In his 1996 doctoral dissertation for the University of Wisconsin, Harkness presents evidence that Ivy was in the courtroom that January day of Leibbrand's testimony, and heard Servatius paint him in a corner about the malaria experiments. Six months later, when Servatius confronted Ivy with the malaria experiments he found a witness who could match him in cunning. Did all these eight hundred prisoners volunteer for exposure to a deadly disease out of patriotism?, Servatius asked.

IVY: I believe that is entirely reasonable, because an individual is a prisoner in a penitentiary is no reason why he should not be patriotic or love his country.

SERVATIUS: Perhaps you will admit that no one would give that as his motive for helping before a German denazification court, namely, that he wanted to help the army.

IVY: I did not get the question. Will you please repeat it?

SERVATIUS: Never mind. Now, witness, of the experiment we have here there were none of those volunteered who were outside the penitentiary, now, why did not persons outside the penitentiary volunteer: business men or such in the malaria experiment, for example? Because we must assume that not only inmates of penitentiary have ideals.

IVY: As I explained yesterday, conscientious objectors were used, and also prisoners were used instead of teachers and business men because these individuals had no other duties to perform. Their time was fully available for purposes of experimentation.

Moments later, Servatius pushed Ivy to admit that the prisoners were not true volunteers because of certain irresistible inducements.

SERVATIUS: If one declares one's self to be a volunteer, must one not weight the advantages against the disadvantages?

IVY: I believe so.

SERVATIUS: The disadvantage here is the risk of a serious disease, the advantage is fifty or a hundred dollars.

IVY: I should say the advantage is being able to serve for the good of humanity.

SERVATIUS: For what reason was the money not paid immediately—but in two payments? So far as I remember from a document yesterday, the hundred dollars was paid as follows: Fifty dollars after the first month, and the other fifty after one year. In other words, a prisoner has to do his job first. Now, why was that so?

IVY: I presume that that is just the common way of doing business in the United States when an agreement is involved. I presume the lawyers had something to do with that.

SERVATIUS: Was the reason not this: that the prisoner would lose his enthusiasm for the experiment and would cease to cooperate? Could that have been the reason for being a little circumspect in the payment?

IVY: I doubt that.

Ivy's stonewalling on the question of appropriate incentives for prisoners in research did not change the fact that there was and is a problem with paying people to be in research. Thirty years later the United States finally all but prohibited prison experiments because of doubts about how voluntariness could be guaranteed in such a setting, especially at a time when minorities were disproportionately represented in the inmate population. But from the prosecution's point of view all that mattered about Ivy's testimony was that his unwaivering testimony that the Nazi experiments were unethical by the medical profession's universal standards supported the prosecutor's case, which was badly needed at that point.

In retrospect, the prosecution's decision to pursue the medical ethics line is questionable. Had these military lawyers known how muddy the reality of experimental ethics was at that time, they might well have adopted a different strategy. As for the defense, compelling as its counterexamples might seem, they distracted from an inconvenient fact that set the Nazi experiments apart: They took place in the context of a mass killing machine. In that context, the death of the subjects, either as a result of the experiments or once they had been returned to the concentration camp barracks, was an acceptable endpoint to the Nazi doctors. It was also true that those who "participated" in the experiments were selected by virtue of their racial or political background. Those of Aryan appearance were carefully excluded. The peculiar depravity surrounding the concentration camp experiments, and not the experimental procedures or maneuvers themselves, truly set them apart. The camp experiments took place in a depraved universe, compared to which subtle moral questions such as "When does an incentive become coercive?" are pathetically academic. Ivy may have stonewalled, but in any event the exchange missed the point.

## THE WARTIME DEFENSE

The other line of defense, that the concentration camp experiments were justified by wartime conditions, also contained landmines for the prosecution. It was a fact that during the Third Reich the exigencies of war easily overcame any actual moral objections to the human experiments. Those who were accused of opposing the experiments reacted as though they were victims of slander. When it was suspected that the Chief of the Luftwaffe's Medical Service, Professor Erich Hippke, had ethical reservations about the freezing research, the accused protested to his superior that he "immediately agreed to the experiments" when Rascher proposed them, "because our own previous experiments on large animals were concluded and supplementary work was necessary. It is also highly improbable," Hippke added, perhaps protesting too much, "that I, in that I am responsible for the development of all types of possibilities for rescuing our flier[s] would not do everything possible to further such works." Any blame for obstacles placed in Rascher's way, Hippke averred, had to do with the usual professional jealousies of those who would like to have achieved important results themselves.

Rudolf Brandt, Himmler's craven personal assistant (and no relation to Karl), explained that concentration camp inmates were used because "volunteers could not very well be expected, as the experiments could be fatal under [the] circumstances." Rudolf Brandt was one of the nonphysicians executed for his role in arranging supplies of victims for the camp experiments. Those who were acquitted at the doctors' trial, like Siegfried Ruff of the Experimental Institute for Aviation's medical department, harbored the same views. Ruff told the court: "Personally I would not consider these experiments as immoral especially in wartime."

But no statement of the wartime defense was superior to that of Karl Brandt. Under cross-examination about using involuntary subjects in an experiment deemed to be of military necessity, Brandt replied:

> In this case I am of the opinion that, when considering the circumstances of the situation of the war, this state institution which has laid down the importance in the interest of the state at the same time takes the responsibility away from the physician if such an experiment ends fatally and such a responsibility has to be taken by the state.

It seems that Brandt had carefully coordinated his reply with his lawyer. In his closing plea for his client, Servatius also located responsibility with the state: "One can condemn the defendant Karl Brandt only by imposing on him the duty of revolution, and the duty of having a different ideology from his environment." On the contrary, Servatius argued, the ultimate responsibility for decisions involving the use of individuals to meet wartime goals must reside with the state, not with any particular officer, and certainly not one in a relatively inferior position to the leaders of the regime.

On its face, Servatius's strategy seems powerful. How could anyone deny the hard truth that individual moral commitments, or moral ideals themselves, must whither before the power of the state? But there were both practical and philosophical problems with this argument. First, the idea that no one could avoid state service is presented as a false dichotomy, for in fact the choice was not so simple as either obedience or fomenting "revolution." There were various ways to avoid duty in the concentration camps, even for physicians, and at least some appear to have pursued those alternatives.

Second, Servatius proposed to lay moral responsibility wholly at the doorstep of the "State." While this may look like hard-headed realism, consistent with Servatius's natural-law philosophy, it is important not to be taken in by his conceptual sleight of hand. For in playing moral idealism off against the idea of the state, Servatius simply traded off one abstraction for another. Obviously the state, as an abstract entity, cannot take moral responsibility in the same sense that an individual or a number of individuals can. To suppose that the state can be a moral agent is to adopt the philosophy of G. W. F. Hegel, the great nineteenth-century German philosopher, who thought of the state as virtually a "person" with its own destiny. Why is the state any more real than the idea of voluntariness? Both are abstractions, imperfectly realized by concrete human actions.

What Servatius was really arguing, dressed up in fancier language, is that the defendants were forced to do the state's bidding by powerful government officials. But as the prosecution pointed out, the defendants' zeal in performing sadistic experiments belied the notion that they were being forced to act.

Finally, Servatius's radically naturalistic legal philosophy reduces the law to a mere codification of the preferences of whatever group happens to be able to force its will at the time. There may indeed be something called "law" in the state of nature, but it is hardly necessary since there is no need for the powerful to appeal to it, and there is no satisfaction to be gained from it by anyone else. What Servatius's view leaves behind is any role for a principle of justice in the law, any sense of decency or fairness. Once again, brute force is the only reality.

In response, the prosecution mainly stuck to a pragmatic approach, arguing simply that "the use of involuntary subjects in a medical experiment is a crime and, if it results in death, it is the crime of murder." The doctor has the responsibility to assure himself that the subject is a volunteer who understands the nature and hazards of the experiment. No allowance or exception was permissible, according to the prosecution, for reasons of national security. While the doctrine of superior orders could mitigate a soldier's guilt in the heat of battle, it could not apply to one far from the heat of battle and with ample time to reflect on his actions.

The prosecution's pragmatic response still had to reckon with some uncomfortable facts about the Allies' own military-medical experiments. Once again, Andrew Ivy did not hesitate to provide the Nuremberg court with a succinct rebuttal of the wartime defense, when he told the court: "There is no state or politician under the sun who could force me to perform a medical experiment which I thought was morally unjustified." Here was another example of Ivy's careful phraseology, for a large part of the defendants' case was that they did *not* find their conduct morally unjustified because of the extreme requirements of war. Taking his statement at face value, however, it appeared that Ivy was denying that respectable doctors would be complicit in questionable experiments, whether under state auspices or for the advancement of science itself.

Again, Ivy's statement did not fit well with historical facts, providing Servatius with another opening. "In all countries experiments on human beings have been performed by doctors," said Servatius in his closing argument, "certainly not because they took pleasure in killing or tormenting, but only at the instigation and under the protection of their state and borne by their own conviction of the necessity in the struggle for the existence of the people."

Decisive in the Nazis' case, however, was the extreme disregard of the subjects' well-being, founded on deep-seated racism, that went far beyond the other cases of medicine in the state's service. Still more damning is the fact that the instigation of many of the experiments, and certainly their enthusiastic pursuit, had little to do with state orders and more to do with the availability of human guinea pigs. The Nazi experiments had as much to do with the pursuit of medical science run wild as with the cause of military superiority. Once the Nazi doctors had access to their victims, even superiors found those doctors hard to restrain.

## BIRTH OF AN ETHICS CODE

Andrew Ivy was shrewd enough to recognize the implications of the defense strategy. Above all, he was concerned that American science be protected from any taint of similarity with the concentration camp experiments. Even before he left the United States for Germany in January 1947, Ivy penned a set of principles to govern research ethics that he presented to the American Medical Association. These statements were lifted from his document word for word by the Nuremberg judges as part of the ethical guidelines included in their decision, the famous Nuremberg Code. Ivy's rules included uncoerced consent, previous experimental work that justified the new research, and the avoidance of needless risk.

But Ivy's craftiness went well beyond even his anticipation that it would be important to be able to testify about an American ethics code. One of the prosecutors, Alexander G. Hardy, kept his key ethics expert, Ivy himself, on the witness stand for three days. Emphasizing Ivy's just-penned ethics rules, Hardy wanted to present them as typically followed in actual practice.

HARDY: Now, [do the rules you have written] purport to be the principles upon which all physicians and scientists guide themselves before they resort to experimentation on human beings in the United States?

IVY: Yes, they represent the basic principles approved by the American Medical Association for the use of human beings as subjects in medical experiments.

Later, Siegfried Ruff's lawyer, Fritz Sauter, cross-examined Ivy. Sauter picked up on the fact that Ivy's rules were of very recent, perhaps even suspicious, vintage.

SAUTER: You told us that . . . an association had made a compila-
tion regarding the ethics of medical experiments on human
beings. . . . Can you recall what I am referring to?

IVY: Yes.

SAUTER: That was in December 1946, I believe.

IVY: Yes, I remember. . . .

SAUTER: Did that take place in consideration of this trial?

IVY: Well, that took place as a result of my relations to this trial, yes.

SAUTER: Before December 1946 were such instructions in printed
form in existence in America?

IVY: No. They were understood only as a matter of common
practice.

Ivy could hardly deny when his rules were written, and he
would have looked foolish if he had claimed that the coming trials
had nothing do with his decision to record them. But he had the
presence of mind to assert that his ethical guidelines were commonly understood anyway, knowing full well that it would be virtually impossible to disprove (or to prove) such a statement.

Yet Ivy appreciated that his mere assertion that there were well
established ethics rules would look hollow in light of the malaria
studies featured in *Life* magazine. Not only was the ethics issue
just his word against the Nazi defendants, there was the rest of
medical research to protect. Ivy dealt with this problem with a
brilliant and typically audacious plan, one that the medical historian Jon Harkness has pieced together. After hearing Leibbrand's
criticism of the prison malaria experiments in January, Ivy contacted Illinois Governor Dwight H. Green and urged him to
appoint a panel to investigate the ethics of the wartime malaria
project, since it took place at Stateville Prison. Conveniently, the
governor named Ivy as the chairman, and Ivy began to recruit several prominent members for his committee.

That was in March 1947. The Green Committee had not yet
met when Ivy returned to Nuremberg in mid-June, near the end

of the trial. Nevertheless, in his eagerness to blunt the damaging testimony of the well meaning Leibbrand, Ivy flirted with perjury in June by implying that the committee had already reached its conclusions. After praising America's World War II prison research, Ivy told the court that he was "chairman of the committee appointed by Governor Green in the State of Illinois to consider the ethical conditions under which prisoners and penitentiaries may be used ethically as subjects in the medical experiments." Ivy then read into the record the text of the contract signed by the experimental subjects. A listener could be forgiven the impression that Ivy and his committee had closely examined the Stateville research, but his rejoinder to Leibbrand certainly sounded as though the matter had been carefully studied over an extended period. Leibbrand was simply wrong, Ivy argued, in his assumption "that prisoners cannot be motivated to take part in medical experiments by humanitarian incentives. This is contrary to our [American] experience."

Since the Green Committee as yet existed only on paper—a fact not generally appreciated in the courtroom—Ivy, when he was cross-examined by Servatius, again had to express himself carefully. Though permitting listeners to assume what they liked about the committee's progress, Ivy framed his answers in personal terms. Meanwhile, Servatius pursued his line of questioning in the dark, his only information about the Green Committee that which Ivy himself could provide. Another game of cat and mouse ensued.

SERVATIUS: In your commission you probably debated how the volunteers should be contacted; is that not so?

IVY: Yes. [Here Ivy simply perjured himself. As the committee had not met it could not have discussed anything!]

SERVATIUS: On this occasion was there not discussions of the question that you should assure yourself that no coercion was being exercised, or that the particular situation to which the person found himself who applied was being exploited?

IVY: Yes, I was concerned about that question.

SERVATIUS: There were discussions about that?

IVY: Not necessarily with others, but there was always consideration of that in my own mind.

Who were the "others" to whom Servatius must have thought
Ivy was referring? Perhaps he and other listeners assumed that Ivy
was here describing a committee that kept its deliberations to
itself. Knowing the facts, though, it is clear that Ivy was using cre-
ative language in answering Servatius's opening question: Yes
there were discussions about the coercion problem, but they took
place in "my own mind." Indeed, there were no other committee
members in the room with whom to discuss it!

Then, under further probing from Servatius, Ivy pushed the
edge of candor still further.

SERVATIUS: May I ask when this committee was formed?

IVY: The formation of this committee, according to the best of my
recollection, occurred in December 1946. . . .

SERVATIUS: . . . Did the formation of this committee have anything
to do with the fact that this trial is going on . . . ?

IVY: There is no connection between the action of this committee
and this trial.

Not content with this distortion, Ivy even went so far as to read
Servatius the "conclusions" of his yet-to-meet committee. These
included the statement that prisoners should not be given an
"excessive reward" for experimental participation, which "would
be contrary to the ethics of medicine and would debase and jeopardize a method for doing good."

How did Ivy justify his public statements to his "colleagues" on
the Green Committee? Back in Chicago two weeks after testifying, Ivy wrote a letter to the other members asserting that "it was
necessary for me to prepare . . . the report . . . in my capacity as a
rebuttal witness . . . , since the German defense attorneys raised
the issue of the condition under which prisoners might be used as
subjects in medical experiments." Ivy offered the members the

opportunity simply to endorse his statements in Nuremberg as the committee's report. They declined and finally issued conclusions that differed somewhat from those that Ivy on the witness stand had represented as those of the committee.

Andrew Ivy left future generations with a complex truth. On the one hand, he was right that the concentration camp experiments were in a different moral category than wartime prison research in the United States, but not because the American research was as ethically pristine as Ivy portrayed it. It was different because, unlike Nazi Germany, the United States was not riddled with a hate-mongering pathology that permitted the systematic injury of certain groups of human beings, injuries that often resulted in their suffering and death for the sake of national security. In fact, death was the endpoint for most victims of the Nazi experiments, for if the "test persons" did not die in the experiment, they were usually killed so that witnesses would be eliminated.

## THE NUREMBERG CODE

Regardless of the medical ethics controversy, in the end the Nuremberg judges accepted the prosecution's contention that the essential issue before the court was murder. This was well for the prosecution, in light of its inability to make a convincing case based on the ethics of research. But once having opened this particular can of worms, those who made the conduct of medical researchers an international issue could hardly put it away. Some resolution was required.

To this day it is not clear exactly how medicine's second-most-famous code of ethics (after the ancient Hippocratic oath) came to be written. Some attribute it mainly to Ivy, others to the court's primary medical consultant, Dr. Leo Alexander of Boston. What seems most likely is that the judges incorporated points made by both of the American doctors, as did chief prosecutor McHaney in his closing statement, who cited as "the most fundamental tenet of medical ethics and human decency that the subjects volunteer for the experiment after being informed of its nature and hazards."

Though their decision finally turned on the murder charge, the judges were obviously disturbed by the apparent absence of clear, universal ethical standards for research with humans. The final section of their judgment includes the ten points that quickly became known as the Nuremberg Code, which begins, "The voluntary consent of the human subject is absolutely essential," and proceeds to establish a number of other requirements, such as prior animal experiments, the avoidance of undue risk to the subject, and the right of the subject to bring the experiment to an end at any time. "All agree," the judges asserted in their preface to the principles, "that certain basic principles must be observed in order to satisfy moral, ethical and legal concepts."

With the judges' bold assertion, those who closely followed the trial's ethics controversy might have perceived a far wider indictment than that directed against the Nazis themselves. For though Servatius and the other defense attorneys failed to defeat the murder charges against most of their clients, they succeeded in raising doubts about the ethics of much medical research, not only German. But these doubts were largely momentary and were soon lost in the pressures of confronting a new postwar world and, for the Americans who tried the Nazi doctors, a new enemy. Besides, the code was inspired by shock at the monstrous cruelties of an evil state. How could it apply to those who had staked everything to crush the devil's dictators, or to those many caring doctors who were the very embodiment of human decency? Looking back at the postwar reaction to the Nuremberg Code, Yale psychiatrist Jay Katz, himself a German-Jewish immigrant, recalled his impression of his professors' reactions from his days in medical school: "It was a good code for barbarians but an unnecessary code for ordinary physicians."

## IMPERFECT JUSTICE

In many ways the doctors' trial was an enormous achievement. Despite the chaos of postwar Germany court officers managed to gather thousands of documents and to conduct orderly proceedings with full representation for both sides. The court heard hundreds of hours of complicated testimony and deliberated for eight months. No one could fairly claim that the defendants did not have every opportunity for a hearing, one that was denied the millions persecuted by them and their regime. Those engaged in mounting the trial were well aware that this contrast between a democracy ruled by law and a dictatorship ruled by fear would probably be their most important legacy. They struggled to avoid providing ammunition for the easy and oft-repeated charge that Nuremberg's was merely a victor's justice.

The seven defendants sentenced to death were hanged at Landsberg prison in the American occupation zone. In an irony that was not lost on the world, this was the institution where Hitler had himself been imprisoned and written *Mein Kampf* two decades before. But what should be history's final judgment of the justice at Nuremberg?

Among those who were hanged were men who had direct responsibility for monstrous suffering. Himmler's old friend Karl Gebhardt, the SS surgeon who did experiments at Ravensbruck Concentration Camp, used young women for studies of bone regeneration, removing portions of bone or whole limbs. Often the same victim was returned to the operating room several times for repeated removals of portions of the tibia, for example. Many died from the lack of antiseptic surgical conditions, others were shot after the operations. Aged 50 at his death, Gebhardt is said to have uttered last words that set a disgusting new standard of haughtiness and hypocrisy: "I die without bitterness but regret there is still injustice in the world."

In hindsight it appears that at least two of the men acquitted, Ruff and his colleague at the Experimental Institute for Aviation, Hans Wolfgang Romberg, were guilty of complicity in the freezing experiments. They were involved in the physical arrangements and design of the experiments and in the assessment of the results. True, Rascher was especially cruel in his performance of the experiments, but he was (from the defendants' point of view) conveniently dead. There was no one to disprove Ruff's defense that he was part of another lab at Dachau that used only true volunteers, not Rascher's. Ruff's personal files on his experiments had disappeared, and the prosecutors could not produce credible eyewitnesses. But apart from Ruff's insistence, there has never been any independent evidence that there was a second lab for human freezing experiments at Dachau.

By far the most controversial of the convictions was that of Karl Brandt. Numerous appeals for clemency were filed, some alleging that Brandt had protected cognitively impaired asylum inmates after the alleged close of the T4 so-called euthanasia program which Brandt himself helped create. Counting for Brandt was the prosecution's inability to tie him directly to culpability for any particular experiments or even knowledge that they were being conducted. Brandt also had a poor relationship with Himmler, who suspected him of loyalty first to the medical profession and only secondarily to the Führer. As Berlin was being pounded on all sides in 1945 Brandt was court-martialed for "defeatism" by an increasingly paranoid Hitler, only to be rescued and then tried by the victorious American forces. Brandt, his defenders said, was trapped between Hitler and his enemies, both of whom reviled him.

Counting against Brandt was the fact that he had been exceptionally close to his leader for most of his career, nearly an adopted son, accounting for the young surgeon's meteoric rise to become the top doctor in the Reich. Brandt was clearly a member of the inner circle in Hitler's mind until late in the war. Though Servatius claimed Brandt was kept at arm's length by skeptical rivals, the prosecution was able to place him at the scene of numerous meetings at which experimental results were discussed. Memoranda from various officials and doctors mention Brandt in connection with jaundice research expected to lead to death and as a consultant on mustard gas experiments. He was surely an advocate of active killing of incapacitated psychiatric patients, even if, as Brandt claimed, he was instrumental in stopping the official program in 1941. But other former Nazi officials testified that it was assumed he was in charge of later initiatives to kill debilitated persons.

Probably the most damning incident concerned Brandt's role in Gebhardt's sulfa drug experiments with female prisoners at the Ravensbruck concentration camp. Gebhardt told the Nuremberg interrogators that he had met with Brandt to plan the project. A high-level conference of all the major German doctors had followed the experiments, but somehow Brandt managed to forget about his attendance and his initial conversations with Gebhardt.

Between a lack of incriminating primary documents showing Brandt's role and his failed memory, the prosecution had trouble connecting him directly to the camp experiments. In his closing argument, Prosecutor McHaney gave himself a low hurdle to clear in making the case against Brandt: "It is not incumbent upon the Prosecution to show that Brandt was familiar with all of the details of all of these experiments. It is sufficient to prove that he knew or should have known of the systematic use of involuntary human subjects for medical experiments by agencies over which he exercised a substantial degree of power and authority."

Responding to McHaney, Servatius argued that "till now nobody has been held criminally responsible for the conduct of a superior or friend; the question of criminal law, however, is the only one the Tribunal has to consider." Servatius dismissed the contention that Brandt should have used his influence to stop the experiments: "Even presuming he was aware of the facts as crimes, his guilt would not be of a legal but only of a political or moral nature."

Ultimately the tribunal found that Brandt's "political or moral" crimes were so grievous as to be punishable at law. As one of Hitler's few intimates for over a decade, Brandt's studied moral blindness was in some ways even more terrifying than the ugly cruelties inflicted by Gebhardt. In this period Brandt rose to the pinnacle of the medical profession in Germany. But his deliberate ignorance cannot be explained wholly in terms of narcissistic careerism.

When Karl Brandt was 15 he was one of tens of thousands of Alsatian Germans who were displaced by the treaty ending World War I. Many Germans had a nearly religious obsession with recovering the territory of Alsace from the French. Brandt converted his resentment into enthusiasm for two nineteenth-century ideas:

the importance of scientific progress and the ultimate reality of the state.

Brandt's warped idealism was shared by many in the desperately depressed 1930s: How could anyone doubt that the claims of science and state far surpassed those of any mere individual human being? In the secular world, the source of individual rights since the enlightenment had been the marketplace, and the marketplace offered only a bitter harvest for the German people after World War I. In the hyperinflationary Weimar economy, war veterans begged in the streets, and wheelbarrows full of inflated German marks were needed to purchase an automobile. The combination of the power of science and the authority of the state simply broke the back of any resistance, moral or political. Together they seemed to represent both idealism and brute reality. Sadly, it fell to relatively few, some in churches and some with left-wing sympathies, to resist the dehumanizing tide. Their resistance was not enough to avoid the catastrophe.

Following his sentencing, Brandt made the American authorities an offer that showed his utter devotion to the twin deities of scientific knowledge and state authority. He proposed that he be subjected to a medical experiment that he could not survive, an act "undertaken in the interests of humanity." Thus, in a single stroke, Brandt proposed to help advance science and to acknowledge the right of the state to execute those it has condemned. Scientific progress and state power would both have been vindicated by Brandt's proposal as, in a way, would Brandt himself.

His offer declined, Brandt was taken to the hangman on June 1, 1948. Among his last words was a reference again to the human experiments conducted by Americans and others, and to the recent Hiroshima and Nagasaki bombings, for which he said the United States would be "forever destined to carry the sign of Cain."

Brandt and his supporters thought him a misunderstood idealist, a martyr to the truth who was rejected by his Führer and his Führer's bitter enemies. But Brandt's last thoughts revealed a moral vacuum, for according to Brandt's own defense, how could any nation be upbraided for wartime actions? Facing death,

Brandt found a moral compass that he had not known before and, even then, did not apply it to himself. Of all people, Karl Brandt was in no position to claim the moral high ground. In the years to come, the nation that executed Karl Brandt would struggle to avoid the blindness he took with him to the gallows.

# DEALS WITH DEVILS

This is to certify that the Joint Intelligence Objectives Agency has examined . . . the Security Report of the sponsoring agency in the United States and finds that there is nothing in his records indicating that he was a war criminal, an ardent Nazi or otherwise objectionable from admission into the United States as an immigrant.

*Security Certificate for Dr. Hubertus Strughold, September 29, 1948*

## WHAT PRICE SCIENCE?

Siegfried Ruff was acquitted by the Nuremberg judges because the evidence of his involvement in the freezing experiments was, in the court's words, "circumstantial." No stigma was attached to those exonerated from accusations of war crimes in the new West Germany. Shortly after Ruff left Nuremberg as a free man, he became the director of a new aviation medicine institute. He also kept in close touch with his old friend, Hubert "Strugi" Strughold, now working at Randolph Air Force Base in San Antonio, Texas.

If Nuremberg was but a brief interruption in Ruff's career, it was not even a threat to that of Strughold, who was secretly singled out for protection by the U.S. Joint Chiefs of Staff when the war ended and lived his life as an honored member of America's military medical fraternity. No one can doubt that the Air Force made an excellent investment. Without Strughold, the first man on the moon would probably have arrived on a Soviet spacecraft.

But today Strughold's special treatment lies under a dark cloud, like that of many other German scientists recruited by the United States after the war. In the mid-1970s his case was reopened by the Immigration and Naturalization Service (INS), but it was closed again after a Texas congressman complained that his background had already been thoroughly checked. An INS official later admitted that Strughold's file did not indicate whether he had ever been asked about the Dachau freezing experiments. When Strughold himself claimed in a newspaper interview that he didn't learn about the concentration camp experiments until after the war, a journalist revealed that his name appeared on the attendance list at the 1942 conference on the low-temperature results. Fifty years since Strughold's departure from Germany, in 1997, the director of the Justice Department's Office of Special Investigations told me that in the mid-1980s his office was preparing to prosecute the much-honored aeromedicine expert as a war criminal. Strughold's prolonged medical incapacity and then his death in 1986 saved him from belated disgrace, and it saved the National Aeronautics and Space Administration (NASA) from some very embarrassing publicity.

The Strughold case is the most prominent saga in a curious chapter in the confused early history of America's encounter with human experiments and national security. As one world war had just ended and another threatened, with different sets of enemies, the hunger for scientific advantages was immense on all sides. Even allies found themselves competing to "exploit" (as the intelligence agencies put it), the intellectual spoils of victory over Germany, and to "deny" those riches to their potential foes. Not only physical science but also medicine had proven itself a growing source of advantage in modern armed struggle.

But how far to go to gain these advantages? Surely proven war criminals and those who presented a demonstrable threat to the United States must be excluded. On the other extreme, no one could object to assisting in the immigration of those who truly resisted the Nazis during those long years, and if they happened to have some skills to contribute to the West, so much the better. What of those who aided, or who actively profited from, the Nazi cause? What about the scientists whose careers were hitched to certain professional advantages? And what, most particularly, about the doctors, sworn to protect human life, who might have been drawn a little too closely to the fires of abject cruelty and perhaps even stoked them a little? Where, in short, is the line of national self-interest to be drawn?

There is a further exquisitely sensitive issue underlying this story. Strughold and some of the other biological scientists recruited to work for the United States were in a position to influence many medical research programs at several military installations. Their personal and political integrity was important not only for reasons of national security but also because their guidance could help shape medical experiments in which American military personnel were themselves used as subjects. Improbable as this nexus of suspect German doctors and abusive research with American soldiers might seem to be, it is an important link in the cold war chain of national security-related medical research.

## THE "FATHER OF AMERICAN SPACE MEDICINE"

Ruff and Strughold had been close associates in Germany. They wrote a textbook together, had similar positions (Ruff was director of the Luftwaffe's Department of Aviation Medicine at the Experimental Institute for Aviation, Strughold directed the Air Ministry's Aeromedicine Institute), and both attended the 1942 conference on the results of the freezing experiments. It was the Luftwaffe's chief surgeon, Erich Hippke, who seems to have come up with the idea for the atmospheric experiments, and who used Rascher to apply to Himmler for permission. Hippke was Ruff's Luftwaffe colleague, and he was Strughold's supervisor. The low-temperature experiments followed, again inspired by Hippke and carried out by Rascher. Not only Hippke and Ruff but also several other scientists above and below Strughold in the medical chain of command were implicated in the human experiments.

In late 1945, while American investigators were piecing these associations together from Himmler's files, Strughold, Ruff, and several others who were later tried at Nuremberg were comfortably set up in Heidelberg doing research for the American occupational forces. But unlike his colleagues, Strughold somehow avoided interrogation, let alone prosecution.

Strughold was born in Westphalia, Germany, in 1898. A brilliant student, he received a Ph.D. in biochemistry from Münster when he was 24, and his medical degree "summa cum laude" from Würzberg a year later. His aeromedical work began almost immediately, and it attracted international attention. From 1928 to 1929 Strughold was a Rockefeller Foundation fellow at Western Reserve University in Cleveland and at the University of Chicago. Upon his return to Germany he was named director of the Aeromedical Research Institute in Berlin, a position held for the next sixteen years, until the end of the war.

Strughold's Rockefeller Foundation fellowship gave him the opportunity to become comfortable with American culture and American English, and he frequently attended scientific congresses in the United States during the 1930s. At one of them, in Washington in 1934, he met Colonel Harry Armstrong.

Armstrong, surgeon for the U.S. Eighth Air Force, was already a pioneer in techniques for protecting aircrews from the primitive conditions of early fighter cockpits, especially the low temperatures and carbon monoxide exposure. Once ridiculed for his conviction that medicine would have to reckon with the problems of flying thousands of miles above the earth and faster than sound, Armstrong was later hailed as a visionary. In Strughold Armstrong found a kindred spirit.

In June 1946 Armstrong included Strughold's name in a list of twenty-two German specialists in aviation medicine to be brought to the United States as part of an operation to secure the Reich's scientific talent for the United States—and to deny it to the Soviets. But in September five who were on Armstrong's list, including Siegfried Ruff, were arrested at the Heidelberg institute by Telford Taylor's war crimes investigators and imprisoned. Four of the five were among those who stood trial, and two of the Heidelberg scientists, Hermann Becker-Freyseng and Oskar Schroeder, were convicted. Becker-Freyseng told a Nuremberg investigator that Strughold provided guidance on the high-altitude experiments and had the authority to stop them if he had wanted to.

One who was arrested but not indicted, Theodor Benzinger, blamed Strughold for his arrest as a means of distracting attention from his own vulnerability to prosecution. In spite of his internment in Nuremberg Prison and a record of Nazi party membership, Benzinger later was brought to the United States in accord with Armstrong's request. Konrad Schaefer, who was prosecuted but not convicted, also came to the United States under U.S. Army protection, his arrest in connection with war crimes having been conveniently overlooked in his intelligence report.

Meanwhile, at the request of the American director of the Heidelberg institute, Strughold was collecting his colleagues' reports of what they had learned in their wartime scientific work. Some, like Becker-Freyseng, mentioned the use of human subjects, so Strughold thought it better to delete those passages. Perhaps because of his importance to the Heidelberg work Strughold was never arrested, let alone prosecuted, or perhaps the prosecutors found even less surviving evidence against him than

they had against several of the others, in spite of Becker-Freyseng's
and Benzinger's accusations. Whatever, the reasons, Strughold
had time to prepare a manuscript describing a wide range of experimental results, later published by the U.S. Air Force as a carefully censored two-volume work called *German Aviation Medicine:
World War II*. He also recruited several dozen other Germans to
work for the Americans before his own departure for the School
of Aviation Medicine in San Antonio, Texas, in 1947. Though his
intelligence report inferred that Strughold, due to his professional success, held a strong Nazi ideology, Armstrong never doubted
his old friend and made certain that he was well taken care of in
the nation he would serve with distinction.

As for Strughold's close colleague Siegfried Ruff, who was
acquitted at Nuremberg, a later effort was made to bring him to
the United States. It failed when reporter Drew Pearson got wind
of it and threatened to tell President Truman, who had signed an
executive order banning ardent Nazis from American shores. Ruff
was condemned to live a comfortable and highly successful professional life in Germany, and the president's order was easily
undermined by those determined to obtain the best German
minds for American science.

## PAPER CLIP

To this day, few Americans know about the special top-secret program that brought German scientists to the United States after
World War II, and fewer still know that their number included
medical scientists. Code-named Operation Paper Clip (because
Army intelligence officers would put paper clips on the dossiers of
German scientists who might be useful to the United States), hundreds of "specialists" and hundreds more of their dependents
entered the United States under special Joint Chiefs' protection,
avoiding regular immigration procedures and requirements. They
were assigned to various military and, later, industrial facilities.
The motivation for these recruitments was straightforward: The
Germans had gathered enormous technical sophistication during

the war, and before 1939 they were surely the most advanced of the military powers in the application of knowledge from such fields as mechanical engineering and metallurgy.

The most famous of the Paper Clip recruits was rocket scientist Werner von Braun, under whom the German rocket program developed advanced fuels, motors, and wind tunnels. The V1 and V2 rockets von Braun's team produced spread death, destruction, and terror in Great Britain. Clearly von Braun's value for the post-war power lucky enough to snag him was incalculable, and all four allied nations were competing for the intellectual spoils of the Third Reich. That von Braun was an attractive and well-spoken man served him well as he and his colleagues from the Peenemünde rocket base negotiated with the Americans for the best possible deal. These personal characteristics were even more important when, in the era initiated by the first Soviet satellite, Sputnik, von Braun became a celebrity of the U.S. space program, appearing at many public events and in the media as a symbol of the brilliant scientists behind the American effort. In the 1960s liberals who doubted the wisdom of the manned space program and the origins of its expertise liked to chide NASA about their famous German, including a famous song parody by satirist Tom Lehrer.

Theoretically, von Braun and all the Paper Clip recruits were cleared of any suspicious political associations by a careful screening process, the goal of which was supposed to ensure that no "ardent Nazis" were permitted to obtain a visa for immigration to the United States, in accord with President Truman's order. A key criterion of "ardent" status was membership in the Nazi party or taking a leadership role in one of the countless Nazi organizations, including professional societies. Although it was known that von Braun had been an SS officer since 1940, and though he had received three promotions during his service with them, he was judged sufficiently important to be brought to the United States under Army custody in 1946. When visa applications were filed for those already in the country, as was the case for von Braun in 1948, the solution to the presence of embarrassing political associations in the record was simple: The record was rewritten to obliterate

certain unfortunate facts and emphasize only the most banal and
benign wartime activities. SS membership was commonly attributed to professional necessity rather than any underlying national
socialist sympathies, as "opportunism" rather than ideology.
Witnesses were found who stated that the individual in question
had been privately critical of Hitler, or at least detached from politics. In von Braun's case, a report labeling him "a potential security threat" was also dropped in favor of a statement in his dossier
that his background could not be investigated because his former
residence was in the Russian occupational zone.

These "adjustments" to the record might be less objectionable
in retrospect were it not for the fact that von Braun's rocket factory in the Harz Mountains was built on the blood of slave labor
from the nearby Dora concentration camp. At least twenty thousand men are thought to have died working in the tunnels of the
former ammonia mine, either from the brutal physical conditions—the old mine shafts exposed the men to sudden and dras-
tic changes in temperature and humidity—or the brutality of SS
guards. No matter how absorbed the scientists might have been
in their work, none could have been unaware of the corpses of
men who had dropped at their workstations from exhaustion, or
those who were left hanging in the factory for days as a warning
to other prisoners.

## NO "ARDENT NAZIS?"

How many Paper Clip recruits were there, how long did the program go on, and how many of the German scientists were suspected of Nazi affiliation? One of the chief chroniclers of the
Paper Clip story, journalist Linda Hunt, has estimated that there
were at least sixteen hundred recruits and several thousand dependents brought to the United States. Hunt maintains that, contrary
to a U.S. General Accounting Office claim, the program did not
end in 1947, but continued through 1973. In her dogged research
on Paper Clip in the 1980s, Hunt found an astonishingly extensive
set of research and development activities, and not a few shocking

embarrassments, associated with the project. Among the embarrassments: The highest-ranking military officer ever convicted of spying, Lieutenant Colonel Henry Whalen, was head of the operation in 1959 and 1960.

How many of the Paper Clip recruits who arrived in the United States were of suspect backgrounds? This question is hard to answer because the Joint Intelligence Operations Agency (JIOA) did a very effective job of censoring the early recruits' files in December 1947. Before then the JIOA had been engaged in a fierce bureaucratic battle with the State Department, represented by Samuel Klaus, who refused to approve visas sight-unseen for a group of Paper Clip recruits, suspecting that at least some of them were barred under Truman's anti-Nazi order. In fact, many on Paper Clip lists had turned out to have disqualifying intelligence reports, and the JIOA was not interested in sharing the information with the obstructive Klaus. Those dossiers that the Justice Department's visa officers did see contained obvious discrepancies between the statements made by the applicants and Nazi records in Berlin.

At this time the JIOA was directed by Bousqet Wev, a Navy captain who was in the forefront of those concerned about the new menace facing the United States. As an early cold warrior, Wev was determined to normalize the situations of the Paper Clip recruits so that their contributions could be maximized. Many of the Germans were dissatisfied being virtual prisoners at places like Randolph Field in Texas or Wright Field in Ohio. As Wev complained in a July 1947 memo, with the Germans soundly and thoroughly defeated and the Soviet threat looming, concern about these valuable scientists' past is "beating a dead Nazi horse."

Dead but not buried. A few months later, in November 1947, Wev's deputy director wrote a "restricted" memorandum along with a list of seven "specialists" whose dossiers were available but problematic. Von Braun's dossier was among them. "It is not considered advisable to submit any of the inclosed dossiers to the Departments of State and Justice at this time. In the case of Werner von Braun the Theater Security Report indicates that he is regarded as a potential security threat to the United States and he will be wanted for denazification trial in view of his party membership. In all other cases the scientists are wanted for denazification."

In spite of their internal reports that cast suspicion on many of their targets, the JIOA searched for a way to circumvent the government lawyers. On December 18, 1947, Wev wrote a letter to the U.S. attorney general. After expressing gratitude for Federal Bureau of Investigation (FBI) reports on several scientists, Wev responded to a suggestion by FBI director J. Edgar Hoover that "the names of the scientists be submitted to the Federal Bureau of Investigation before they are brought to the United States." This procedure "will not be necessary," wrote Wev, "in view of the fact that this program was officially closed on 30 September 1947, with the provision that only special cases would be considered after that date." These "special cases" would only involve those people who had to leave Germany rapidly. All others, Wev wrote reassuringly, would of course be submitted in advance.

Having thus crafted an exception through which could be driven truckloads of desirable scientists in the future, Wev still had to deal with a backlog of specialists he wanted to maintain in the program and deny to the Soviets. Thus, around the same time he wrote to the attorney general, with not only the Justice Department but also the FBI, the State Department, and journalist Drew Pearson all breathing down his back, the Paper Clip managers under Wev's leadership began to systematically alter security reports. Those reports that concluded an individual was an "ardent Nazi" were revised to "not an ardent Nazi" but an "opportunist." Among the revised documents were those of von Braun. Americans walked on the moon before the man around whom the American space program was built admitted what had been rumored for nearly twenty-five years, that he was a member of the SS.

As for Strughold, the documents accompanying his visa application file are all dated 1947, including his visa affidavit itself. But in the typed year on the affidavit the 7 has been altered by hand to an 8, reflecting perhaps the JIOA's decision to delay efforts to process this and other applications until matters settled down a bit at the civilian agencies. Strughold's "Revised Security Report" about his conduct from 1933 to 1945 states: "Subject was regarded as an absolute professional man whose main interest was aero-medicine. He was a bachelor who led a retired life. His social life was confined to that entertainment sponsored by fellow Institute members. He was considered to have a pleasing personality and was generally well liked. There is no evidence that he was ever politically active." His security evaluation concluded that he "was not a war criminal, was not an ardent Nazi" and unlikely to be a threat to the United States. No mention is made of his wartime work with the Nuremberg defendants. Several character references attest to Strughold's monastic lifestyle and utter devotion to his scientific work, as well as his lack of sympathy to Nazism.

Only the most credulous could fail to note the convenience of this benign profile for American authorities, much like that attributed to von Braun. Yet for those who hold a different theory about Strughold's character and sympathies there is an amusing and somewhat chilling slip in his visa application, one from his own statement about the reasons for his wish to immigrate. Strughold wrote that "the United States is the only country of liberty which is able to maintain this liberty and the thousand-year-old culture and western civilization." It is news indeed that American civilization dates to the first millennium, but perhaps Strughold was thinking of the racial legacy of certain Aryan tribes. Strughold seems not to have traveled as far in his worldview as his American sponsors might have wished from the "thousand year Reich."

Strughold continued as an active recruiter for Paper Clip in Germany and Austria, and was named head of the new Department of Space Medicine at the School of Aviation Medicine in 1949. His work included research on the effects of weightlessness, decompression, and lack of oxygen, all critical to the manned space effort. When a reporter inquired about his wartime experiences, Strughold said that he "was against Hitler and his beliefs." "I sometimes had to hide myself because my life was in danger," he claimed. If this was true, then Strughold did a very poor job of concealing himself, considering that throughout the war he occupied a high-level position in the military medical establishment and was present at very sensitive briefings about concentration camp experiments.

Strughold retired in 1968 and died in 1986. A year before his death the state of Texas declared his birthday, June 15, Hubertus Strughold Day. Strughold's likeness was part of a mural of heroic figures in the history of medicine at the Ohio State University medical school, and a library at Brooks Air Force Base was named after him. In 1993, when Jewish groups protested his inclusion in the medical school mural, the image was removed. The Strughold Library at Brooks remains.


## THE CASE OF WALTER SCHREIBER

Harry Armstrong had another German protégé, one who created the most embarrassing public episode for Paper Clip (or its technical successor, code-named Project 63). Walter Schreiber had been chief of the Department for Science and Health for the German High Command, with a specialty in infectious diseases. Schreiber not only had a hand in funding human experiments, as a member of the Reich Research Council, and assigned doctors to conduct epidemic jaundice experiments that deliberately resulted in prisoners' deaths but also was a hands-on participant. At Buchenwald he was present for the injection of five prisoners with phenol to see how long it would take them to die.

As the Third Reich disintegrated, Schreiber was captured by the Red Army. Though capture by the Soviets was generally bad luck for most Nazis, it was good luck for Schreiber, whose reports based on the camp experiment results were thought to be of scientific value. Instead of being indicted for war crimes, he was indoctrinated in communism in Moscow and put to work as chief of sanitation for the East German police. In 1946 the Soviets sent him to Nuremberg to testify against his former political and military leaders, which came as a shock to American prosecutor Alexander Hardy: Schreiber's name was on a list of 200 persons suspected of medical war crimes, along with those who were later to be the twenty-three defendants at the doctors' trial. When the Soviets were informed that Schreiber was wanted for interrogation they quietly explained to Hardy that he was needed for an important assignment and could not be released for possible prosecution. Later, several of those sentenced to death at the doctors' trial identified Schreiber as the officer responsible for concentration camp experiments with bacteria that led to horrible deaths.

In 1948 Schreiber presented himself to American authorities and the press claiming to have somehow escaped to West Berlin. Many suspected that he was really a Soviet spy, but the Joint Intelligence Operations Agency and the Central Intelligence Agency (CIA) valued his expertise. After working at an American military base in the occupied zone he was brought to Randolph Air Force Base in San Antonio in October 1951, where he joined Strughold, among many others. Schreiber's arrival was considered important enough to be announced with a photograph in *The New York Times*, accompanied by a brief, sanitized account of his war record and postwar activities.

Almost immediately, questions began to be raised about Schreiber's background by medical and Jewish groups, especially by a liberal organization called the Physicians' Forum, which counted Leo Alexander, the Nuremberg court's expert, among its members. Nuremberg prosecutor Hardy joined Alexander in the effort. The group petitioned Armstrong for Schreiber's "immediate expulsion" from the United States, providing citations from Nuremberg testimony about his role in experiments at Dachau, Buchenwald, Ravensbruck, and other camps. Armstrong replied that Schreiber was "the only qualified person" to provide classified information to the American military (presumably having to do with his World War II reports of the experimental results), and that he was not engaged in teaching at the School of Aviation Medicine.

Not satisfied, the doctors' group announced that it was petitioning President Truman directly for Schreiber's removal. A spokesman for the Physicians' Forum said that Schreiber's Air Force assignment was "a reflection on the moral standards not only of the medical profession, but (also) of the entire country." At about the same time, in February 1952, New York Supreme Court Justice Meier Steinbrink, who was also chairman of the Anti-Defamation League of B'nai B'rith, called on Secretary of Defense Robert Lovett to investigate. Adding still more heat to the case, a young Polish woman who had been a gas gangrene experiment victim at the Ravensbruck concentration camp, and who had been treated at Beth Israel Hospital in Boston, said that she wanted to face Schreiber and identify him as her tormenter. Schreiber denied all the charges, suggesting that there may have been another Schreiber in the Waffen S.S. Wehrmacht and that the accusations were communist-inspired. Armstrong stonewalled, telling the Physicians' Forum that "there is not a shred of evidence we know of that he is guilty of any crime other than serving his country during the war the same as I served mine."

All this publicity must have caused considerable consternation at project headquarters. Within two weeks of the Physicians' Forum appeal to Truman, the secretary of the Air Force announced that Schreiber's contract was being terminated. The contracts of at least two other questionable recruits were cancelled, and arrangements were made to send Schreiber to join his daughter in Argentina, a country friendly to Nazi war criminals. These negotiations took some time, however, and in the spring of 1952 another story surfaced that the U.S. Air Force was trying to help Schreiber find a teaching job. In his contacts with the academic world, the Randolph Field commander attributed Schreiber's troubles to persecution by "medical men of Jewish ancestry." New York Congressman Jacob Javits and Senator Herbert Lehman threatened to seek further action if Schreiber's announced expulsion were not carried out in short order. In a secret May 6 cable, Washington informed an American officer in Germany: "Schreiber's immediate departure U.S. extremely urgent." Finally, the Air Force booked passage for Schreiber, his wife, his son, and his mother-in-law on May 22, 1952, along with a generous travel allowance.

The Schreiber affair threatened to blow the lid off the entire German project. By now, according to those who have investigated it, Paper Clip and its successors had become virtually a rogue operation of the Joint Intelligence Operations Agency, its leaders having committed themselves to the recruitment of too many questionable individuals. When Secretary Lovett asked for an historical brief on Paper Clip after Schreiber's departure, he was given a carefully worded account that flatly denied that any "known war criminal, ardent Nazi or profiteer or notorious supporter of Nazism or militarism is eligible under the project."

## WHO DID WHAT TO WHOM?

Though it is easy to criticize U.S. military officials for engaging the likes of Strughold and Schreiber, they were likely exceptional among the hundreds of Paper Clip and Project 63 recruits in their close ties to Nazi atrocities. Yet a significant number of other German scientists employed by the American military in the years after the war were more enthusiastic supporters of Nazism than government immigration standards were supposed to allow. The emerging conflict with the Soviets in the wake of a brutal world war explains the determination of a few officers to stake the American claim in the scientific spoils of war, but it does not justify it. The evasions and outright lies of a few officers amounted to insubordination, to resistance of a democratically elected government's policy by well placed military authorities. While their goal was not to embrace the Strugholds and Schreibers, it was an irresistible outcome of their determination that the United States should dominate the postwar era.

If the Paper Clip story is not mainly a medical ethics story, it surely has implications for governmental attitudes toward the importance of ethical standards in medicine. These attitudes might well have come home to roost far more directly than could have been anticipated at the time. For what if some of those with suspicious pasts had engaged in abusive experiments upon American soldiers in the United States, brought here courtesy of our own military?

The evidence that this might have occurred is indirect. So far as is known, no documents survive linking specific scientists with

Nazi associations to specific military research in the United States involving human subjects. But considering that there was a great deal of such research being done at some of the bases that hosted the Paper Clip recruits, the possibility cannot be ruled out. Paper Clip historian Linda Hunt found that a number of chemical warfare experts arrived at Maryland's Edgewood Arsenal in the late 1950s. One of them, Albert Pfeiffer, worked on the airborne dissemination of chemical warfare agents. His job during the war was to develop various weapons for the German navy, including chemical weapons detectors. While I worked for President Clinton's Advisory Committee on Human Radiation Experiments I discovered that large numbers of German ophthalmologists were assigned to the School of Aviation Medicine in Texas at a time that research on flash blindness from atomic weapons was a significant operational concern. Again, these facts do not amount to evidence that any suspect Paper Clip scientists were directly involved in abusive research with human subjects in the United States, but it is hard to escape the conclusion that many of the German recruits were for decades important consultants on a myriad of military-medical projects.

## THE INFAMOUS DR. ISHII

In 1947 and 1948, while the Nuremberg trials concluded and the situation of the Paper Clip recruits was being secretly debated in the United States, the implications of yet another set of wartime human experiments were known to a still smaller circle of American officials. Unlike the Nazi atrocities and American military-related research, Japanese exploitation of tens of thousands of people in China in horrid biological warfare experiments has received precious little attention in the West. The inattention is partly due to high-level decisions among a few U.S. officials to avoid a war crimes investigation of Japanese doctors and officials. Instead, it was decided to guard the Japanese biological warfare information and expertise as closely as possible; the Japanese were, after all, wholly under American supervision, unlike the Germans, who were occupied by four powers.

Because the Japanese story has been hidden from all but a few it did not influence cold war policy on military medical experiments with human beings in the United States. But the shocking tale—only now coming to light through the efforts of a few intrepid historians—is instructive about the postwar atmosphere that also shaped Paper Clip. Credit for uncovering a massive quantity of information about Japan's biological "factories of death" goes to Dr. Sheldon Harris, a senior California State University professor who has dedicated more than ten years to a monumental detective job. His account centers on one especially compelling personality.

In the summer of 1932 a 40-year-old Japanese army officer named Ishii Shiro arrived in Manchuria, recently invaded by Japan and now being reconstituted as Manchukuo, a puppet state of the militarists in Tokyo. Ishii's mission was to establish a bacterial warfare laboratory in the conquered province, or rather to turn the whole region into a laboratory, with its population as guinea pigs. A man of exceptional intellect and energy, Ishii had graduated about a decade before from the medical school in Kyoto, entered the army, and worked in the First Army Hospital in Tokyo. While in Tokyo he also gained a reputation as a big spender, drinker, and womanizer in the red-light district, attracting the attention of many young geishas.

Ishii impressed his superiors, and he was assigned to postgraduate studies back in Kyoto, where he had the kind of lucky stroke that so often proves decisive in preparing the way for professional success. An epidemic had broken out on the island of Shikoku, and Ishii was assigned to locate and isolate the virus. The causal agent was later identified as an encephalitis strain called Japanese B. On the island Ishii gained considerable experience in public health measures that complemented his laboratory studies of bacteriology.

With this practical experience and his advanced training completed, and having married the daughter of Kyoto Imperial University's president, Ishii was well positioned for an influential career. Stationed at the army hospital in Kyoto, he continued his biological research, published a number of scientific papers, and set out to persuade his skeptical superiors that biological warfare had much to contribute to Japanese military prowess. From 1928 to 1930 he undertook a virtual world tour that included a number of countries involved in biological warfare research, including the United States, where, according to the Japanese military attaché, he visited MIT as part of his quest for useful bacteriological information.

Back in Japan, now appointed a professor of immunology in Tokyo's Army Medical School, Ishii gathered important allies among important military and academic leaders. Though apparently disliked by his peers for his arrogance and ruthlessly competitive personality, Ishii convinced the medical school dean to provide him with a building for his exclusive use. Ishii used this Tokyo headquarters to prepare for branching out to field testing, and he got his chance following the Manchurian invasion. Now thoroughly dominated by ultranationalists and anticipating conflict with the Soviets over Siberia, the army welcomed his biological warfare research proposal. Ishii was well funded and given a 300-man unit to begin his work.

## THE WATER PURIFICATION BUREAU

For his human experiments Ishii used Chinese laborers to construct a prison and laboratory complex of 100 brick buildings outside of Harbin. Up to 1,000 prisoners could be held in the main building, a mixed group ranging from criminals to political rebels to innocents picked up from the street. They were given a relatively good diet to keep them healthy while awaiting their experimental use, shackled in tiny cells. Then they were inoculated with various diseases, in the early years, mainly anthrax, glanders, and plague, but also cholera. Blood was drawn regularly and sent for study. When the subjects became too weak to be of further value, they were killed by a poison injection. There were also experiments with cyanide, phosgene gas, and deadly electrical shocks.

Pleased with Ishii's preliminary results, his commanders authorized the construction of a much larger facility, capable of manufacturing large quantities of bacteria as well as continued human experiments. By 1939 the new death factory was ready, located on hundreds of acres that had been clear-cut and taken from Manchurian peasants, in Ping Fan. The huge complex was made up of 150 buildings, including administrative offices, laboratories, worker dormitories, barracks, barns, stables, a farm, greenhouses, a power plant, furnaces to incinerate human and animal remains, a prison for human guinea pigs, and recreational facilities for the Japanese personnel who numbered several thousand. High security was maintained, including constant aerial surveillance above the site. Officially, this was the local Water Purification Bureau installation, with Ishii as its head. In fact it was a site that became the home of the infamous Unit 731.

The Ping Fan prison complex included two buildings that housed the experimental subjects, again drawn from a variety of sources and local populations, among them White Russians and Russian Jews as well as Han Chinese. The victims were commonly called *murutas* ("logs"), following a cover story told to the locals that the heavy construction was for a lumber mill. These human "logs" were usually charged with capital crimes but often not tried, and then they were consigned to Unit 731 for extermination. Transported in heavy irons, they were processed at the compound in an enormous administration building, deprived of their remaining possessions, given prison clothing, and assigned numbers. Thousands died there, but records were kept in such a way that more precise estimates are impossible, numbering prisoners from 1 to 1500 and then starting again with the delivery of fresh specimens to replace those who had been poisoned.

Besides the experiments on individuals, activity on an immense scale was devoted to the manufacture of pathogens for field testing. Equipment included four 1-ton capacity boilers and fourteen autoclaves, each of which held thirty cultivators Ishii designed himself. At its peak production the Ping Fan complex apparatus could produce enough cells to provide 40 *million* billion pathogenic bacteria over several days. In his exhaustive account,

Sheldon Harris includes the following list of ailments cultivated and applied to human victims: "plague, typhoid, paratyphoid A and B, typhus, smallpox, tularemia, infectious jaundice, gas gangrene, tetanus, cholera, dysentery, glanders, scarlet fever, undulant fever, tick encephalitis, 'songo' or epidemic hemorrhagic fever, whooping cough, diphtheria, pneumonia, bysipelas, epidemic cerebrospinal meningitis, venereal diseases, tuberculosis, salmonellas, frostbite, and countless other diseases."

Various delivery systems were tested, including using several kinds of bombs in the creation of bacterial clouds. From 1939 to 1942 Unit 731 personnel tested their weapons on Soviet soldiers and local populations using a vast array of methods. Over a thousand wells were poisoned with typhoid bacilli, for example, and Ishii created a cholera epidemic by "vaccinating" locals in Changchun. He dumped typhoid and paratyphoid bacteria into wells and marshes in Nanking and left sweet cakes laced with the stuff where they would be found by poor inhabitants. Rats were released carrying plague-infested fleas, and in Ning Bo the reservoir was stocked with pathogens of cholera, typhus, and plague that were also being sprayed on wheat fields from the air. There were also chemical warfare experiments on Chinese prisoners with mustard gas, and, in experiments reminiscent of the Nazi atrocities, altitude experiments in low-pressure chambers, and even frostbite studies. Once again, certain questions were of universal interest.

Beyond the thousands who died in agony from the direct violence of Ishii's experiments (sometimes combining puncture wounds from exploding shells with infections, for example), the subsequent effects on people in Manchuria and others elsewhere in China are incalculable. Unit 731 ran several branch camps besides the huge Ping Fan headquarters. Others were exterminated in sites as far afield as Beijing and Canton, probably even Shanghai and Singapore. Not only does the extent of the enterprise at the time defy rational imagination, so do its lingering traces. The epidemic effects of biological weapons field trials were felt for many years. To this day, the Chinese government is trying to locate and destroy the chemical warfare munitions left behind, numbering about 2 million pieces buried in now-rusting and rotting containers and amounting to over 120 tons of toxic agents.

In May 1997, pots with quite different contents surfaced after heavy rains in Southern China, far from Ishii's territory in Manchuria. The remains of victims of yet another Japanese unit, 8604, had been buried in earthen containers, each containing the bones of two or three people. No one knows how many other burial sites there are, nor how great the toll of suffering from Japan's biological weapons experiments will turn out to have been.

## THE CAVE OF HELL

Over the years there have been persistent allegations that American prisoners of war (POWs) were subjected to Japanese biological weapons experiments. Another investigator of Japanese war crimes, Yuki Tanaka, has gathered recently released documents that detail the use of Australian POWs on the South Pacific island of Rabaul, a major holding center for Allied soldiers captured by the Japanese. In 1944, Tanaka reports, about thirteen men who had been held in an air-raid shelter-cave were put on a diet consisting entirely of boiled cassava root. Allied bombings had disrupted supply routes to the island so the Japanese wanted to determine if soldiers could manage on this kind of diet. These thirteen were the survivors of a larger group, the others having been either massacred or dead of malnutrition or disease. Nine survived the root-diet experiment, only to be subjected to attempts to demonstrate immunity against malaria by being inoculated with malaria-infected blood. Two more of the men died of malaria.

Tanaka also reports larger human experiments. About one hundred Australian POWs on Ambon Island were inoculated against typhoid and paratyphoid and some were used in a diet experiment. Fifty who continued to do hard labor died. Perhaps the most controversial of the POW experiments that have been alleged is said by Tanaka to have been conducted by Ishii's Unit 731 in Mukden, Manchuria, between January 1943 and March 1945. In what would be the largest such incident, 1,485 American, British, Australian, and New Zealand POWs are said to have been forced to take inoculations of typhoid-parathyroid, cholera, and dysentery, and to drink liquids carrying various pathogens. Tanaka's source for these allegations is interviews conducted by the Australian Broadcasting Corporation in 1983, including one with a former Unit 731 member. But Harris finds himself unable to conclude that these claims are accurate (though he does not disagree that the POWs died in large numbers). Among other things, the Red Cross was given rather easy access to Mukden inmates, and in all the camps where human experiments are known to have been performed all prisoners were killed as the war ended. In Mukden nearly seventeen hundred survived. What actually happened to all those men may never be conclusively known.

## UNSETTLED ACCOUNTS

Harris devoted much of his research to uncovering the greatest mystery about the cruel and calculated Japanese experiments: how they were so successfully hidden from postwar public view that none of the perpetrators suffered for their actions. In fact, the leaders of Unit 731, their sponsors in Tokyo, and those responsible for other biological weapons experiments on human beings remained prominent members of Japanese society after the empire's defeat and through the extraordinary recovery of a modern, democratic Japan. Including Ishii himself, they continued distinguished medical careers with impunity, some rising to the highest positions in the Japanese medical establishment.

In the beginning of the conflict with Japan, American authorities were at first so infected with racist attitudes about Japanese that characterized the rest of the country that they could hardly believe they were capable of sustained intellectual activities like a biological warfare program. Toward the end of the war, acting on a growing body of evidence, POW interrogations turned up some accurate information amid many convincing denials of knowledge. By June 1945 military intelligence was able to prepare an incisive memorandum on the subject.

Though alarmed by the extent of the Japanese program, American officials did not want to publicize their concerns because to do so might compromise their own biological weapons efforts at Fort Detrick in Maryland. There and at other installations like Edgewood, where the mustard gas studies were proceeding, the Chemical Warfare Service maintained a force of nearly four thousand. With $60 million in funding, the combined American biological warfare / chemical warfare program was second only to the Manhattan Project itself. While the work was mainly on defensive measures for military and civilian populations, steps were taken to produce bombs containing infectious organisms. At the same time, the Detrick scientists produced a great deal of valuable data for human and veterinary medicine and agriculture. Just as defensive and offensive weapons potential can rarely be segregated, so also the same knowledge can often improve the human condition as well as maim and kill.

With the American occupation of Japan, war crimes investigators did prepare charges against Ishii and others. Information poured in from so many sources that the story leaked to the American press. Ishii was apprehended and interrogated about many subjects, among then-persistent rumors that he had experimented on American POWs, but he was amazingly successful in standing up to psychological pressure and misleading his inquisitors, enormously downgrading the scale and success of his activities. Others also performed well in evading and confusing the Americans. Even so, Harris concludes that by late 1947 the investigators had plenty of evidence to indict the principal figures. The main obstacle to a war crimes trial was not evidentiary, but political.

For all their success, the Fort Detrick scientists had not been able to answer important questions about the delivery and field testing of biological weapons. The kinds of experiments that the Japanese performed on their "logs" and on the general Manchurian population could not be approved in the United States. Relations with the Soviets were deteriorating and Manchuria was under Stalin's control, adding to fears of communist hegemony in Asia. A Detrick division chief named Norbert Fell, who held a doctorate in microbiology, promised immunity to several important Japanese biological warfare scientists, and he held lengthy interviews with Ishii. Fell did bring home some useful information and was able to see through the lies and evasions of Ishii and his colleagues. However, the Japanese scientists succeeded in both avoiding any description of the full scope of their crimes and letting the Americans know that they had much important experience that they could share with the Americans rather than the Soviets. In thus tantalizing the visitors from Maryland they gained an important psychological beachhead for later negotiations.

When the Soviets started pressing the United States for the right to interrogate Ishii and others as part of their preparation for a war crimes trial, as well as to add to their own knowledge about the weapons, the Americans became as uncooperative as possible without creating an outright break with their putative allies. Interrogations did take place, but Ishii was in his usual clever form and gave his Soviet interviewers even less than he gave the Detrick representatives.

Finally, Ishii himself was granted immunity. Military intelligence accepted his tough negotiating position in light of the U.S. need for information about biological warfare uses for crop destruction and human experiments. In May 1947 a joint State Department-Armed Forces working group for the Far East recommended that all such information be referred to intelligence channels rather than the Tokyo War Crimes investigators. General MacArthur's headquarters forwarded this recommendation to the Joint Chiefs of Staff at the Pentagon. Interminable discussions then took place between the upper echelon of the occupational forces in Japan and Washington, and by March 1948 it was too late to organize materials for additional indictments in the war crimes prosecutions about to begin. By default, Ishii and his peers had escaped prosecution.

In summing up the history, Harris notes that ethical issues were not raised in deliberations about the fate of the Japanese biological warfare experts. In a theme that will become familiar, the main concern expressed was the embarrassment for the U.S. government if the deal became public. It has been suggested that the information finally provided by the Japanese added little to what had already been learned by the massive CWS effort at Fort Detrick and elsewhere from 1942 to 1945. The American scientists, Harris concludes, "hungered after forbidden fruit" because they were unable to go as far in their experiments as the Japanese did with such awful impunity. In fact, the American interest in biological weapons experiments was widely recognized as the great worldwide conflict raged. In 1942 Secretary of War Henry Stimson said that:

> The value of biological warfare will be a debatable question until it has been clearly proven or disproven by experiences. The wide assumption is that any method which appears to offer advantages to a nation at war will be vigorously employed by that nation. There is but one logical course to pursue, namely, to study the possibilities of such warfare from every angle, make every preparation for reducing its effectiveness, and thereby reduce the likelihood of its use.

As the Japanese experience attests, the evils of biological warfare are not so easily confined to its use in combat.

## ROUGH JUSTICE

Justice of a sort was meted out to some Japanese biological warfare scientists from an unlikely source. In December 1949 the Soviet Union conducted a war crimes trial in remote Khabarovsk for twelve of Ishii's associates who were unfortunate enough to be captured by the less forgiving of Japan's principle adversaries. In the fashion of Soviet justice the trial was remarkably efficient, requiring only five days to determine the guilt of all of the defendants, who were all given light sentences. If the trials were not a model of judicial deliberation, they did provide a wealth of detail about Ishii's operations that would otherwise have been lost. The testimony of Major General Kawashima Kyoshi, a Unit 731 division chief, was typical of the exchanges on human experiments:

QUESTION: Will you tell us what you knew about the experiments performed by the 1st Division on living people?

ANSWER: The prisoners kept in Detachment 731's inner prison were used for various researches in preparation of biological warfare. The object of the researches was: to increase the toxic effect of the lethal germs of various infectious diseases, and to study methods of employing these germs on human beings. I myself was never present at any of these experiments, and I am not in a position to give any details.

QUESTION: How were these experiments performed?

ANSWER: They were performed in the prison. In addition to the prison, there were special laboratories in which experiments were also performed on human beings.

QUESTION: How many prisoners was the prison designed to hold at one time?

ANSWER: From 200 to 300, but it could hold up to 400.

QUESTION: How many prisoners were sent to the detachment's prison in the course of a year?

ANSWER: I have no statistics on this point and do not know the exact figures, but roughly from 400 to 600 a year.

QUESTION: After a person had been infected with a particular germ, was he given medical treatment in the detachment's prison, or not?

ANSWER: He was.

QUESTION: And after he recovered, what happened to him?

ANSWER: As a rule, after he was cured he was used in other experiments.

QUESTION: And this went on until the person died?

ANSWER: Yes.

QUESTION: And every person who got into Detachment 731 was bound to die?

ANSWER: Yes. I know that in all the period the prison existed, not a single prisoner emerged from it alive.

QUESTION: What was the nationality of the people who were subjected to these dreadful experiments?

ANSWER: They were chiefly Chinese and Manchurians, and there were also some Russians.

QUESTION: Were there any women among the prisoners experimented on?

ANSWER: There were.

QUESTION: Did you see any women in the prison when you visited it in April 1941?

ANSWER: I did.

QUESTION: What was the nationality of these women?

ANSWER: I think they were Russians.

QUESTION: Were there any women with children among the prisoners?

ANSWER: One of the women had a baby in arms.

QUESTION: She was brought to Detachment 731's prison with her infant?

ANSWER: I heard that she gave birth to it in the prison.

QUESTION: And this woman was not destined to leave the prison alive?

ANSWER: Such was the rule when I served in the detachment, and that is what happened to this woman, too.

Each defendant's testimony was concluded with a ritual self-denunciation that referred to his medical background, as in the case of Kawashima:

QUESTION: As a doctor, you realized of course the inhumanity of experimenting on living people?

ANSWER: I did.

It is not known what influence the Nuremberg trials had on the Soviet decision to pursue a judicial proceeding, but the prosecutions in West Germany might well have given the Soviets an idea for disposing of the Japanese in their custody while also picking up some propaganda points abroad. Unlike Nuremberg, however, the Soviet trials engaged in none of the reflection on the ethical rules that should govern human experiments, nor did they provide an opportunity for the defendants' attorneys to put Soviet research on the record. Although the Khabarovsk trial's justice was too rough to deserve an honorable place beside Nuremberg, the facts revealed were not so inconsequential to deserve lumping it in as just another Soviet show trial.

## UNFINISHED BUSINESS

Ever since the end of the Korean War there have been persistent rumors that the United States applied its captured Japanese biological warfare information in that conflict. Those rumors have proven resistant to evidence and have been heatedly denied by U.S. authorities. Recently, however, two Canadian investigators have built a compelling, if not conclusive, case that America's secret deal with Ishii and his colleagues had concrete consequences only a few years later.

York University professors Stephen Endicott and Edward Hagerman have identified newly released documents from the United States, Canada, and China that undermine long-standing denials that the Japanese lessons were applied during the Korean War. Some of the most provocative evidence comes from Chinese memoranda at the highest governmental levels. In March 1952 outbreaks of suspicious diseases occurred in several Chinese provinces, and captured American soldiers were found to have been inoculated against plague—not standard operating procedure then or now.

Endicott and Hagerman cite a memorandum from the acting chief of staff of the Chinese army to Chairman Mao Zedong and Premier Zhou Enlai, reporting medical experts' view that cholera, typhoid fever, plague, and recurrent fever were the agents that could have had the effects seen. Meanwhile, the North Korean foreign minister lodged a protest at the United Nations about U.S. germ warfare. The Chinese formed a committee to centralize strategy for epidemic prevention, with Premier Zhou as its chair. Also in March 1952, the committee sent a top-secret telegram to local government officials:

> Since 28 January, the enemy has furiously employed continuous bacterial warfare in Korea and in our northeast and Quingdau areas, dropping flies, mosquitoes, spiders, ants, bedbugs, fleas . . . thirty-odd specimens of bacteria-causing insects. . . . They were dropped in a very wide area. . . . Examination confirms that the pathogenic microorganisms involved are plague bacillus, cholera, meningitis, paratyphoid, salmonella, relapsing fever, spirochaeta bacteria, typhus rickettsia, etc. . . . Now that the weather is turning warm, contagious disease and animal vectors will be active without restraint, and serious epidemic diseases from enemy bacterial warfare can easily occur unless we immediately intensify nationwide work on the prevention of epidemic disease.

According to a Chinese army document from March 13, 1952, five U.S.-trained agents of Korean origin dressed in North Korean army uniforms were captured and interrogated. "Their main task is to know the effect of the bacterial war, the army and civilian epidemic disease situation, how many days it takes for people to die and the number of deaths."

To be sure, information gained from the Japanese connection proved important for benign, public health purposes during the Korean War. Japanese biological warfare experts helped U.S.

Army doctors deal with an outbreak of hemorrhagic fever among American troops in 1952. Though its source remained a mystery, the disease was successfully treated. In spite of this constructive use of Japan's biological warfare expertise, Endicott and Hagerman note that work on hemorrhagic fever began a year before the epidemic, indicating an effort to transfer research results from the notorious Unit 731 to the U.S. biological warfare program.

It seems that the Chinese and North Koreans believed that their American enemy was using biological agents against them. But were they? Wartime Korea and post–World War II China were ripe for naturally occurring epidemics, but it is clear that Chinese public health experts thought their unusual disease outbreaks—which were successfully controlled—were not natural events. The rest of the case built by Endicott and Hagerman may be dismissed as circumstantial because there is no declassified "smoking gun" memo from the American side. However, they note a huge increase in spending on biological warfare development, from $5.3 million in 1950 to $345 million in the years 1951 to 1953. If nothing else, the Japanese experience helped stimulate American interest in rapid expansion of a biological warfare program.

At the end of 1996, the U.S. Department of Justice's Office of Special Investigations added yet another chapter to the Japanese biological warfare experiments. In a move that was necessarily more symbol than substance, the department announced that sixteen Japanese citizens were being put on a "watch list" of aliens who are ineligible to enter the United States. Some were involved in the operation of "comfort women stations," where women from Korea and other conquered territories were forced into prostitution to service Imperial Army forces during the war. Others were attached to Ishii's Unit 731, called by the Department of Justice "an infamous Japanese Army detachment in Manchuria that conducted inhumane and frequently lethal pseudo-medical experiments—including vivisection—on thousands of nonvolunteer prisoners of war and civilians." Though its modest force and language fails to capture the horror of the crimes, this announcement at least begins to close a circle in American history. The government embarrassment feared by American operatives who bargained with the biological warfare experts after the war has come to pass.

As was the case for the Paper Clip recruits, the trade-off for observing moral niceties at home was to make deals with those who had been devils abroad. At the risk of tarnishing American honor, moral compromises were viewed as necessary for survival in a new and bitterly divided postwar world. The hunger for forbidden fruit proved hard to quell as American scientists and defense officials placed on the drawing boards still more innovative weapons that created unknown and often undue risks for their handlers.

# THE RADIATION EXPERIMENTS

With one exception, the historical record suggests that these patient-subjects [who received plutonium injections] were not told that they were to be used in experiments for which there was no expectation that they would benefit medically, and as a consequence, it is unlikely that they consented to this use of their person.

*President Clinton's Advisory Committee on Human Radiation Experiments, 1995*

On March 24, 1945, a black, 53-year-old cement worker named Ebb Cade had a car accident near Oak Ridge, Tennessee. Suffering from broken bones in his right arm and both legs, Cade was taken to the nearby Manhattan Project Army Hospital. Because Cade's injuries required several operations to properly set the bones, he was kept in the hospital for a few weeks. It was long enough, also, for Cade—code-named "HP [human product] 1"—to become the first of eighteen patients to be injected with plutonium, 4.7 micrograms, on April 10, 1945.

In October 1995, President Clinton's Advisory Committee on Human Radiation Experiments concluded that Cade and all but the last of the plutonium subjects probably did not know they were being used in a study sponsored by the same top-secret agency working on the atomic bomb. These seventeen unaware patients had placed their trust in some of the most distinguished medical institutions in the country, at the University of Rochester, the University of Chicago, and the University of California. They had no reason to suspect their role in a military experiment, nor even a basis for understanding what such an experiment might be about. The very word *plutonium* was classified until after the bombings of Hiroshima and Nagasaki.

In spring 1997 President Clinton, following the advice of his expert committee, offered several hundred thousand dollars each in compensation to the one surviving subject and to the families of the others who had been secretly injected. Before this point was reached, the war that inspired the plutonium injections began to fade into history books, its successor cold "war" had finally ended, and the nation's nuclear complex and military establishment were being transformed to operate in a new world order. It had taken more than fifty years for the country to face its transgression, and still it might not have happened were it not for the efforts of journalist Eileen Welsome of *The Albuquerque Tribune*.

The cases of Ebb Cade and those who followed him in the plutonium injection series illustrate the pressures and tensions that surround military-medical research when a liberal, democratic society goes to war. The problems raised by the handling of plutonium were novel and important, and the amounts received by Cade and the others did not seem to do them any harm. In fact, the president's offer of compensation was based on the apparent failure to inform Cade and the others, and on later attempts to cover up the experiment, not on any evidence of injury. Nonetheless, the government concluded that the patients had been wronged. Adding insult to moral injury, there is controversy about the quality of the plutonium studies' design. They were mounted quickly, due to overwhelming concern about the risk faced daily by the laboratory workers exposed to a hazardous and unfamiliar substance while doing work of great patriotic importance.

## THE PLUTONIUM PUZZLE

The idea for the plutonium injection experiment did not originate at Oak Ridge but thousands of miles away, at Los Alamos, New Mexico, where radiobiologists were puzzling over the health effects of a new metal, introduced to the world by human hands. Plutonium got its start when the atomic bomb was being developed. There was great doubt that enough uranium-235 could be obtained from natural uranium to power more than one weapon by the January 1945 deadline the White House had given the Manhattan Project scientists. Glenn Seaborg and his team at the University of California at Berkeley had hit upon a likely answer to this problem in 1941, one for which Seaborg won the Nobel Prize. They found that a new element could be derived by first bombarding uranium-238 with neutrons to produce neptunium-239, and then isolating the product's emissions, or "daughters." The final result of that process was named plutonium, after the planet Pluto. "It should have been called 'Plutium,'" Seaborg said, "but we liked how 'plutonium' rolled off the tongue."

Plutonium's alpha-wave activity indicated that it could support an explosive chain reaction necessary for an atomic bomb. The production of sufficient quantities of plutonium was assigned to Enrico Fermi at the University of Chicago, who built an "atomic pile" that would sustain a chain reaction, enabling the uranium-238 isotope to absorb neutrons and create uranium-239, which would in turn decay to plutonium.

The substantial quantities of plutonium that would be handled raised questions about the well-being of the laboratory workers. Alpha waves do not penetrate the skin, but what if plutonium were ingested or inhaled? How much plutonium in the body is too much, and how can this be known? In all the history of the planet there was no experience with this element, isolated by human inventiveness. Previous experience with radiation sources, like that of early radiologists who died from X-ray exposure and young women who ingested liquid radium while painting watch dials, alerted physicians to potential problems. The challenge of answering these questions fell to a small fraternity of fairly young men in the new field of "health physics," the study of the effects of radiation upon the human body. Some of them were in close professional contact before the war, then they were given responsible positions all over the country at Manhattan Project facilities. Their concerns about plutonium converged as they went about their respective duties.

In 1942, radiologist Robert S. Stone was selected to run a new Health Division at Chicago. Several years before, Stone had done pioneering work on the use of cyclotron-produced neutrons in cancer treatment. Stone played a key role in the unfolding attitudes toward human radiation experiments, both during and after the war. His colleague in the radiation therapy studies at the University of California was Joseph Hamilton, who remained at The University of California at Berkeley in charge of the cyclotron. Both were hired by Ernest Lawrence, for whom the lab was later named. Early in 1944 Seaborg sent Stone several memos with the same theme. "I am seriously worried about the health of the people in my section, for which I am responsible," Seaborg wrote on January 15, "since they will soon handle such relatively large amounts of plutonium. I wonder whether some plutonium should be made available to Dr. Hamilton for his distribution studies sooner than the couple of months or more indicated in your memorandum." The shipment to Hamilton for animal studies at Berkeley was approved for February, when more "product" would be available. Meanwhile, Stone wanted plutonium to be regarded as "potentially extremely poisonous," with a very low, 5-microgram, tolerance limit.

Louis Hempelmann was a young Washington University-trained physician who worked at the Berkeley lab with Hamilton. Hempelmann was on his way to becoming one of the great experts on radiation epidemiology and health physics. In 1949 he published a paper that stopped a dangerous shoe-store marketing craze: the use of simple X-ray machines called fluoroscopes to fit children's shoes. In the 1960s he and a University of Rochester colleague identified X-ray treatment of mastitis as a cause of breast cancer in some of the treated women.

Shortly after Seaborg's worried letters to Stone, Hempelmann went to Boston to study safety measures in the radium industry. At around the same time, Joseph Kennedy of the Los Alamos Chemistry and Metallurgy Division (and another Berkeley cyclotron alumnus), was getting ready to receive quantities of plutonium from the project's Clinton, Tennessee, reactor. He asked Hempelmann about ingestion or inhalation risks to his personnel, and Hempelmann replied that the effect would be confined to local tissues.

There followed a period in which workers at Chicago and Los Alamos were regularly checked for plutonium levels, mainly by "nose swipes" in which samples were taken from each nostril using moist filter paper. These confirmed that workers could be exposed to fairly high levels of plutonium dust, especially when they failed to follow protocols. At Berkeley, Hamilton started his animal experiments to answer questions about the relationship between the mode of exposure and retention, and how rapidly the plutonium would be excreted from the human body. Though much was learned about plutonium from rodents and dogs—that it is a bone seeker like radium, that excretion rates are low, that the main absorption routes are through puncture wounds and inhalation—uncertainty about toxic levels in humans remained. Once again, the scientists noted, only so much can be gleaned from animal experiments when the organism of primary interest is the human being.

As though timed to trigger the next logical step in the experimental process, on August 1, 1944, a 23-year-old Los Alamos chemist named Don Mastick was opening a sealed tube containing 10 milligrams of plutonium when the vial suddenly burst. Gases that had built up in the tube caused the solution to spew out, splattering the wall. The acid taste in Mastick's mouth told him that he had been exposed to some of the plutonium vapor. Though his face and mouth were immediately scrubbed, for days thereafter just by blowing out of his mouth Mastick could cause an ionization chamber's needle to go off the scale from across a room. Hempelmann also pumped Mastick's stomach and retrieved plutonium he had swallowed. Mastick seemed none the worse for the exposure, however, even though tiny amounts of the plutonium were detected in his urine thirty years later.

Coming on the heels of five other accidents in which wounds were exposed to the product, this was enough for Hempelmann. Two weeks after the Mastick incident Hempelmann wrote to J. Robert Oppenheimer, head of the Los Alamos lab, recommending human experiments to answer the questions remaining from the animal work. The project should not be undertaken at Los Alamos, he said, but at a site with proper medical facilities. The fact that the Los Alamos staff was working almost constantly, trying to meet a deadline for the explosion of a prototype weapon less than a year later, lent urgency to the proposal.

## THE INJECTIONS CONTINUE

It is easy to assume that class differences separate those who conduct human experiments and those who are subjected to them. Ebb Cade was a working-class black man in Tennessee, surrounded by professionals with fancy credentials. But at least one of the key figures in the plutonium injection project was a talented biochemist who hailed from circumstances that were at least as modest as any of those who were injected with plutonium. Wright Langham was born in 1911 in Winnsboro, Texas. He emerged from his hardscrabble childhood a self-taught, and certainly self-motivated, aspiring scientist who graduated from Panhandle A&M College and received a doctorate from the University of Colorado. Langham was given a job with the Plutonium Project at Chicago, then was transferred to Los Alamos in 1944, where he remained until his death in a plane crash in 1972. By the time of his death, Langham was well recognized in international radiation science as the singular authority on the effects of plutonium on the human body, though in a world of large egos he retained his perspective. "I have not made any great contributions to science," he once said. "I have never been a scientific bride—so to speak—but I have been a bridesmaid at some of the biggest and most interesting scientific weddings in history." "Mr. Plutonium" was often called upon to advise authorities on contamination problems in the civilian and military nuclear energy programs. It was Wright Langham who arranged for 5 micrograms of plutonium to be sent from the Los Alamos Health Division to Oak Ridge, and it was Langham who analyzed the data received from the plutonium injections.

Ebb Cade received 4.7 of the 5 micrograms Langham provided, less than Robert Stone recommended as the maximum tolerance limit. The dosage was designed to mimic the excretion rate in a lab worker, with blood and bone samples analyzed hours later, and urine and stool samples collected and analyzed over the next six weeks. Fifteen of Cade's teeth were seriously decayed, and they were extracted and also sampled for plutonium. Whether they were extracted specifically for the study is not known, but that, too, would raise serious ethical questions.

Although Cade's injection level was low, the presidential advisory committee stated in 1995 that the cancer risk for the plutonium could not be ruled out for a 53-year-old man who might live another twenty years. In their own 1995 review of the plutonium injections, the Los Alamos lab argued that life expectancy would not have been that long for a man Cade's age in the 1940s. In fact, Cade died eight years after the injection from unrelated causes.

But the potential harm to Cade was not the main point, for even if the dose had deliberately been set low enough to avoid any possible injury, one could still ask whether a citizen should have been used in this way, apparently without his knowledge or consent. The matter of what Cade knew has not been entirely resolved. In 1974 an army doctor named Joseph Howland told Atomic Energy Commission (AEC) investigators that he had administered the injection without Cade's consent, on the written orders of a superior, Dr. Hymer Friedell, the Manhattan Project's deputy medical director. But Friedell told the presidential advisory committee that he did not order the injection, and that it was administered by another doctor at Oak Ridge, not Howland.

The action then shifted to Billings Hospital at the University of Chicago, where three more patients were injected with plutonium from April to December 1945. On April 16, a 68-year-old man with advanced cancer of the mouth and lung became the second subject. Then a 55-year-old woman with breast cancer was injected on December 27, and a young man with Hodgkin's disease on the same day, possibly at another Chicago area hospital.

The older man with cancer received only 6.5 micrograms, but the breast cancer patient and the man with Hodgkin's disease received 95 micrograms, far more than the others but still too little to produce effects right away. By the time the studies of samples from these patients were completed there was at least one surprising and useful result: The excretion rate of plutonium from human fecal material was far less than that of animals. Therefore, checking human stool turned out to be an unreliable method of determining the acceptable body burden of plutonium.

## WHO KNEW WHAT?

When AEC investigators spoke with one of the Chicago physicians in 1974, he claimed that the patients were told a radioactive substance was going to be injected that would "not necessarily" be for their benefit but might help others. If the three Chicago patients were informed in this fashion (and there is no documentary evidence to corroborate the story), then that would have been admirable as far as it went. However, to leave open the hope that they might have benefited from the injection would have compromised the ethics of the consent obtained; there was no hope that these patients would benefit from the injections. In fact, the man with lung cancer and the woman with breast cancer both died within eight months of being exposed to plutonium.

Meanwhile, Joseph Hamilton in California selected a 58-year-old man named Albert Stevens as the first California subject. Stevens had been admitted to the University of California's hospital in San Francisco with a diagnosis of stomach cancer, and he was injected on May 14, 1945. Shortly after Stevens' plutonium injection a large portion of his stomach was removed. Unfortunately, a lab analysis of the tissue showed that it was not cancerous; Stevens actually had a gastric ulcer.

In spite of the misdiagnosis (about which Stevens may never have been told), he was still a valuable subject for the collection of information about human plutonium excretion. When Stevens considered moving out of the Bay Area two months after the operation, Howland apparently attained approval for a small monthly payment to keep him there. The arrangement aroused the suspicion of his sister, a nurse, but, again, Stevens seems to have been in the dark about why his excreta were of such enormous interest to the university doctors.

The odd circumstances of Stevens' story pale in comparison to those of the second California subject, a 4-year-old boy from Australia named Simeon Shaw. Shaw's case came to the attention of the San Francisco researchers following newspaper stories about his rare case of osteogenic sarcoma. With great fanfare in the press, Shaw was flown in a U.S. Army transport to California, and in late April 1946 he was injected with a solution that included plutonium. A month later Shaw was discharged from the hospital and returned to Australia, where he died in January 1947.

The San Francisco researchers, led by Joseph Hamilton, may not have been embarrassed by the hopeful publicity aroused by Shaw's case because they had more in mind than just getting information for the Manhattan Project. Then and later, they expressed the hope that the evidence might help them treat future cancer patients. However, when the University of California at San Francisco (UCSF) did its own investigation fifty years later, an

expert committee found that Shaw himself could not have benefited from the injection and was not expected to.

Still more damning, the UCSF's internal investigation turned
up a 1946 memorandum from a Manhattan Project Research
Division officer, who said of the California team: "These doctors
state that the injections would probably be made without the
knowledge of the patient and that the physicians assumed full
responsibility." The 1995 report from the president's Advisory
Committee on Human Radiation Experiments found no evidence
that consent to the plutonium injections had been obtained from
Stevens or from the parents of Simeon Shaw.

The plutonium injections did not end with these first two
California patients. Elmer Allen, a 36-year-old African-American
railroad porter, was also injected in San Francisco following amputation of his left knee for bone cancer. Eleven more hospitalized
patients were injected at the University of Rochester, including
48-year-old Eda Schultz Charlton, who was suffering from a rash,
hepatitis, and a blood disease. John Mousso was 44 when he was
injected during treatment for Addison's disease, and Fred C. Sours
was 64, the town supervisor of Gates, New York, who was admitted
to Rochester's Strong Memorial Hospital for generalized dermatitis
and weakness. They all died years later of conditions seemingly
unrelated to their radiation exposure.

But suffering has been attributed to the injections themselves,
or at least to the circumstances surrounding them. In her discovery
of the story of Eda Charlton, for instance, Eileen Welsome of *The
Albuquerque Tribune* learned that after the injection Charlton suffered from nausea, vertigo, and severe weight fluctuations for the
rest of her life. In 1974 she was apparently told about the plutonium by Rochester physicians, who for years monitored plutonium
levels in her system. As she aged, Charlton became increasingly
cancer-phobic and depressed. She died of cardiac arrest in 1985.

Mousso and Charlton, along with the last of the plutonium
subjects, Elmer Allen, were admitted to the University of
Rochester's metabolic ward in 1973 for a follow-up study sponsored by the Argonne National Laboratory. Apparently they were
still not told the purpose of the studies, but they were given the

impression that this was part of their long-term care. The bodies of several deceased subjects, including Fred Sours, the Gates, New York, town manager, were exhumed to check plutonium levels in their skeletal remains. The families, too, were not told the true purpose of the exhumation, only that the U.S. Atomic Energy Commission wanted "to determine the microscopic distribution of residual radioactivity from past medical treatment," even though the plutonium injections were not conducted mainly to treat disease.

In 1972, before the follow-up study got started, the AEC decided not to use the word *plutonium* with the patients of the families of those who were deceased. "I protested that they must be given a reason for our interest in them," Argonne's Robert Rowland told the presidential advisory committee in 1994. "And I was told to tell them that they had received an unknown mixture of radioisotopes in the past, and that we wanted to determine if it was still in their bodies. Further, we were not to divulge the names of the institutions where they received this unknown mixture."

Argonne's Human Use Committee was informed of the follow-up study in 1973, after it had begun. Afterwards, the AEC did tell Eda Charlton and John Mousso about the plutonium injections, but the documents they were asked to sign did not include information about the possible risks of the injections. The AEC also decided that any further exhumations of remains should proceed with full disclosure to the families.

## SECRECY AND MEDICAL SCIENCE

Secrecy and deception among rival nations are not twentieth-century inventions. Military powers have always sought to keep the details of their war planning hidden from those who would do them harm. Espionage is perhaps the most ancient capital crime, even more universal in the severity of its consequences than defiling the gods. For the power to mete out punishment for threatening the state is crucial to its authority, and no threat to the state is greater than subversion.

Like other areas of modern warfare, such as the development
and manufacture of complex weapons systems, secrecy in science
poses problems that did not confront history's earlier generals.
Information about the tactical placement of fighting forces, and
even the strategic aims of a nation, could largely be protected by
the few who needed to know the big picture. More importantly,
command decision making does not demand or lend itself to the
participation of many different contributors working far afield of
one another. As the battle is unfolding, military leaders may well
consult with a few trusted advisors, but rarely will they engage in
an extended give-and-take.

The same cannot be said of modern science, which in its cre-
ative phase often demands the complementary or sometimes competing efforts of many disparate individuals. The sheer complexity
of scientific questions requires a degree of openness, while at the
same time scientific workers are jealous of their priority and, like
anyone else, want due credit for their breakthroughs. Either way,
scientists like to talk about their work and often chafe at external
constraints.

Many documents that became part of the Nazi doctors' trial
record at Nuremberg demonstrate the Reich leaderships' concern
to keep the concentration camp experiments under wraps. The
primary motivation for secrecy was the public relations problem
that knowledge of the experiments could cause, both at home and
abroad. Germany's enemies could exploit the information as propaganda, and the country's Catholics would be disturbed and
might even succeed in shutting down or at least slowing the effort,
as they had the "euthanasia" program. Although most of the camp
experiments seem to have been scientifically crude as well as
morally bankrupt, the German military establishment also gleaned
at least some useful information from the low-temperature and
altitude experiments that they did not want to share with their
enemies. After the war, medical advisors to the U.S. military
advised that air-sea rescue services should adopt the techniques
that had been found advantageous in the concentration camps.

It is not always easy for national security officials to decide
what medical research should be kept secret. At the extremes,

offensive weapons development seems a good candidate for high
security, but research for purely defensive purposes might not be,
depending upon how much information about offensive capacity
the defense-oriented research might betray. Similarly, research on
naturally occurring diseases in a region where combat might take
place might not be worth classifying—unless of course that
research would tip off an adversary about military objectives.

Specific cases belie general rules about state secrecy and medical
research, however. The malaria experiment organizers welcomed
publicity, but the venereal disease research was not trumpeted,
perhaps because of a wish not to offend puritanical sensibilities
rather than to protect national security. That the Navy did not
relieve the mustard gas "volunteers" of their oath of secrecy so
they could seek medical care, even decades after the experiments,
suggests a fear of publicity as much as of compromised national
security. On the other hand, World War I-era chemical warfare
activities were shielded from public view so far as possible.

The atomic bomb project was the greatest test of the now-
familiar marriage between science and state secrecy. This monumental effort not only called on the restraint of many brilliant and
highly independent physicists, it also demanded the employment
in massive industrial projects of many other skilled individuals
who hadn't the foggiest idea what their particular jobs were helping to create. In Los Alamos, New Mexico, for instance, 4,800
men and women maintained the device that separated uranium
radioisotopes for the first atomic weapons, without knowing what
the thing was for. The bomb itself was commonly referred to as
"the gadget," and the crucial uranium component as "tube alloy."
Considering the highly individualistic character of many of the
European physicists who were so important to the Manhattan
Project—a matter of some concern to government officials early
in the war—it is remarkable that they were finally willing to submit themselves to constraints on their professional discourse.

The experience with nuclear weapons design became the modern template for secrecy in national security research, one that
brought medical research into its domain, as well. No better example of this evolution is available than the plutonium injections.

From the beginning in 1941, plutonium was a closely held secret and was referred to in classified documents as "product" or "49" (its number on the periodic table is 94). But the plutonium injections were not the only case of medical research on radioactive substances brought within the ambit of national security, and they were not the last.

Nor were many such experimental programs officially secret; sometimes they were just too complicated in their purposes and arrangements to arouse public interest. Further, generally the results of sensitive medical experiments were published in the medical literature, but the circumstances or sponsoring agencies were often not mentioned in the articles. So if the government's investment in the research was not exactly secret, neither was it presented in such a way that attention would be drawn to any but its medical aspects.

The "Boston Project" is a nice illustration of these complicating factors. Plutonium was not the only radioactive substance being investigated during and after the war. While the plutonium injections were being done, studies were also being pursued with radioactive strontium, polonium, radium, and uranium. From 1953 to 1957, eleven terminally ill patients at Massachusetts General Hospital in Boston were injected with uranium in a project sponsored by the Oak Ridge National Laboratory. All but one had brain tumors, as the eleventh was misdiagnosed and instead suffered from a severe brain hemorrhage. The scientist in charge was Dr. William Sweet, a brilliant Harvard medical graduate and former Rhodes scholar. Sweet is an eminent neurosurgeon who received the prestigious Harvey Cushing Medal from the American Association of Neurological Surgeons.

Like the plutonium injections, the uranium experiment was motivated mainly by the need for safety standards for nuclear workers. In recent work on the project, historians Gilbert Whittemore and Miriam Bowling have found that the selection of brain cancer patients as the subjects, and of uranium as the radioisotope, was driven by the AEC's worker safety problem, not by the patients' needs. Nor was Sweet's team familiar with safe handling procedures for uranium, a fact that concerned AEC officials and that suggests animal work had not been done before the human exposures.

A secondary purpose of the project was to see if uranium would localize in the brain as a possible future cancer treatment. Even so, it could not have helped the patients with brain cancer because the rest of the theorized treatment (activating the uranium in the brain with a neutron beam) was never done. Unlike the plutonium injections, however, all the uranium injections were very high doses, and all the patients were severely ill, with many dying. Interviewed in 1995, Dr. Sweet maintained that he received consent from the patient and family members. "We relied on communication with the family, because even an individual who is much of the time alert and cognitive function to understand yes, it's a dangerous situation, we had no way of proving that. We felt the next of kin responsible—relative or relatives—had to be the ones who were told what we were up to." The patients and their families had already been given the terminal diagnosis. Dr. Sweet continued, "They were all extremely grateful, and assumed that what doctors already had told them [sic], that the situation was totally hopeless. If you're willing to spend some time trying to help them out, they're just too grateful for words."

Without intending to take advantage of their patients' gratitude, medical researchers sometimes do just that. Were the families told that their dying relatives were to be used in experiments that would do them no good, and that might actually hurt their kidneys with a high burden of uranium? There is no record, and anyway, as the president's Advisory Committee on Human Radiation Experiments said of the uranium studies, "there was no justification for using dying patients as mere means to the ends of the investigators and the AEC."

## THE SECRET POSTWAR RESPONSE TO THE PLUTONIUM INJECTIONS

Elmer Allen, the 36-year-old African-American railroad porter, was the last of the eighteen subjects injected with plutonium, on July 18,

1947, and probably the only one who was told anything about the experiment before it was done. The difference in procedure was the result of the fact that the war had ended, and many Manhattan Project activities were turned over to a new civilian agency, the AEC. When the AEC administrators learned about the plutonium injections they were surprised. When they learned that more were proposed they were, to put it mildly, alarmed. The complex secret debate that ensued about using one more human subject in an ongoing experiment might be unique in the annals of medical science. Certainly the confrontation that ensued between civilian authorities and research physicians was virtually unprecedented.

Elmer Allen's accidental role in postwar military-medical research began when he hurt his left knee getting off a train. Company doctors in Oakland diagnosed a fracture but it wouldn't heal, and the railroad refused to accept liability. After six months out of work, and with his leg too swollen to walk, in June 1947 Allen was referred to the University of California's clinic in San Francisco. Pathologists concluded that the failure to heal could be attributed to bone cancer. Amputation was recommended, and with his cancer diagnosis Elmer was the sort of patient who would fit into the plutonium injection series.

While Elmer Allen was suffering with his injury, administrators at the new, civilian-controlled AEC were puzzling over one of their inheritances from the atomic weapons project. The AEC opened its doors in January 1947, taking over most atomic-energy-related activities from the Department of Defense and the Manhattan Project. As the government entity most involved in the development and use of atomic energy, the AEC was uniquely situated to establish and promote policies for radiation-related research with human subjects. The AEC was the primary supplier of radioisotopes used in research during the 1940s and into the 1950s. In the shadow of Hiroshima, Nagasaki, and the 1946 nuclear bomb tests in the Bikini Atoll, the AEC moved quickly and cautiously in its dual role of promoter and protector in the field of atomic energy.

Just before the official dissolution of the Manhattan Engineer District, in December 1946, its officials ordered a halt to the injection of radioactive substances in California. A month later

Stafford Warren, the project's medical director who had become head of the AEC's medical advisory board, recommended further "clinical testing" of radioactive materials to the AEC's first chief, Carroll Wilson. In keeping with the AEC's engineering culture, Wilson's title was General Manager. In the months to come the new agency's deliberate, efficient hands-on manager would be locked in a struggle for control of the nation's human radiation research enterprise, but not with the military. Rather, Wilson's struggle would be with some of his medical colleagues within the AEC's circle of advisors, with himself cast as a member of the laity.

Carroll Louis Wilson was a pioneer in the field of nuclear power management and an important junior member of the small science policy fraternity of the 1940s. Wilson, was also a member of the "MIT mafia" that was so important in establishing America's science policy, and worked closely with the most distinguished members of that group. He had been an assistant to MIT president and Manhattan Project czar Karl Compton, and to Vannevar Bush. He had also helped David Lilienthal, former head of the Tennessee Valley Authority and the first AEC chairman, in preparing Lilienthal's landmark 1946 *Report on the International Control of Atomic Energy*. Wilson was as well prepared as anyone for the enormous task he faced at the AEC in producing, controlling, and promoting the use of atomic energy.

Wilson's main antagonist that spring was Stafford Warren, a colorful first-generation health physicist with a bit of a swagger who prided himself on being at the center of the action. Tall, handsome, and mustachioed, the California-bred Warren had been among the first physicians to inspect the damage after the atomic bombing of Japan. When the U. S. military conducted its famous and well-publicized atomic bomb tests at the Bikini Atoll in 1947, Warren was the head of radiation safety for the sailors who were charged with checking the target ships. An outsized character who relished the adventure that fate had provided his generation of atomic scientists, Warren arrived for his first day of work at the Manhattan Project packing a sidearm.

Wilson authorized Warren's January request for further radiation experiments, but only on an interim basis, and the AEC's lawyers set some conditions after a meeting with Warren. One of the conditions was that "it be susceptible of proof that any individual patient, prior to treatment, was in an understanding state of mind and that the nature of the treatment and possible risk involved be explained very clearly and that the patient express his willingness to receive treatment." The lawyers also wanted a written, patient "release," but Warren rejected this point and won. After all, these were still the days in which it was accepted that doctors may determine what their patients knew. Instead, Warren got the agency to agree that at least two doctors would "certify in writing" that the patient had received an explanation and had agreed to the experimental "treatment." Round one belonged to Stafford Warren.

While these negotiations were going on, the Manhattan Project deputy medical director, Hymer Friedell, recommended that a report about two of the Chicago plutonium injections be declassified. An AEC declassification officer (whose name is unknown) immediately saw the implications of the experiment. His February 28, 1947, memo is one of the most prophetic statements ever made about national security and human subjects research.

> The document appears to be the most dangerous since it describes experiments performed on human subjects, including the actual injection of the metal plutonium into the human body. . . . It is unlikely that these tests were made without the consent of the human subjects [perhaps a diplomatic statement to the writer's superiors], but no statement is made to that effect and the coldly scientific manner in which the results are tabulated and discussed would have a very poor effect on the public. Unless, of course, the legal aspects were covered by the necessary documents [presumably patient permission forms], the experimenters and the employing agencies, including the U.S., have been laid open to a devastating lawsuit which would, through its attendant publicity, have far-reaching results.

Perhaps it was this anxious declassifier's memo that forced Warren back to the table. In early March Warren attended a meeting with Major Birchard Brundage, chief of the AEC's medical division, and two agency lawyers. The session might have been a bit tense, if not testy. The lawyers again wanted to require researchers to obtain a "written release" from patients. Warren would not cede doctors' authority to decide how to practice, however. Finally, the lawyers accepted his "recommendation" that, instead of a patient's signature, two doctors would "certify in writing to the patient's state of mind to the explanation furnished him and to the acceptance of the treatment." Not wishing to trust entirely Warren's memory about the agreement's details, the legal advisors did make a point of writing a memorandum for the record about their conviction "that the patient must express his willingness to receive the treatment."

Though Warren had succeeded in protecting the self-determination of medical researchers, by allowing nonphysicians (the AEC legal advisors) to set a standard for disclosure he made an important—and in some ways historic—concession. This concession meant that, unlike the previous plutonium injection patients, Elmer Allen would be told about the experimental nature of his "treatment" in July, even though it was really a "clinical test." In an April 30, 1947, letter to Warren, who had returned to California to become dean of the UCLA medical school, Wilson confirmed the deal, which meant that several medical schools would continue to receive grant funds under the new AEC, including UCLA. But another part of that letter was not honored in Elmer Allen's case. It required that the "treatment" has some "therapeutic effect," but there was no reason to believe the plutonium would help Allen.

Now what to do about the previous injections? Because there was no evidence that consent had been obtained from the seventeen subjects, it was decided to maintain the injections' secrecy. On March 19, 1947, the chief of the AEC's medical division gave the rationale for keeping the Chicago plutonium report classified.

> The Medical Division also agrees with Public Relations that it would be unwise to release the paper . . . primarily because of medical legal aspects in the use of plutonium in human beings

and secondly because of the objections of Dr. Warren and General Cooney [of the AEC's Division of Military Applications] that plutonium is not available for extra Commission experimental work, and thus this paper's distribution is not essential to off Project experimental procedures.

In spite of the agreement to keep the previous injections quiet, the AEC's physician-scientists and nonphysician officials had some more tense meetings in early April. "The Commission does not intend to influence in any way the exercise of judgment by the doctor as to the administration of any particular treatment authorized under the approved program," Wilson wrote to Warren on April 30. Then he added a facetious remark that said much about his relations with the AEC's medical advisors. "Indeed, from the discussion at the meetings of April 3-5, it seems evident to me that doctors would not allow their judgment on this matter to be influenced by anyone." The AEC's chief had run up against the solid wall of the medical profession's self-determination.

Wilson's requirements for documented consent and therapeutic intent were not exactly widely broadcast at AEC labs or among their contract researchers. Despite its combing of old AEC archives, the Advisory Committee on Human Radiation Experiments couldn't find any evidence that "the letter or its contents" (as their report put it) were communicated to anyone other than Stafford Warren. There is only one instance in which Wilson's letter seemed to make a difference: in the paperwork for Elmer Allen's plutonium injection at the University of California at San Francisco in July. According to Allen's medical record, "the experimental nature of the intramuscular injection of the radioactive nature was explained to the patient, who agreed upon the procedure. The patient was fully oriented and in sane mind." In accord with Wilson's directive, three doctors signed as witnesses.

Elmer Allen never recovered from his medical problems following his amputation. In spite of a loyal and loving wife he suffered from various medical and emotional problems and sank into a long life of despair and alcoholism. His troubles cannot be attributed to the plutonium injection, but the experiment took advantage of a poorly educated, working-class black man with a grave diagnosis in the racist environment of midcentury America. Regardless of the importance of the information that might have been obtained, the selection of Elmer Allen did not bring honor to the medical research community. The only tangible result of the Wilson-Warren debate, the minimal "consent" form signed by others, was not enough to ensure that Allen was truly a volunteer.

Inadequate though the consent was in Allen's case, it was more consideration than was accorded the seventeen others who preceded him. Surely one crucial difference was that the first seventeen plutonium injections took place during wartime. So far as is known, there was never an explicit directive that, due to the national emergency, some individuals could be unwitting experimental subjects. Rather, it was assumed that some things could be done because they were necessary for the war effort. And when there was explicit consideration of policies on human experiments, as in the Committee on Medical Research, it was unclear exactly what the limits were. There was at least formal agreement that only "volunteers" could be used. As the AEC lawyers realized early in 1947, the first seventeen plutonium subjects did not meet even this modest standard.

With the end of the war, and especially before the marked deterioration in relations with the Soviet Union, there was no national emergency to rationalize a failure to use only "volunteers." Hence the perceived need for Elmer Allen's "consent." In another sense, though, the. national security establishment that grew up almost overnight just before and during the war, and that continued into the postwar period, never shed the culture of secrecy that accompanied its creation. At least in its early years the civilian-dominated AEC seems to have been aware of the complexities posed by secrecy for the medical experiments it sponsored, so much so that worries about human subjects continued into late 1947, even after the deal with Stafford Warren.

The final tragedy of the plutonium injections lies in the fact that the purpose they were to serve—helping to protect nuclear workers from radiation exposure—was an abject failure. In spite of an intention to follow internal radiation sources that might have been inhaled or swallowed, the major federal effort turned out to focus on "external emitters," by requiring workers to wear radiation badges. In 1997, a nonprofit and nonpartisan organization called the Institute for Energy and Environmental Research, reported that "large numbers of nuclear weapons workers have received information which systematically understates their actual exposures, because the dosages were not combined." The Department of Energy denied that many people would have had high exposures once the data was recalculated, but the very fact that the internal sources of radiation damage were dropped from calculations until the late 1980s points to the fact that the plutonium injections were a road to nowhere.

## DISCOVERING "INFORMED CONSENT"

Still troubled by the issues raised by the plutonium injections, in June 1947 Wilson convened a three-day meeting of an independent, blue-ribbon Medical Board of Review to advise on policy for the new agency's medical research. Composed of distinguished physicians and scientists, many of whom were intimately involved in the work of the Manhattan Project, AEC-sponsored human experiments were on the agenda. Their conclusions were endorsed by the Advisory Committee on Biology and Medicine but are known only because Wilson communicated them to Robert S. Stone in November. Stone was the Chicago health division chief to whom Seaborg had worried about his staff working with plutonium, and who had advised on plutonium exposure limits.

After the war Stone became professor of radiology at the University of California at San Francisco. In the fall of 1947 he asked the AEC to declassify some of his reports so they could be published in scientific journals, apparently the same documents that had started the whole human research debate in the first place a year before. Carroll Wilson wrote to Stone, again denying the declassification request and reporting the new AEC policy, that no "substance known to be, or suspected of being, poisonous or harmful" should be used in human subjects unless all of the following conditions were met:

(a) that a reasonable hope exists that the administration of such a substance will improve the condition of the patient, (b) that the patient give his complete and *informed consent* in writing, and (c) that the responsible next of kin give in writing a similarly complete and informed consent, revocable at any time during the course of such treatment. [emphasis added]

This was an amazing statement. Not only did it mark the first time anyone is known to have used the term *informed consent* (even the Nuremberg Code, written around the same time, used the then-conventional *voluntary consent*), it also required that one's "next of kin" consent to one's being in an experiment! That was a far higher standard than had ever been set before or since, and neither practical nor ethically necessary. Wilson also quoted his blue-ribbon Medical Board of Review's justification.

Were it not for the extreme value and pressure for securing reliable information on the limits of human tolerance of radioactive substances there would be no need for explicit reference to this subject [human testing]. . . . We believe that since secrecy must of necessity mark much of the medical research supported by the federally-sponsored AEC, particular care must be taken in all matters that under other circumstances would be open to investigation and publicity.

The continuing efforts of Stone and others to have the plutonium papers declassified were denied because the studies did not meet the criteria newly articulated by the AEC. No doubt Stone and his colleagues regarded this as a highly unfair ex post facto arrangement, requiring experiments to satisfy conditions that were not stated at the time the experiments were planned or executed. In Nuremberg a similar argument was being made by Servatius on behalf of Karl Brandt. Experiments that had already been done and did not meet the stated criteria, the AEC decided, would have to be kept secret. In spite of his failure in 1947, Stone continued to be an aggressive advocate of human radiation experiments.

The Medical Board of Review's concern about the implications of a federal agency doing such work was shared by others in the nuclear bureaucracy that fall. In September 1947 the Oak Ridge manager asked Carroll Wilson "what responsibilities does the AEC bear for human administration of isotopes?" Two weeks later Oak Ridge sent its own memorandum to the AEC's Advisory Committee on Biology and Medicine listing "pros and cons" of human experiments. Among the latter were:

> (1) Moral, ethical, and medico-legal objections to the adminis-tration of radioactive material without the patient's knowledge or consent; (2) There is perhaps a greater responsibility if a federal agency condones human guinea pig experimentation.

"Human guinea pig experimentation" was a fairly vivid state-ment of the problem facing the agency. The risks of bad publicity should word of the experiments leak, including the prospect of lit-igation, were aggravated by the public trust that government agencies enjoy when they are permitted to work in secret. All the more important to attain the most thorough documentation of subject consent possible. In a formalistic, legal sense, having the subject sign a consent form would have been far more convincing than just having doctors sign their own statement in the patient's record. All this was clear even to those working at the AEC's var-ious facilities, like Oak Ridge, and they wanted some guidance from the top of the agency. Wilson and his administrative col-leagues backed down on that issue in the spring of 1947, but they seemed to have had their resolve stiffened by the Medical Board of Review report.

Nonetheless, Wilson's letter to Stone had even less distribution than his letter to Stafford Warren the previous April. It appears to have been mailed and the policy promptly forgotten, since there is no evidence that it was ever applied anywhere. By 1951 a member of the AEC's biology and medicine division asserted that the agency has not established "a general policy concerning human experimentation," and letters between Los Alamos and the AEC central office in 1956 were written as though the 1947 statements had never been made. Carroll Wilson and his AEC managers tried to take action to resolve a thorny problem, but they were no match for a powerful medical establishment that, at the end of the day, called the tune.


## THE NUCLEAR-POWERED AIRCRAFT DEBATE

There was another "Dr. Warren" to advise the AEC about medical matters, Shields Warren, a very different person from Stafford Warren and unrelated, though they were often confused with each other in their shared field. The confusion was ironic, since they were often at odds, especially concerning the propriety of human experiments. But though highly principled and reflective, Shields Warren was not nearly as strong a personality as his antagonist on this issue. He was a mild person who spoke with a stutter, an impediment that mysteriously disappeared when he lectured about health physics.

Shields Warren had been a professor at Harvard Medical School. An authority on cancer pathology, he became a leading light in the early movement for peaceful uses of atomic energy. In his role as the AEC's first director of its biology and medicine division and a subsequent agency advisor during the cold war, he was frequently torn between his sense of duty to the nation and his other personal ideals. Warren was a tragic figure in the history of human radiation experiments. Though he was often scrupulous about the use of human subjects, he was also gradually worn down in the 1950s by demands from all sides to lessen radiation protections, especially in the case of Native American uranium miners.

Shields Warren played a key role at a September 1949 meeting of officials from Britain, Canada, and the United States in Chalk River, Ontario, where "permissible body burdens" of plutonium were being discussed in the context of continued work on atomic weapons. Because, as Warren pointed out, very little was known about the effects of plutonium on human beings, a conservative standard of 0.1 microgram body burden was set, the same as for radium. But Wright Langham of Los Alamos complained that such a low standard would make his lab's work impossible; they had been using a 1.0 microgram permissible body burden. Apparently under pressure to raise the Chalk River standard, a group that included Langham met in Warren's Washington office in January 1950. They decided to split the difference between the Chalk River and Los Alamos standards. Though given various rationales over the years, 0.5 is still the level in use for the permissible body burden of plutonium.

Did this episode demonstrate Shields Warren's skill as an administrator or his willingness to be moved by national security interests? In fact, there wasn't much human data to support any particular level, as Warren himself knew. But unlike some of his colleagues, Warren was no fan of high-dose radiation experiments on humans. His cautious attitude was reflected in a controversy two years after the last plutonium injection and right around the time he was working through the problem of the permissible body burden. In 1949 the AEC and the Pentagon formed a Joint Panel on the Medical Aspects of Atomic Warfare. Among other things, they were to help plan a project called Nuclear Energy for the Propulsion of Aircraft, or NEPA. Just as the Navy was working on its nuclear submarine, so also the idea that an airplane could have an unlimited power source with a crew that could stay aloft indefinitely, protecting the skies from the Soviets, was compelling. But what about shielding the crew from the nuclear power source? How much protection was needed in exchange for what margin of safety?

The NEPA project was advised by a who's who of radiation safety experts: Stafford Warren, Robert Stone, Joseph Hamilton, Hymer Friedell, Shields Warren, and Alan Gregg, chair of the AEC's biology and medicine advisory group. Stone and Shields Warren were the principal players. In January 1950 Stone submitted a nine-page paper to the joint panel arguing that only by conducting human experiments would it be possible to predict the biological effects of radiation exposure and that it would be ethical to do so. Stone argued that such experiments were needed, not only because of the nuclear-powered aircraft then being researched but also owing to the prospect that soldiers and sailors would be exposed to radiation from weapons as a result of international hostilities.

From a scientific standpoint, Stone noted the wide disagreement among radiologists about doses that would produce "specific effects" in humans. Thus Stone recommended that some people be exposed to 25 roentgens and observed. If there were no "significant" changes, then the dosage should be doubled, and then repeated a week later. If there were again no significant changes, the amount should be at least doubled, to 150 roentgens. Based on experience with the ill at these levels, Stone writes, "it seems unlikely that any particular person would realize that any damage had been done to him by such exposure." Stone argued that the small risks of "undetectable genetic effect" on the life span or possibly on the blood must be weighed against the advantages of actual human exposure, such as reassuring pilots who would carry out a particular mission.

Stone did his homework on the history of human experiments. He noted that the use of human subjects in medical experiments was not new, mentioning Edward Jenner's development of a smallpox vaccine (using his own son and neighborhood children as subjects), Walter Reed's yellow-fever work, the use of federal prisoners by the Public Health Service, and the CMR's malaria studies in state penitentiaries. In a section called "The Ethics of Human Experimentation," Stone cited Andrew Ivy's view that the most important ethical requirement is that subjects be volunteers who are under no "undue pressure" to participate. Stone also cited the American Medical Association's code of ethics, and the analysis by the Illinois committee appointed by Governor Dwight H. Green of Illinois that Ivy chaired.

Stone concluded that the proposed radiation experiments met all ethical criteria. He recommended that a subject population be identified that can be followed years after exposure: "Life prisoners are the one group of people that are likely to remain in one place where they can be observed for a great many years." To obtain "short term results," other types of subjects might be used. "Patients with incurable cancer such as those having multiple metastases might volunteer. . . . Certain scientists might be willing to volunteer for specific doses," as well as some in the "general population," but again they might be hard to follow. Those under 21 should be ruled out because they cannot legally volunteer, as probably should "those below the menopause (unless they have incurable cancer) . . . because of psychological factors." The significance of the latter remark is unclear. Perhaps these "psychological factors" had to do with adding yet another stress to their situation, or perhaps Stone was referring to the unfairness of raising their hopes of a cure.

At first the NEPA Medical Advisory Committee approved in principle the need for further human experiments, and the Pentagon's Committee on Medical Sciences endorsed the proposal, but at a late January 1950 meeting the Pentagon committee revoked its endorsement. The transcripts of this and many other Pentagon advisory meetings survive, having been declassified in 1994. They constitute an extraordinary window into the history of the debate about human experiments and national security.

At the Pentagon's committee meeting, some argued, as did Stone, that there was a need for human experiments under "safe" conditions using "volunteers," and others were clearly opposed. A revered senior professor of physiology from the University of Rochester, Wallace O. Fenn, warned that human experimentation "is a very dangerous route to get started on and that we shouldn't sanction human experimentation without careful consideration. . . . I think we will get the information that is required from animals, animal experimentation and accidental exposure and shouldn't approve routine experimentation on volunteers."

Also on the Committee on Medical Sciences was the Air Force's legendary Harry Armstrong, the man who sponsored Hubertus Strughold and dozens of other German medical scientists. Now with the rank of general, Armstrong defended human experimentation. If they were to be blocked in the specific case of radiation, where would a prohibition end?

I don't believe we can adopt that stand because if we do it for that we should do it for all areas of research, and certainly, many of our valuable findings in the past have been based on volunteer human experimentation. I think that the actual research should be evaluated in each individual case and certainly given every possible safeguard but if we go on record as being opposed to human research experimentation in this field we should apply it, I believe, to all fields.

Attempting to defend his position from Armstrong's critique, Fenn responded, weakly, "I wouldn't make it quite as broad as that. I'd qualify that a little." But Armstrong hit him with both logical barrels: What makes the risks of being in a medical experiment any different from other risks encountered in the armed forces?

I don't see there is any great difference in principle in undertaking a hazardous [medical] procedure [as compared with dangerous training conditions]. It seems to me it doesn't make much difference whether it's an atomic energy [*sic*] or using an ejection seat at 530 miles an hour. They are both likely to kill you, and I don't see any particular reason why we should include any area, or if you include one you must include them all. I don't see where you should make any distinction.

Of course, Armstrong added, "I certainly don't think we should advocate widespread and superficial plunging into this thing by any means, but I don't think we can solve that by simply saying we are not in favor of any human experimentation."

Then Shields Warren's name came up. What is the view of the AEC's medicine and biology division, a member asked. "I talked with Dr. [Shields] Warren and he agreed with me," said Fenn, whose impression of Warren's view was confirmed by another member. Warren was indeed strongly opposed to Stone's proposal, and he had company. In April, when the joint panel backed off the use of military personnel and endorsed prisoner volunteers, the AEC's Alan Gregg asked a Pentagon official if the proposal didn't "fall in the category of cruel and unusual punishment?" To which

Shields Warren added, "It's not very long since we got through trying Germans for doing exactly the same thing."

Another possibility was to observe the effects of radiation on cancer patients. This idea was attractive because, in theory, these people were being exposed to radiation anyway, for therapeutic reasons. The question was posed at a May 1950 meeting of the Pentagon's Committee on Medical Sciences. It was agreed the AMA principles of medical ethics, authored by Ivy, would have to be respected. But could the needed information be obtained this way? Rear Admiral F. C. Greaves of the Navy Medical Corps expressed doubt on the eminently practical grounds that cancer patients might not survive long enough.

> I agree with Colonel Stone in that there certainly is a need for this type of information, particularly in view of the fact that we are going to be confronted with the problem of protecting personnel, not only in airplanes, but also in submarines, of this type of thing. . . . But this is a long-range think [sic], and people who have types of diseases in which it is necessary to give them X-ray therapy may not be with us long enough to make the information we get valid.

An Army colonel named Stone (unrelated to physicist Robert Stone) then candidly expressed the reality of the military's needs, which did not necessarily resemble the kind of information that could be gathered from treating a serious illness.

> Admiral Greaves, I'd like to point out that from the Army's viewpoint, at least, the levels that we are particularly interested in are those of relatively short duration. In other words, a man may develop a cancer 20 years later but if he is in the middle of combat we don't think that would actually deter from actually something [sic], so that what we are interested in is what level is going to make this man sick or noneffective within a period of 30 days, in all probability. Now we are very much interested in long-term effects but when you start thinking militarily of this, if men are going out on these missions

anyway, a high percentage is not coming back, the fact that you may get cancer 20 years later is just of no significance to us.

Callous though it may have sounded, this was an honest statement of the military perspective.

The discussion then returned to the practicality of using cancer patients, and Stone continued.

I think it would have to be a selective study. For instance, take any of our big centers where we have quite a lot of cases of carcinomas; (you can't pick lymphomas, but carcinomous types of metastasis) a number of those individuals will live in varied states of health from a period of six to eight months and X-ray therapy was indicated in epilating measures, and I think when we study our material on the population in Japan, plus our combined animal work, then we might logically draw up a series of bracketing experiments in which you probably get 30 to 50 such cases in a hospital like Memorial Hospital, for instance, in New York, or certain hospitals in other cities, by carefully selecting the cases and getting the amount of radiation from that bracket we might be able to get a very satisfactory answer.

Admiral Greaves agreed with that plan, but then his frustration with delays in answering important national security questions surfaced. "I am wondering if we are not being a little too skiddish [*sic*] about this. We have a problem on our hands and I think we should consider it very seriously, but whether it is enough of a problem to go ahead and take a chance." But others, such as Colonel Elbert DelCoursey of the U. S. Army Medical Corps, alluded once again to the recent experience with Nazi experiments. "I must say that in my own mind I realize that all of these things are important to know and we must know them," DelCoursey said, "but it is difficult for me to come to a decision of whether or not you should go into human experimentation on this because of the world opinion on the experimentation in Germany. That bothers me." Admiral Greaves concurred. "I find it very difficult, too," he admitted.

Wallace Fenn then expressed further discomfort with attitudes that might permit prisoner experimentation:

> I think the important thing is whether you take the decision to go down this road of human experimentation and work on prisoners, even though they are volunteers, and start the idea that as long as they are prisoners it really doesn't matter very much what you do to them, and it is no great loss to society, which I think it isn't, but it is a bad decision.

But Greaves emphasized that it is not because prisoners are less valued as human beings that they are good candidates for experimentation. The important thing about them is that they are available. "I don't think the reason for the proposal to use prisoners is because they were prisoners to society, or little use to society," he argued. "The reason was that they would be there and you can put your finger on them and observe them for a long period of time. That isn't true of volunteers from the rest of the world, either Armed Forces or otherwise. They are here maybe this year and gone next. You lose track of them. This is a long-term thing."

Among other considerations, the burdens of secrecy were a continuing source of discomfort. At their September 1950 meeting, the AEC's biology and medicine advisors concluded "that human experimentation at the present time is not indicated, that it would have serious repercussions from a public relations standpoint if undertaken by an agency that has to do a portion of its work in secret;. and that adequate data can be obtained from animal exper[iments], from the Los Alamos accidents, from certain observations which have been made by clinical radiologists, and from the studies at Hiroshima and Nagasaki." Though they weren't on this list, the Nazi example kept reemerging. In the end it might well have been the crucial factor in sinking the NEPA human experimentation proposal. Even one of Robert Stone's colleagues, Berkeley's Joseph Hamilton, wrote Shields Warren in December 1950 that the idea of using prisoners "would have a little of the Buchenwald touch."

One alternative that was rarely mentioned in the NEPA debate, or indeed in the entire postwar history of human experimentation, was that researchers themselves should volunteer to be subjects. Self-experimentation not only became unfashionable as the twentieth century went on, it was less useful as more complicated experiments involved a wider array of variables and required subjects in various conditions.

Tragically, one who died from years of reckless exposure to radiation sources was Berkeley nuclear medicine enthusiast Joseph Hamilton. To demonstrate to students the value of radioactive tracers for medicine, Hamilton liked to drink water laced with radioactive iodine and then hold a Geiger counter up to his neck, which clicked wildly. Hamilton died of leukemia in 1957 at the age of 49.

## THE PENTAGON'S DRESS REHEARSAL

The NEPA debate turned out to be a transitional episode, one in which the human experiments problem passed from the Atomic Energy Commission to the Department of Defense. Several of the Pentagon's secret councils would spend a great deal of time on the issue over the next few years. One high-level body that subsequently played an important role in the promulgation of the draft human experiments policy was the Armed Forces Medical Policy Council (AFMPC), to which the NEPA experiments issue was referred in 1951. Shortly before that, at the end of 1950, Shields Warren expressed his opposition to Stone's proposal in no uncertain terms: "I am very much opposed to human experimentation when it isn't good for the individual concerned and when there is any other way of solving the problem."

Apparently Warren's view carried the day, in both the AEC and the Pentagon. According to the AFMPC's 1951 annual report, the official position of the Department of Defense on human experiments was to wait for AEC approval because, as the report delicately stated, "the research program required to develop necessary scientific information concerning radiation doses involves both civilian and military problems." The "problems" were not only medical questions, but also policy issues about human experiments. To buttress its position, the AFMPC quoted the opinion of the AEC's Division of Biology and Medicine:

> that human experimentation at the present time is not indicated, that it would have serious repercussions from a public relations standpoint, particularly if undertaken by an agency that has to do a portion of its work in secret; and finally that adequate data can be obtained from animal experimentation, from Los Alamos accidents, form certain observations which have been made by clinical radiologists, and from the studies at Hiroshima and Nagasaki.

For the fledgling AEC, the plutonium injections helped lead to some of the cold war's most carefully drawn procedures in the use of human subjects. Not the Carroll Wilson letters of 1947, which were all but forgotten nearly as soon as the ink was dry, but rules created in 1948 and 1949 that controlled which researchers got access to radioisotopes and that barred certain populations from being used in experiments, mainly children and pregnant women. So long as these requirements were followed, patients receiving radiation in medical studies were among the best-protected research subjects in the country until the mid-1960s.

For the Pentagon, the NEPA discussions were an opportunity to learn from the AEC's experience with the problem of human experiments. The ethical, legal, and public relations issues, compounded by the burdens of secrecy, were all inherited by the Defense Department as it faced its own early cold war concerns. But the scale of the problem for defense planners was far greater than it had been for the atomic energy administrators. Unlike the AEC, radiation was only one of the topics of concern to the Pentagon, though anything associated with radiation had a special status because of public interest in the much-touted dawn of the Atomic Age. Although the culture was preoccupied with the Bomb, the Pentagon was also concerned about the possibility of radiation warfare from nondetonating sources. Hence the infamous "Green Run."

## THE "GREEN RUN" AND ITS CHILDREN

In 1997 American baby boomers were confronted by headlines about their unsuspecting exposure to radiation as children: "40 Years Later, Bomb Test Fallout Raises Health Alarm," "Thousands Have Thyroid Cancer from Atomic Tests," "U. S. Alerted Photo Film Makers, Not Public About Bomb Fallout." Growing up in New York's Hudson Valley (amid a steady diet of disaster movies about giant ants and other fictional A-bomb mutations), I was exposed to measurable amounts of radiation wafting its way east from the Nevada blast sites, as were my friends. These exposures were as nothing compared to some counties in the Plains states, which probably accounted for at least some "excess" deaths.

It is disturbing to think that A-bomb blasts might have compromised one's health as a child living hundreds or even thousands of miles away from detonation sites. But at least the environmental radiation was a by-product of the tests rather than their purpose. What Americans did not know for decades was that radioactive fission products were being deliberately released on and over U.S. soil by our own government.

On December 3, 1949, a plume of radioiodine 131 and xenon 133 drifted into the atmosphere over Washington State from the stacks of a government nuclear plant. The cloud sat over the area for days until dispersed to the north by a storm. Local vegetation absorbed up to 400 times the then-permissible level of radiation, and animals about eighty times the standard safety limit. Called the "Green Run" because of the young or "green" fuel that was used, the release was no accident. It was part of a series of tests conducted by the Hanford, Washington, nuclear facility.

When in 1942 the boss of the Manhattan Project, General Leslie Groves, went in search of a site for the manufacture of plutonium, he chose one of the loveliest and most pristine spots in the country. Set on the Columbia River, Hanford enjoyed both remoteness and plenty of fresh water needed to cool the nuclear reactors. The area soon began to buzz with activity as a major secret facility came to life, providing the raw material that was used in the plutonium injections and in several of the first atomic weapons.

On September 23, 1949, the Soviet Union detonated it first atomic bomb. After the war, knowing that the Soviet atomic bomb program was well under way, the Air Force had been assigned the job of detecting nuclear tests from great distances, and now the project had more urgency. Telltale atmospheric gases from production facilities could tell the United States the rate at which the Soviets were able to produce plutonium. Air sampling from airplanes produced disappointing results, as instruments detected radioactive material only within a few miles of the site, so other techniques had to be tried. The Green Run was conducted to enable trials of novel detection methods.

It took more than forty years for the whole story of the Green Run to be brought to light, and it surely seems to provide a suitable occasion for outrage at government irresponsibility, as felt by many who live in the surrounding community. But the moral of Green Run is far more complicated. First, it was by no means a unique event. By 1995 the Department of Energy determined that between 1944 and the 1960s there had been several hundred secret intentional releases of radioactive material. Besides Hanford they took place at the Army's Dugway Proving Ground in Utah, in Bayo Canyon, New Mexico, at AEC sites in Nevada and Idaho, and in the Alaskan wilderness.

Second, the sum total of radiation released by all these episodes was dwarfed by the emissions accidentally produced. Hanford in particular was a shockingly "leaky" facility. From 1944 to 1947 the plant released around eighty times the amount of radioiodine vented in the Green Run. The AEC recognized that wartime laxity was no longer justifiable. By 1949, emissions were reduced to a thousandth of their previous levels. The cleanup of the Hanford site now taking place will cost far more than building it, and it may never be fully accomplished.

Third, the Green Run and its cousins probably had minimal health effects, if any. The most serious "pathway" of exposure, milk from cows that graze on contaminated pastures, was not known at the time. But in general, dose reconstruction studies of radiation releases have not presented cause for alarm. The Green Run increased expected fatal thyroid cancers in the exposed population by 0.04, implying far less than even a single death. At Los Alamos the RaLa tests of radiolanthanum (lanthanum 140) for measuring atomic bomb implosion also involved intentional releases. About 0.4 excess cancer deaths in Los Alamos County could have been expected from the RaLa tests.

But numerical estimates are cold comfort to people who have lived and raised their children on contaminated soil. Making matters worse, after decades of secrecy and grudging release of bits of information, a government's credibility is badly undermined. Often the exposed populations were members of minority groups. One Los Alamos activist has alleged "a callous disregard for the well-being and lives of the Spanish and Native Americans in our community."

An Inupiat Indian from Point Hope, Alaska, worried about the radioactive materials that were spread on soil near her home from 1958 to 1962 as part of Project Chariot. "I have to wonder about my health, what impact the poison on the earth will have all through my lifetime, emotionally, physically, and most of all for my children and my grandchildren."

The top-secret "field tests" and "intentional releases" present problems different from traditional medical experiments, which are usually conducted on individuals. Field tests by definition affect large populations. There can be no informed consent for this kind of research, even in theory. But there can be disclosure that permits the "consent of the governed" to being part of military experiments that affect the environment. That way, if most citizens don't want to take the (usually very small) chance of being harmed by a test in return for some information that could protect us from aggressors, they can say so. The top-secret status of the radiation field tests ruled that out, of course, so here we are confronted head-on with the problem of secrecy in a democratic society: Is the government permitted to take chances with the public health—or at least the public trust—if the trade-off is data that might help the nation defend itself? Undue or not, the risks associated with radiation field testing fell on America's unwitting body politic.

# THE PENTAGON MEETS THE NUREMBERG CODE

During the war we more or less made our own policies on this,
but I am not sure that this is possible today.

*John R. Paul, Director of the Armed Forces, Epidemiological Board,*
*February 18, 1948*

## A FORMIDABLE PRESENCE

As the powerhouse of the postwar era, the atomic bomb had a competitor: a diminutive, stylishly bejeweled woman named Anna Rosenberg. An unlikely senior Pentagon official from 1950 to 1953, she secretly played a key role in getting the Pentagon to adopt a human experiments policy that was far ahead not only of the rest of the U.S. government, but of civilian medical research as well.

The 10-year-old Anna Marie Lederer emigrated to the United States from Hungary, became a feminist and political operative in New York City's Tammany Hall political machine, married businessman Julius Rosenberg (whom she divorced at age 60 to marry a prominent Republican), and developed a knack for settling labor disputes. Though her name and that of her husband coincided amazingly with those of Ethel and Julius Rosenberg, the couple executed in 1953 as atomic spies, they were not related.

The colorful Rosenberg was a favorite of the press. *Time* cited her "technique of mowing down disputants with a machine-gun delivery of tough, sensible talk, backed up with hair-trigger thinking." In 1938 she helped the young Nelson Rockefeller deal with a labor problem at the family's new monument, Rockefeller Center in midtown Manhattan. According to Rockefeller's biographer, Carey Reich, Rockefeller was fascinated by this feminine woman who wore exotic hats and elegant perfumes but could curse like a sailor at the bargaining table.

With her dramatic personality Rosenberg also collected a singular array of powerful friends, and it was these connections, not just her labor expertise, that became important to Rockefeller. According to Rockefeller biographer Carey Reich, "He had never met anyone like her: tenacious, street-smart, with a web of contacts that permeated the innermost depths of City Hall and ranged up to the highest levels of Washington." Rosenberg caught the attention of Franklin Roosevelt while he was governor of New York and became a close friend and confidante of Eleanor. With FDR in the White House, Rosenberg was able to sponsor a few future luminaries, including young Nelson Rockefeller, whose introduction to Roosevelt by Rosenberg won him a place in the administration and launched his political career.

During the war Rosenberg was a senior official at the War Manpower Commission, where her understanding of returning soldiers' needs helped lead to the G.I. Bill. After victory in

Europe, General George C. Marshall convinced President Truman that Rosenberg should be appointed Assistant Secretary of Defense for Manpower and Personnel, "to . . . solve the manpower problem" in the Pentagon. That such a position would be awarded to a female civilian in those days was simply extraordinary, and Truman had to tolerate a great deal of criticism from military traditionalists. Truman stuck to his guns. As a result, a person with an exceptionally keen understanding of personnel issues was in a key role at a time when America's defense establishment was undergoing the stresses of paring down its forces from a world war while also adjusting to a cold war.

Of Anna Rosenberg New York's Mayor Fiorello LaGuardia said, "She knows more about labor relations and human relations than any man in the country," high praise in that un-self-consciously sexist era. In the Pentagon, the Hungarian-émigré dynamo who understood labor issues so well was in a crucial position to get the defense establishment to adopt, at least on paper, a state-of-the-art policy on human experimentation, one crafted in a trial of Nazi war criminals. Still more remarkable, the defense secretary who gave the ultimate order was one of the few people in the country as familiar with labor relations as Anna Rosenberg was, a former chairman of executive operations of General Motors named Charles E. Wilson. Wilson had once breezily told Congress, "What's good for General Motors is good for America," and with that memorable equation of capitalism and patriotism, became one of the few auto executives whose name was ever a household word. Together they saw the issue of human experimentation through the lens of personnel management and—almost—made a revolution in medical ethics.


## PANIC!

The destructive power of the bombs that fell on Hiroshima and Nagasaki startled even the highest ranks of the American military. Wishing to learn more about the implications of atomic weapons for air and sea forces, the armed forces conducted the first two

peacetime tests in 1946 in the Pacific Marshall Islands, code-
named Operation Crossroads, only months after the defeat of
Japan. Unlike later bomb tests, Operation Crossroads was widely
publicized and attended by many dignitaries and journalists.
Reminiscent of the genteel picnic staged by local gentry on a bluff
overlooking a field called Bull Run nearly a century before, the
social and scientific event heralded by the military at the Bikini
Atoll left defense officials in shock at the results.

The not-so-hidden agenda of the Crossroads exercise was a
competition between the Navy and the emergent Air Force about
what role each would play in the atomic age. Dedicated flyers
believed that modern fighter aircraft would render naval power
obsolete, especially if equipped with atomic weapons. Navy brass
were determined to show that this theory was, at the very least,
much exaggerated. What did happen led officials to an entirely
new concern, for target ships that had been placed around ground
zero of an underwater blast, though not pulverized, were rendered
uninhabitable by radioactive tidal waves. At first the admirals
refused to believe in this invisible threat, for all they could see was
intact vessels from the captured Japanese fleet. Defiant, they
ordered sailors onto the ships.

It fell to Crossroads' chief medical officer, Stafford Warren, to
persuade them that the contamination danger was real and profound. Recently returned from Hiroshima and Nagasaki, where he
had been under orders to downplay bomb radioactivity, Warren
was less willing to play a submissive role this time, and he insisted
on heightened safety measures for Crossroads. Warren engaged in
a pitched battle with the admirals about having men board the target ships, one that could only have been won by a man with his
amiable self-confidence. Indeed, the chastened Warren concluded,
the ships still posed a threat, even as empty shells off-limits to
human beings. "Difficult and expensive medico-legal problems
will probably occur if previously contaminated target ships are
'cleared' for constant occupancy or disposal as scrap," he warned
the Navy commanders.

Though unaccustomed to this imperceptible enemy, top
Pentagon officials came quickly to appreciate the nature of the

new challenge they faced, one that had as much to do with the psychology of the atomic age as it did with the actual destructive force of the new arms. Years before Hollywood discovered the appeal of radiation-induced monsters to a public at once thrilled and fearful of the unleashed power of the atom, defense planners saw that the insidious national security threat posed by the Bomb was as much panic among fighting forces and the civilian infrastructure as it was injury and death.

And so, by the late 1940s, the impetus for human radiation experiments had shifted from protecting laboratory workers to preparing soldiers for the future of combat: atomic battlefields in which nuclear weapons would be as common as traditional armaments. How could our troops best be taught to fight in such an unfamiliar environment? How could their fears about radiation hazards be controlled so they could function? How much radiation exposure was in fact too much? And how could our fighters be equipped so that the danger could be minimized, at least while they were engaged in combat? Pentagon strategists faced a difficult set of questions as midcentury approached. One thing they were sure about: A powerful and implacable new enemy was asking the same questions.

Concerns about preparedness were not limited to radioactive weapons; they also included other unconventional forms of warfare. In December 1951 President Truman's secretary of defense, Robert Lovett, secretly expressed concern about "our lack of readiness in chemical and biological warfare," and ordered the three services to increase their activities in these areas. On February 11, 1952, a joint meeting of representatives of all three service branches discussed "increased emphasis on CW and BW." The minutes of that meeting include the summary statement: "That we have a serious need for increased testing of these weapons, in particular, experiments involving humans."

Reporting on these meetings to the secretary of defense on April 25, 1952, the assistant for special security programs emphasized the problem by stating: "if the signal to retaliate were given tomorrow, or even within the next year, the United States could make little more than a token effort." To concerns about what might be called the "biochem gap" were gradually added similar worries about radiation preparedness, and by sometime in 1952 all three areas were routinely considered together. "ABC warfare research" was a crying need of the research effort, and human experiments were a critical component of that effort.

## IN SEARCH OF A POLICY ON HUMAN EXPERIMENTS

Defense officials believed that human experiments would once again be necessary, but they also knew that experiments with people had unsavory, if somewhat vague, associations with the Nazis. There were also legal concerns. Fear of suit by aggrieved service personnel was probably not the primary motivation for these concerns, since that kind of action was considerably less likely even to be seriously considered then than is the case today. Rather, difficult insurance questions arose concerning indemnification of civilian volunteers in case of injury related to an experiment. Military personnel were automatically covered for injuries incurred during service, and at this time the armed forces did not require that experiment volunteers from their ranks give up their rights to be compensated. Further complicating the picture, Department of Defense administrators were engaged in an extensive reorganization process in the early 1950s. During that process it became evident that the Pentagon lacked the technical authority to conduct human experiments according to its own operating policies, experiments that many planners thought highly desirable. The lack of a set of formal rules on human experiments became another important impetus to introduce some kind of formal policy. More difficult was just what kind of policy to introduce.

As would be expected, in the absence of a policy, various medically relevant experiments continued during the postwar era. There were always new materials under development that needed to be tested. As we have seen, one expedient that is discouraged today was for researchers to use themselves as their own subjects, especially in the very early stages of a project. Lawrence Altman reports the case of John P. Stapp, an Air Force flight surgeon who became interested in safety issues. During the late 1940s Stapp participated in his own ejection seat experiments. "I saw no difference between doing a human experiment and leading a military charge to take a military objective," Stapp said, "because all of this was in a military context. I was expendable." In 1954 he became the "fastest man on earth" when he was strapped into a rocket sled at Holloman Air Force Base in New Mexico and reached the speed of 632 miles an hour in five seconds.

Stapp's attitude that the risks of medical experiments were analogous to other military obligations was widely shared. While Stapp was engaged in using himself and other volunteers in flight safety tests, biomedical experts were putting pressure on other officials to include medical issues in their planning for future bomb tests. In late February 1951, the chairman of the Pentagon's Armed Forces Medical Policy Council, Dr. Richard L. Meiling, convened an ad hoc meeting within seven military representatives to discuss his concern about the lack of medical participation in atomic bomb tests. Although the group allowed that "adequate biomedical coverage was arranged for the next tests" (nuclear blasts code-named Operation Greenhouse), the medical policy group recommended that other planned tests be expanded to "include medical studies if any knowledge can be gained thereby." Meiling then asked the Department of Defense's Research and Development Board to agree that a "determined effort be made to arrange for necessary and practicable biomedical participation in all future atomic weapons tests." This request was immediately forwarded to the commander of the tests scheduled to follow Greenhouse, Operation Windstorm. Meiling also took his case to Robert LeBaron, the chairman of the Military Liaison Committee to the Atomic Energy Commission, who also appealed to the research and development staff "recommending biomedical participation in future tests."

The pressure bore fruit. On March 5, 1951, the planners of Operation Windstorm met with other representatives of the military, including three of the seven who had met with Meiling, to consider expanding the biomedical program according to

Meiling's request. In describing the project plan to the sixteen
other participants, Dr. Spilhaus, of the Armed Forces Special
Weapons Project (AFSWP), asked them to either: "(a) Agree that
in view of the limitations, the present program is sufficient in
scope and content or (b) Make positive suggestions regarding necessary additions to its program to bring it to an acceptable level of
sufficiency."

The group discussed several possibilities. The conduct of "controlled experiments" was "in general discouraged because it was
felt that these could be conducted with greater confidence limits
in laboratories." The suggestion of thermal experiments like those
already planned for Greenhouse met with mixed reactions. Some
argued that it was unnecessary to conduct such experiments
because reliable data had already been or was going to be obtained
by other means, including exposing large animals to detonations.
Another proposal, supported by Spilhaus, was to examine the
effects of missile debris. It was agreed that the latter two areas
would be useful if feasible means to conduct experiments could be
found. However, the group's final ruling was that the previous
AFSWP operation plan, which did not include human experimentation, was "satisfactory."

But the medical experts continued to press their case. In
June 1951, Meiling again raised the issue of medical participation in radiation weapons tests, this time with an emphasis on
the one problem he must have known had haunted the
Pentagon leadership since Crossroads: panic. In a memorandum addressed to the deputy secretary of defense and other
important officials, Meiling argued that the "almost universal"
fear of radiation posed an "urgent" need for troop participation
in scheduled test shots. Describing a plan in which the Medical
Policy Council would "cooperate . . . and provide the necessary
coordination of the medical services," Meiling wrote: "A tactical exercise of this nature would clearly demonstrate that persistent ionizing radiation following an air burst atomic explosion presents no hazards to personnel and equipment and
would effectively dispel a fear that is dangerous and demoraliz-
ing but entirely groundless."

This time Meiling had pushed the right button. The Military Liaison Committee to the AEC supported Meiling's proposal. In July the committee indicated that the Army planned to conduct a maneuver with approximately five thousand troops during one upcoming test. The action was intended to provide "valuable information on the psychological implications" of atomic weapons use. Responding to Meiling's proposal, Colonel Roper, the executive secretary of the Pentagon's liaison to the AEC, noted that "a medical problem such as you suggest could undoubtedly be worked into the maneuver." Roper cautioned, however, that "final plans for this action had not been made."

The general issue of human experiments was not confined to radiation studies, but also had implications for research on biological and chemical warfare. Indeed, it was biochemical warfare worries that finally pushed the Pentagon establishment to get moving on a human experimentation policy. On December 17, 1951, the Medical Policy Council endorsed the principle that "final realistic evaluation of biological warfare must await appropriate field trials in which human subjects are used." At a special meeting of high-ranking Department of Defense officials on progress in chemical and biological warfare on February 11, 1952, Army Secretary Pace made remarks that were summarized in the secret record:

> That we have a serious need for increased testing of these weapons, in particular, experiments involving humans. Mr. Foster [deputy secretary of defense] said the Armed Forces Medical Policy Council had this problem under consideration. General Bullene [the Army's chief chemical officer] stated that he also has a study group working on this problem, which study he will expedite and report to the Secretary.

At its September 8, 1952, meeting the medical policy experts heard a presentation from the chief of preventive medicine of the Army Surgeon General's Office concerning the medical services' role in the development of defensive measures and devices. It was pointed out that the research had reached a point beyond which essential data could not be obtained unless human volunteers were utilized for such experimentation. Following detailed discussion, it was unanimously agreed that the use of human volunteers in this type of research be approved.

## ENTER THE CODE

By the fall of 1952 the matter of a human experimentation policy was coming to a head. The declassified records of the Medical Policy Council, under its new chairman Dr. Melvin Casberg, include a seemingly innocuous entry.

> The Armed Forces Medical Policy Council again considered the subject [of human experimentation] at their meeting on 13 October 1952, in view of certain changes in the conditions under which experiments were to be conducted. It was resolved that the ten rules promulgated at the Nuremberg Trials be adopted as the guiding principles to be followed.

It is not clear what the "certain changes in the conditions under which experiments were to be conducted" were, but they may have included the Pentagon's legal exposure in the absence of a formal, written policy. To the medical council's legal advisor, Stephen Jackson, the solution was obvious: an internationally sanctioned tribunal composed of American judges and operating according to American legal rules had made a clear statement of the matter only five years before. Jackson was no authority on health law but a journeyman attorney whose previous assignment was director of the film industry's self-policing decency review board. Long before the days of advisory labels for foul language, sex, or violence, Hollywood engaged in a vigorous self-censorship program. It might be said that Stephen Jackson is the only person in history to have had a crucial part in both medical and cinematic ethics. The pivotal role destiny assigned him to find a solution is vividly documented in a letter written months later by a Pentagon administrator: "It was on Mr. Jackson's insistence that the 'Nuremberg Principles' were used in toto in the document, since he stated, these *already had international juridical sanction*, and to modify them would open us to severe criticism along the line—'see they use only that which suits them'" [emphasis added].

What is remarkable about Jackson's recommendation is that a senior administration legal advisor found that the 1947 ruling by the judges at the Nuremberg medical trial set international legal precedent to which American researchers—and the U.S. government—should be held. Never before nor since then has the code received such high-level recognition as a valid law. But Jackson's proposal faced rough waters outside the Medical Policy Council. Over the next few months Jackson won the day, but he could not have done so without support from a higher power. Who that was is revealed in a memo Jackson wrote to medical council chair Casberg on October 22, 1952, nine days after the AFMPC passed the Nuremberg Code recommendation:

> I discussed the attached with Mrs. Rosenberg on Saturday. She concurred in the conditions except that she recommended that a provision be added to 1. requiring that the consent be expressed in writing before at least one witness.
>
> I have added such language in the appropriate place under number 1. The new matter is underlined. Mrs. Rosenberg has approved this language.
>
> Mr. Kent the General Counsel, has approved this addition from the legal standpoint.
>
> I recommend that the conditions be so amended.

The meager record of these important events reveals some tantalizing details about Rosenberg's influence, for not only did she obviously concur with the idea of employing the code as the Defense Department's human experiments policy, in insisting on written subject consent, but she also went much further than the code itself. As a seasoned labor negotiator she obviously valued getting a signature on a contract. Nothing could replace ink on paper as evidence of a meeting of minds. Perhaps Rosenberg didn't fully appreciate how alien this sort of thinking was to medicine and medical research, which had traditionally relied on the good intentions of physicians and the trust of those under their care. Yet her support considerably strengthened the chances for the proposed policy to be adopted. The proposal would need it, for it received a very lukewarm reception.

## AN UNWELCOME PROPOSAL

In the minds of those who opposed the proposal, the problem was not necessarily with the Nuremberg Code itself. Rather, the medical and military critics in the Pentagon were opposed to any written policy that threatened to restrict human experiments for national security needs, or that questioned the moral integrity of physicians and commanding officers and their ability to make tough ethical calls. These concerns were not usually put so bluntly, but were couched in rationalization. The statement of the Pentagon's Committee on Medical Sciences was typical. Asked to comment on the proposal at their meeting in October 1952, the members argued that

> human experimentation has been carried on for many years by capable investigators. . . . To issue a policy statement on human experimentation at this time would probably do the cause more harm than good; for such a statement would have to be "watered down" to suit the capabilities of the average investigator. Thus, it would be restrictive to the exceptional research worker.

This was an odd statement. At first the Medical Science Committee seemed to be saying that a written policy would not be strong enough in practice, but then it seemed it would be too strong for the "exceptional research worker." In other words, scientific merit trumps other ethical considerations. The view is respectable, even if flawed, but the committee seemed reluctant to state it plainly. Revealing its concern for physician autonomy, the committee also asserted that "human experimentation within the field of medical sciences has, in years past, and is at present governed by an unwritten code of ethics [which is] administered informally [and] considered to be satisfactory. . . . To commit to writing a policy on human experimentation would focus unnecessary attention on the legal aspects of the subject."

A few days later, on November 17, 1952, the Research and Development Board's vice chairman wrote to the chair of the Armed Forces Medical Policy Council that the medical science group's chair was "reluctant," but "realizes the probable need for such a policy and said he would not oppose it." It appears that the Research and Development Board's vice chairman successfully urged the medical science chair to abstain rather than oppose the Nuremberg-like policy draft.

When the Nuremberg Code proposal was not criticized, it was ridiculed. At its November 10, 1952 meeting, the chairman of the Committee on Chemical Warfare read aloud a draft of the Armed Forces Medical Policy Council proposal. The draft included all ten statements of the original code as well as an eleventh, added by Jackson, reaffirming a policy not to use prisoners of war in research. After the reading, one member remarked dryly, evoking general laughter, "If they can get any volunteers after that I'm all in favor of it."

On November 13, the chemical warfare advisors reported that they had arrived at their own recommendations. The first was that "the need for arrangements to use human test subjects in the CW [chemical warfare] program in toxicology and medicine be brought to the attention of the Armed Forces Medical Policy Council." The chemical warfare committee also suggested that a British-style system of rewards for volunteers be employed, one in which whole units "volunteered" for research. Attempting perhaps to gain support for the chemical warfare committee's alternative, on December 9, 1952, the executive director of the committee wrote the Assistant for Special Security Programs in the Office of the Secretary of Defense about the chemical warfare group's rec-ommendations. He argued that they go "a step or two beyond the AFMPC recommendation in calling for a system of rewards for volunteers, and for recognition of government liability in case of accident." The memo continued:

The whole need of the CW program for human volunteers, in the judgment of this Committee, cannot be met by an arrangement that allows acceptance of volunteers from personnel normally on duty at installations engaged in such research. For this purpose the permissive statement [apparently a reference to the consent form] should be subject to the interpretation that uniformed volunteers could be assigned to temporary duty at the experimental installation for the purpose of engaging in the program as test subjects. This is the essence of the British system, which we are advised has worked quite well.

But the chemical warfare advisors' proposal involved significant problems of its own. For example, the suggestion that paid volunteers be assigned to temporary duty at special sites raised the question whether such arrangements would have been in practical compliance with the principle that human subjects must be free to terminate their participation in an experiment at any time. Just how did this plan square with medical ethics? It sounded very much like the arrangements that had been made for the mustard gas experiments ten years before, the secrecy of which was still being maintained, even among those veterans who felt abused by the research.

Whether all the other players in the debate knew it or not, the Medical Policy Council proposal had already been endorsed by the general counsel and an assistant secretary, Anna Rosenberg. That top officials were committed to the eventual adoption of the Nuremberg Code-based draft (perhaps regardless of the reaction of other Pentagon advisory panels), is dramatically evidenced by a handwritten note from "gvu"—George V. Underwood, Director of the Executive Office of the Secretary of Defense—to Deputy Secretary Foster dated January 4, 1953. Underwood was trying to put the proposal into effect, but he was somewhat hampered by the fact that a new administration was about to take power. Dwight D. Eisenhower had been elected, and his nominee for secretary of defense, Charles E. Wilson, awaited congressional approval.

Said Underwood: "I believe Mr. Lovett has a considerable awareness of this proposed policy. It has been under development for some time. Because of the importance and controversial character of the policy, I strongly recommend advance clearance with Service Sec'ys [*sic*] thru Joint Sec'y's [*sic*] group. If you agree, we'd like to recapture the case so that copies can be made available to Service Sec'ys [*sic*]."

But the final call had to be that of the new Pentagon chief: "Since consequences of this policy will fall upon Mr. Wilson, it might be wise to pass to him as a unanimous recommendation from the 'alumni.'"

A new administration was about to take power in Washington. The top echelon of the Pentagon wanted to make sure that an important but controversial matter was placed before the new secretary of defense with all the support needed to make it easier for him to approve the proposed policy. This was to be done in spite of the opposition or patent lack of enthusiasm, and even blatant opposition, of Pentagon advisory groups. To maximize support, Underwood's plan was to mobilize heavy artillery in the form of the service secretaries.

But Underwood's plan failed. On January 8, 1953, Casberg briefed Foster and the three service secretaries on the policy. The secretaries did not object but also were not enthusiastically in favor. It was decided only to refer the matter to Secretary Wilson since it was controversial and since it would be up to him to administer it, if it were approved.

Presumably Underwood was somewhat frustrated that he was having so much trouble getting this policy put on the books. His only alternative was to explain the situation to the new Department of Defense leaders. On February 5, 1953, he wrote a letter to a new deputy secretary under Wilson: "This question involves the establishment of a Department of Defense policy prescribing conditions which will govern the use of human volunteers in experimental research in the field of atomic, biological and/or chemical warfare. There is no DOD policy on the books which permits this type of research."

Underwood went on to describe the meeting of the service secretaries one month before, and concluded: "Mr. Foster informed me that he had discussed this question with you and suggested that I should submit the papers to you as soon as you opened for business."

Underwood failed to get the enthusiastic endorsement he had hoped for from the service secretaries at the January 8 meeting. One reason might have been the absence of Secretary Lovett. He was testifying before Congress that day. It is possible that Foster had impressed on his successor, Kyes, the importance of moving on the recommended policy early in the administration of Secretary Wilson. Whatever the explanation for the delay, Underwood found the new defense chief open to the proposal.

## THE WILSON MEMORANDUM

In the years during and after his stewardship of the Pentagon, Charles E. Wilson was largely regarded as a superficial bungler who lacked the cleverness needed to navigate Washington politics. His famous line equating the interests of General Motors and the United States was taken as typical of his inappropriate blunders. But more recently Wilson has been compared with another straight talker from America's heartland, Harry Truman. Besides, Wilson was a role player for Dwight Eisenhower, a president with a strong military background who wanted his secretary to reduce Pentagon expenditures and make it more efficient. Wilson did these things, and he possessed the personal political courage to refuse to appear before Senator Joseph McCarthy's hearings on allegations of communists in government, which he dismissed as "damn tommyrot."

Wilson was also familiar with personnel issues and therefore sensitive to the same kinds of labor-management concerns as was Anna Rosenberg, having dealt with them at the behemoth General Motors, which for many years was the bellwether company in labor disputes for the rest of American industry. Shortly before Wilson was confirmed by Congress, the Armed Forces Medical Policy Council put a memo on his desk that "strongly recommended that a policy be established for the use of human volunteers (military and civilian employees) in experimental research at

Armed Forces facilities," and that such use "shall be subject to the principles and conditions laid down as a result of the Nuremberg trials."

It would be reasonable to assume from the declassified memoranda of that period that Wilson was briefed on the controversy surrounding the proposal. Unlike his predecessors in office, he brought deep familiarity with personnel issues that probably disposed him to clarity in agreements with the "workforce," in this case the soldiers, sailors, and airmen who might be used in medical experiments. Rosenberg's recommendation that a signed contract be included in the policy would have been consistent with the attitude of a former CEO of an automobile manufacturing giant. Since Rosenberg stayed on through the early months of the new administration, Wilson would have had an opportunity to consult her directly on the subject.

On February 26, 1953, the new secretary did sign off on the council's proposed policy. The memorandum was given the number TS-01188, the prefix standing for "top secret." Why the highly classified designation? Perhaps because of a reference to the sensitive subject of unconventional warfare in the document's preface, which would have triggered automatic classification. While I was working for the president's Advisory Committee on Human Radiation Experiments, a government classification officer (whose job had suddenly turned into that of a *de*classification officer after the cold war) told me that any document with the word *atomic* in it was probably automatically classified at that time.

Whatever the reason, the memo's top-secret status later caused not only delay in implementing its requirements but also great embarrassment for the Pentagon decades later. Critics asked how it was expected that scientists, including many university professors on contracts whose careers depended on publishing their results, could be guided by a top-secret document! Pentagon officials did recognize the problem, as evidenced by the fact that subsequent documents attempting to implement the secretary of defense's order were of lower security status, but the content of the memorandum seems not to have been well recorded for public consumption until nearly ten years later.

In the distinguished tradition of modern bureaucracies, the opening paragraphs of the Wilson memorandum were carefully crafted by Jackson to say much that was not said:

1. Based upon a recommendation of the Armed Force Medical Policy Council, that human subjects be employed, under recognized safeguards, as the only feasible means for realistic evaluation and/or development of effective preventive measures of defense against atomic, biological or chemical agents, the policy set forth below will govern the use of human volunteers by the Department of Defense in experimental research in the fields of atomic, biological and/or chemical warfare.

Like all experiments involving human beings, the research contemplated in this paragraph raised a sticky problem: Even if the work is done "under recognized safeguards," that is no guarantee of safety, since the need for standards of acceptable exposure levels is one motivation for human experiments in the first place. But the Pentagon planners were convinced of the moral superiority of their intentions compared with those of other nations. Not only the circumstances in which the experiments are done and the way the human beings are used would be morally different from the way others had done them but also America's goals—freedom and democracy—were seen as warranting tough measures. One way to emphasize our superior ethical standing is by noting, as Wilson's memo does, that the weapons in question are being studied for defensive purposes. Also of more than passing interest is that the paragraph does not appear to apply the policy to offensive studies (can one assume that no research was to have been done for offensive purposes?) or to human experiments involving conventional warfare. Again, atomic, biological, and chemical weapons occupy a more sensitive public relations category than more familiar sorts of arms.

The second introductory paragraph begins by reiterating the defensive nature of the proposed research, applying the policy also to "civilians on duty" at military installations. Then, inserted into the first statement of the Nuremberg Code, is the passage that Rosenberg recommended:

The consent of the human subject shall be in writing, his signature shall be affixed to a written instrument setting forth substantially the aforementioned requirements and shall be signed in the presence of at least one witness who shall attest to such signature in writing.

The next portion of text also was introduced to the code for obvious technical reasons:

In experiments where personnel from more than one Service are involved the Secretary of the Service which is exercising primary responsibility for conducting the experiment is designated to prepare such an instrument and coordinate it for use by all the Services having human volunteers involved in the experiment.

There are two other changes from the original text of the Nuremberg Code. A passage permitting experiments involving "death or disabling injury" to the subjects if the experimenter includes himself as a subject was eliminated. Even the Walter Reed myth could not induce the Pentagon leadership to accept such an arrangement. At the end Jackson also added an explicit prohibition of the use of prisoners of war as research subjects, interesting in light of the fact that the use of prisoners as research subjects in the civilian world was escalating.

## POLICY POSTMORTEMS

On the following day, February 27, 1953, the Director of Administration of the Office of the Secretary of Defense asked for permission to reproduce the memorandum for the three service secretaries, and he asked for three copies for the Research and Development Board's committees. As the Committee on Medical Sciences began its meeting on February 27, the members did not know about the new secretary's action. During a discussion of the potential harms of hepatitis studies, when it was mentioned that there had been three deaths in the program, another debate about the use of human subjects broke out. As in other excerpts from verbatim transcripts of Pentagon policy meetings, not all the participants can be identified from the record, beyond a rank and last name.

COLONEL WOOD: I think if we have men volunteer who are satisfied that they are taking a full risk and they fully understand what this risk is, then we are justified in going ahead on the basis of absolute necessity and there being no alternative whatsoever. So I have mixed feelings about this thing. I would not be willing to be a volunteer. However, on the other hand, there is no other way to do this work.

CAPTAIN SHILLING [Medical Corps, U.S. Navy]: In connection with the human volunteer problem in general, I think we have all discussed this for the last six months at all levels in the Department of Defense. There is one thing that disturbs me a great deal, and that is at the DOD level and at the Medical Policy Council Level [sic] there is a strong urge to try and set up an over-all policy for the conduct of human experimentation. They even go back to the Buchenwald trials, and they are trying to work ought [sic] an over-all pattern that will, if you meet this pattern—To me, this is utterly fantastic as a method of approach.

This naval officer's reference to "the Buchenwald trials" was correct in spirit if not in substance. The trials in Buchenwald did not yield a code like the one at Nuremberg, but the reference indicates an awareness of the events in Germany among the medical officers. Little did Shilling and the others know, of course, that the "utterly fantastic" approach had already been adopted by their boss, and so he continued:

CAPTAIN SHILLING: As far as the Navy is concerned, I have cleared this with policy, and we want to strongly urge that human research be conducted as it is now outlined from a policy standpoint; namely, that the field or the individual or the groups who want to do the research prepare a complete experimental design, showing exactly what they want to do, what the safeguards are going to be, what the program is, why it has to be human rather than animal, and so forth, and then come in and be evaluated by the Surgeons General involved in the Army, Navy, and Air Force, and then that it go up to the Secretary informed for final permission. This is the way we do it now and I think we are going to get into a horrible mess if we try to set up an overall standard for every type of research. What happens is that you put so many safeguards on that we cannot do the multitude of things we are tying to do.

Moments later, the chairman broke in:

THE CHAIRMAN: We have here a document which was just brought in which is signed by Mr. Wilson, dated February 26th. With your permission, I would like to release this information. However, in order to do so, it will be necessary for any member of the audience to excuse himself if he does not have a top secret clearance.

After the letter was read to the committee the transcript pointedly notes that an off-the-record discussion ensued. Of the many transcripts of high-level Department of Defense advisory meetings I have read, there were hardly any other unrecorded discussions. After all, these were already classified and closely held documents. Clearly the medical science committee members were upset and frustrated at the turn of events, having been basically frozen out of the ultimate decision-making process. They must have realized that their input was irrelevant to the outcome. One can imagine that they wanted to ventilate.

Whatever took place off the record, the members decided to pursue some substantive concerns about the new policy. On March 12, the chairman, Dr. Coggeshall, wrote a memorandum to the chairman of the Research and Development Board in which he reported that the Committee on Medical Sciences had passed the following resolution concerning the Wilson policy: "The Committee on Medical Sciences is desirous of receiving the official legal interpretation of all the clauses of the document and the rationalization of apparent discrepancies."

Unfortunately, we do not know what "discrepancies" this resolution refers to, nor if the committee received a reply from the
Research and Development Board counsel. Clearly the members
were looking for problems in hopes of at least modifying the new
policy. Though they failed, it is clear from this document that the
Wilson memo did not immediately quiet the controversy over
human experiments in the Department of Defense.

## A PARTIAL VICTORY, A FAILED POLICY

Routine efforts to pass the defense secretary's order down the
chain of command started almost immediately. At the end of June
the secretary of the general staff of the Army sent a memorandum,
called CS [Chief of Staff] 385, to the chief chemical officer and the
Army surgeon general reiterating the content of the Wilson
memo. The Army secretary's message also added various opinions
from the judge advocate general, including:

> that disability compensation is available for civilian employees;
> that there is no authority to pay life insurance premiums for
> military or civilian personnel; that the services of private citi-
> zens could not be accepted because they could bring a claim
> against the Government; and that contractors may decide to
> permit the participation of their employees, but "The terms of
> the contract must insure that the contractor will observe the
> conditions and safeguards set forth in this directive."

The Army memo ended by noting that the secretary of the
Army must approve all such proposals in writing, that the surgeon
general of the Army will review and comment on such proposals,
and that he may seek the advice of the other service surgeons general and the Public Health Service.

Thus the Army at least required that the consent standards set
out in the Wilson memo apply to its research contractors, and not
only to its own physicians. It is not clear how those standards were
to be communicated to contractors or what kind of follow-up was

intended, if any. As we will see later, when the Army proposed in 1962 to insert a slightly different restatement of the Nuremberg Code into extramural clinical research contracts some medical school officials reacted in a fashion which strongly suggests that they had no knowledge of the 1953 directive.

In at least some cases, then, the Army Chemical Corps successfully implemented the new policy for which it had been preparing. For example, the Chief of the Plans and Evaluation Office of the Chemical Corps, in a memorandum dated July 24, 1953, forwarded a copy of an Army implementation memo to the commanding officer of the Cal C Medical Laboratories at the Army Chemical Center, Maryland. The Chemical Corps administrator asked that plans for experiments using human volunteers be submitted by August 7, 1953. Seven research projects were in fact submitted by the medical laboratory commander on that date. On November 5, 1953, the secretary of the Army wrote to the Army chief of staff granting approval for the experiments and directed that the same principles and safeguards that apply to Army laboratories be observed by contractors.

Unfortunately, the process was not always successful, even in the early days. According to a report published by the Army inspector general in 1975, one operation called Top Hat took place at the Chemical Corps School at Fort McClellan, Alabama, between September 15 and 19, 1953. As described in the inspector general's report:

> This research project, which was termed a "local field exercise," involved the use of Chemical Corps troops in testing methods of decontaminating biological warfare agents, mustard gas, and nerve gas. A review of the scant literature available on the exercise indicated that it was conducted in contravention of the intent of the Department of Defense and Department of the Army policies.

In what would prove to be the single greatest bureaucratic and philosophical problem with the Pentagon policy, the 1975 army report concluded that Operation Top Hat was probably thought to fall within the "line of duty" of a Chemical Corps exercise and was not regarded as an experiment. On the whole, the Army inspector general reported in 1975 that there had been a "startling . . . lack of consistency in the interpretations" of Secretary Wilson's policy, citing several other examples. The inspector general's report turned out to be a key document in the growing awareness of research ethics problems in the military during the 1970s, and we will meet up with it again later.

There were other obstacles to implementing the Wilson policy, including other problems about exactly what kind of studies it was meant for. A 1953 Army study examined soldiers' performance in cold environments and the effect of vitamin supplements on 128 personnel. The experiment proposal states that consent was solicited from the men, but it is not clear what they were told; no written consent form seems to have been used. The participants are called "selected volunteers" on page 2 of the memo. A specific unit was recommended for the test, but Puerto Rican and "Negro" personnel were excluded; no rationale was given. Perhaps the scientists excluded these groups from the study because of the widely accepted belief—which is now recognized as racially biased—that members of these minorities were significantly less able to withstand cold. Whatever the reasoning behind the exclusion, various Army officials signed off on the proposal.

Should this study have followed the rules set out in the secretary's memo? The study was not an atomic, biological, or chemical warfare experiment, but a nutritional study. Even so, it would seem odd not to apply the same ethical standards to a human experiment just because it happened to fall into a different scientific field. One could attribute the lapse to simple bureaucratic inertia, but there is at least one other partial explanation: the ethical rules based on Nuremberg were never really embraced by the military-medical establishment, never really penetrated that culture. Thus, unless it was specifically applied by top brass, the ethics policy was easily forgotten.

Or it was never known in the first place. The top-secret status of Wilson's original memo caused problems with communication of the policy to subordinates in the armed forces who actually had to implement it. A memorandum dated "3-5-54" from the acting chief of staff of the Air Force to the assistant secretary of defense (Health and Medicine) indicates that an Armed Forces Special Weapons Project technical report "mentions the fact that human volunteers were employed during atomic weapons tests conducted in 1951." The memorandum continues:

Subsequent reports from later tests on the same subject contain comparable references as well as referring to at least two instances in which volunteers were injured as a consequence of taking part in field experiments. Because of the implications involved due to these injuries, it is felt that a definite need exists for guidance in the use of human volunteers as experimental subjects.

Then, in a memorandum for the record of the same date, the same officer wrote of his discovery in November 1953 that there was a "T/S" [top secret] document signed by the secretary of defense on requirements for the use of human volunteers in experiments. The memorandum for the record goes on:

Since this information was of particular importance to this office in classifying and/or releasing information on the Flash Blindness programs at weapons tests, attempts were made to learn of the nature of these requirements. On 14 January 1954, Lt. Colonel Browning [the author of the memo] and Major Miller had a conference with the Executive Assistant to the Assistant Secretary of Defense (Health and Medical) at which time it was learned that although this document details very definite and specific steps which must be taken before volunteers may be used in experimentation, no serious attempt has been made to disseminate the information to those experimenters who had a definite need-to-know. . . . It was suggested that this office prepare a letter for the Assistant Secretary in which was detailed our need for this information and the manner in which we were handicapped through ignorance of the provisions of this document. It is intended that this letter shall point up the need for some relaxation of the grip in which this document is now held.

In fact, the Pentagon's "grip" on the code was not wholly relaxed. It seems that by 1956 the Wilson memo was forgotten in the Air Force. A supplementary agreement between Kelly Air Force Base (San Antonio) and Tulane University dated August 20, 1956, includes only the following paragraph on "Human Subjects":

It is hereby understood and agreed that any and all treatments and observations involving human subjects in connection with this contract shall be carried out within the limits of the accepted code of ethics of the American Medical Profession [sic] for clinical and laboratory investigations.

Perhaps the intended reference is to the American Medical Association's code of ethics, but it is notable that the Air Force's own extant policy, one that was based on the Wilson memo, is not cited.

Similarly, a September 12, 1958, letter from the Deputy Commander for Research and Development of the Air Research and Development Command instructed various Air Force units on the policy for the use of humans in "inherently hazardous experiments." The 1953 Pentagon policy is not referenced. The accompanying ten-point "evaluation guide" includes "1. All necessary preliminary exploratory laboratory, dummy and animal tests have been conducted and evaluated? Human subject testing is the only remaining means of providing the final validation?" and "5. The subject is a volunteer who understands the degree of risk involved in the experiment?"

There is no mention of signed and witnessed consent forms, and no reference to the original 1953 policy. Yet a memorandum dated March 10, 1953, from the deputy assistant for atomic energy conveys the Wilson memo to the inspector general of the Air Force, so at least it is clear that the chain of command was informed.

Perhaps, it could be argued, the policy was applied only to "ABC warfare" research. But documents related to at least one series of radiation experiments that took place under Air Force auspices from 1951 to 1956 fail to reveal any influence whatsoever of that service's implementation of the Pentagon's ethics policy. The impetus for the experiments was the nuclear-powered aircraft project.

The research was conducted by the School of Aviation Medicine (SAM) on a contract with Houston's M. D. Anderson Hospital for Cancer Research. Though the study was motivated by a need for information relating to the national security, it could not be done directly. Again the stumbling block was the ethics of exposing healthy people to high doses of radiation. But there was an alternative. A document called Project Specifications, dated October 19, 1950, stated:

It is desired to measure certain mental and psychomotor abilities of patients who are undergoing radiation therapy in order to evaluate any differences in performance that may result from radiation effects. This information is urgently required by the U.S. Air Force in connection with the NEPA [Nuclear Energy Powered Aircraft] Project. It is clear that before attempting to operate its proposed nuclear powered aircraft, the U.S. Air Force must evaluate its radiation hazards. There are no scientific data with which to assess these dangers of the NEPA aircraft in terms of their probable effects upon crew performance and well-being. Since the need is pressing, it would appear mandatory to take advantage of the investigation opportunities that exist in certain radiology centers by conducting special examinations and measures of patients who are undergoing radiation treatment for disease.

Unable to escape the ethical problem of using healthy airmen, the fallback position was that of using people who were getting radiation treatment anyway as part of cancer treatment. The subjects were patients at M. D. Anderson, but the testing was done by physicians from SAM. Three psychomotor tests were given to subjects, called "the complex coordinator, the hand coordination test, and the rotary pursuit test." All had "a proven relationship to the skills required in basic pilotry." At first the data were not promising because the tested patients had received very low doses of radiation, but then high-dose radiation treatment up to 200 roentgens came into favor among oncologists at M. D. Anderson. Then the investigators began to feel that they got some worthwhile results. A total of 263 patients are believed to have participated in these studies.

How were the subjects selected and how did the hospital staff motivate them for the testing? To help insure that the subjects were healthy and cogent enough to perform the psychological tests, outpatients were used, but the nature of the testing required that they be boarded in the hospital. Hospitalization obviously required a significant level of commitment on the part of the participants. Though they were ostensibly volunteers, nothing is known about what the patients were told.

## LEARNING FROM FAILURE

These were only a few of the studies that should have qualified for coverage under the Pentagon's Nuremberg Code-based policy but seemed to escape its requirements. Anna Rosenberg's written-consent rule prevailed within the civilian hierarchy of the Department of Defense but had little traction within the military-medical culture. Even her considerable political skills only went so far. Had Secretary Wilson's policy been more efficiently dispersed, it would have had an excellent chance of gaining more influence, because it represented a direct order from the highest official in the defense establishment. But its original top-secret status and the ambiguities about its range of application crippled it from the beginning.

Here is a lesson from Bureaucracy 101: Policies are one thing, practices another. The whole issue of the use of human beings in important scientific experiments is complex enough. Add to that national needs in a patriotic era, medical scientists who believe in their work and their own integrity, and an officer corps uncertain about the meaning and scope of an order in an unfamiliar field, and you have a recipe for failure. The folks in the field did not identify with and embrace the approach settled upon by the Pentagon leadership, if they even knew about it. As the Army's 1975 investigation pointed out, the problems that dogged the Wilson rules exemplify "the extreme difficulty of attempting to implement a complex policy by means of a relatively simple, but highly classified directive."

Another problem with the Wilson policy was that it answered only part of the human experiments dilemma. It was clear that there had to be subject consent but vague about how much risk people could be asked to accept in the name of national security research. Declassified files of the Army Chemical Corps from 1955 and 1956 show that the corps wrestled with this problem. Like the earlier discussions about medical ethics in the Pentagon, this one was also motivated by a need to do research. At a 1955 meeting the corps' advisory board issued a recommendation: "Tests on human subjects with biological agents be given a high priority." The immediate concern was the need for improved protection against aerosolized microbes.

The recommendation evidently provoked another internal debate, this time in the Chemical Corps. About a year later, A. R. T. Denues, a physician at Sloan-Kettering Cancer Center in New York City and a lieutenant colonel, was asked a pointed question by the chief of the Chemical Corps' research division: "How can we develop and standardize BW and CW agents when higher authority requires human dose-response data [information about what reactions are created at various exposure levels], yet these agents are considered by medical authorities to be too dangerous for human experimentation?" The familiar ethical paradox of doing important human experiments in new scientific territory was transparent.

Denues supplied a short, five-page response that essentially begged the question. "With only general background to draw on," he wrote, "an off-hand response to this implied impasse would simply be that one cannot do so [that is, conduct potentially dangerous human experiments], yet obligations exist to do so, specifically to maintain R&D efforts and field test [*sic*] in BW and CW." He noted that "widely-recognized moral, professional and legal principles and practices govern experimentation with humans and preclude their use if there is prospect of death or of disabling injury." Nevertheless, "competent medical opinion, on the hazard of any proposed human evaluation and an overall medical evaluation must be accepted as part of a regular, productive system of Research and Development."

Beneath the bureaucratic mumbo-jumbo, what Denues seems to be saying is that risky experiments can be done only if "competent medical opinion" approves of them. "The difficulty implied in the question thus appears procedural and formal, rather than technical, and it should respond to treatment by forceful leadership and tactful education." In other words, if authoritative and persuasive voices pronounce an experiment to lie within reasonable bounds of risk, then the problem can be managed. Risks can be minimized.

Denues' solution was a little too pat. Risks cannot always be foreseen, and there is always going to be a margin of uncertainty in any experiment. The uncertainty is especially great when the textbook theories and the animal experiments can't predict much about the human effects. LSD experiments with animals would give little or no information about the potential harm to a human being from what turns out to be a high dose.

## MIXED MESSAGES

In fairness, though, it is important to remember that the chemical corps was trying to deal with the problem, one that haunts any potentially dangerous experiment with humans. A paradox of human experiments is that they often must be done to learn about the dangers of some agents, in spite of the general ethical obligation not to expose people to harm. It's a problem that researchers and ethicists still struggle with every day. And the Denues memo did explicitly recognize the ethical and legal problems with very dangerous experiments. The document strongly suggests that thinking about this problem had improved since the late 1940s, but not that the Wilson memo made much of an impact. Once again, the ambitious solution that Stephen Jackson and Anna Rosenberg pushed through a reluctant military-medical bureaucracy failed to change the culture.

There is a mundane political explanation for the Wilson policy's failure. Both of the era's defense secretaries, Truman's Lovett and Eisenhower's Wilson, were locked in a struggle to wrest power from the Joint Chiefs of Staff and collect more clear authority in the Office of the Secretary of Defense, a battle that the chiefs finally lost. But in the early 1950s the Joint Chiefs were in a strong position, and they sent out competing policy messages, as they had during Operation Paper Clip in spite of Truman's official denunciation of importing suspected Nazis. A September 3, 1952, memorandum from the secretary of the Joint Chiefs of Staff urged that "responsible agencies should . . . [i]nsure, insofar as practicable, that all published articles stemming from the BW or CW research and development programs are disassociated from anything which might connect them with U.S. military endeavors." There would be no peaceful coexistence between secrecy and signed consent forms for military experiments.

The Wilson policy's failure was a tragedy, not only because of the confusion that was wrought concerning medical-military experiments during the next twenty years. For all their inadequacies, the policy and the debate that swirled around it were the most serious and sustained discussion of human research ethics from the end of the Nazi doctors' trial to the mid-1960s. The Pentagon's policy and the issues it exposed could have served as a model of discourse on the subject, in both the national security and academic sectors. Instead, they must be remembered as a missed opportunity.

Whatever the reasons for the Wilson policy's failure, far from establishing a bulwark of principles according to which medical experiments would have to be conducted by federal security agencies, it was the last important attempt of its kind in a government agency for a dozen years. The policy appeared as a formal regulation in 1962, as AR 70-25 in the Army, and it was no longer restricted to atomic, biological, and chemical warfare research. However, it did not apply to "clinical research," the studies that would usually be done in Army hospitals.

At first AR 70-25 remained largely opaque in its meaning, was largely irrelevant to the national security establishment, and met with resistance among university researchers on Army contracts. But within a few years of AR 70-25's publication those attitudes would be forced to change. Renewed attention to ethical problems with human experiments came about because of abuses that occurred during the decade between the Wilson memo and the late 1960s. During that time federally sponsored human experiments seemed to career out of control in just about every direction.

# IN THE WILDERNESS

Two former CIA employees separately recalled the same incident in a bar in San Francisco where a hostess/singer in the employ of the bar had been surreptitiously given a small dose (neither of the participants recalled the exact quantity) of LSD in a cocktail. One of the participants recalled the name of the bar, the position of the subject, that she had blonde hair and a "fairly good voice," and that the incident occurred about 1958. . . . They reported that she was able to continue the performance of her duties for the remainder of her shift but was treated at a hospital after she went off duty. A follow-up conversation with her several days after the incident reportedly revealed that she apparently had suffered no harmful aftereffects, but had given up drinking.

*From a 1970s' investigation of CIA activities in the project known as MKULTRA*

## THE ACID TEST

With his clubfoot and stammer, Sidney Gottlieb was no James Bond. Yet in the 1950s, as a key member of the CIA's Technical Services Staff (TSS) at the height of the cold war, he was perhaps the most influential of America's spy masters, second only to CIA chief Allen Dulles. The Bronx-born Gottlieb lived a retiring life with his wife and four children on a farm, drank only milk from his own goats, and sold the Christmas trees he grew himself by the side of the road. Brilliant and thoroughly dedicated to his craft, Gottlieb held a Ph.D. from Cal Tech, overcame his physical disability by learning how to folk dance, and shared with Dulles a certain awe in the potential of mind-altering substances to shift the balance of terror with the Soviets.

Like the technical wizard Q in Ian Fleming's novels, most of the TSS staffers were concerned with developing and implementing newfangled electronic devices, mainly for surveillance purposes. But the mission of Gottlieb's MKULTRA project in the Chemical Division was mind control, an idea that had become popular following suspicions that defendants in postwar Eastern European political show trials had been "brainwashed" into confessing. During the Korean War reports of glassy-eyed allied prisoners surfaced. Then the CIA wondered if some of its agents were being controlled by a kind of secret force. Perhaps it was possible to create what one student of the agency has called a "human robot" with drugs. A prime candidate was a drug that, a decade later, would symbolize the breakdown of the social order for which the CIA stood.

Lysergic acid diethylamide, or LSD, had been discovered quite by accident in 1943 by Dr. Albert Hoffman, a Swiss chemist, who absorbed a chemical he had been working with one day in his laboratory, a derivative of the fungus ergot. The discovery was quite timely because there was great interest in the strategic possibilities of hallucinogens during the war. Not far from Hoffman's Basel, Switzerland, lab, SS doctors at the Dachau concentration camp were using prisoners to experiment with mescaline as a mind-control device, or perhaps to disrupt enemy combat forces. After the war, when the CIA learned about the Nazi concentration camp experiments with mescaline, and then about the potential of LSD, its leadership took an immediate interest. Americans had already made their own efforts in this area. In 1943 the Office of Strategic Services recruited Manhattan Project officials to try marijuana as a possible "truth drug." At first the twelve subjects tried it in a liquid concentrate but promptly threw up. Then they hit upon the technique already well known to jazz musicians and other hipsters: They smoked it. Sure enough, the experiment succeeded in "loosening the subject's tongue."

Gottlieb's LSD work led directly to the most infamous tragedy to befall the MKULTRA project, the death of one of its own scientists, Dr. Frank Olson. Olson was on the staff of the Special Operations Division (SOD) at Fort Detrick where, ironically, he specialized in the airborne delivery of disease as a biological weapon. He and his wife were University of Wisconsin graduates with three children. Olson was a well-liked colleague who had a particular fondness for practical jokes, but he spent most of his time with his family.

Without obtaining proper clearance, Gottlieb decided to try LSD on men from SOD, with which TSS had a contract to infect enemies with disease. During a SOD retreat in western Maryland in November 1953, Gottlieb spiked some Cointreau with LSD. Several of the men drank it, unaware, including Olson. They promptly dissolved into an all-night session of odd behavior, but Olson was especially disturbed by what was happening to him. One of his companions described him as turning psychotic. The next few days he was deeply depressed and barely communicated with his wife. Olson's undisclosed LSD experience seemed to have tripped a psychiatric crisis. Gottlieb arranged visits to a New York physician who had a top-secret clearance but who was not a psychiatrist. The consultations were of no avail and Olson's depression and paranoia increased. Just before he was to return to Maryland to be checked into a Maryland sanitarium with CIA-cleared psychiatrists, Olson crashed through the window of his hotel room on the tenth floor of the Statler Hilton and fell to his death.

Olson's connection to the agency was immediately covered up and it was arranged that his widow receive a government pension. Gottlieb and others who were involved in the experiment received a mild reprimand from CIA chief Dulles. In 1975, when the truth was revealed through congressional hearings on CIA activities, the Olson family appeared on television to make a powerful statement, urging that Olson's death "become part of American memory and serve the purpose of political and ethical reform so urgently needed in our society." President Ford personally apologized to the family and in 1976 Congress passed a bill to pay them $750,000 in compensation. As his family hoped, Frank Olson's death did become a crucible for the outrageous abuse of American citizens in mind-control experiments and many other projects during the 1950s.

As for Gottlieb, who died in 1999, he remained unrepentant, believing that the era justified his actions. A one-time socialist, his devotion to the American cause during the cold war led to self-experimentation, including taking LSD hundreds of times, according to a family friend. Gottlieb lent his talents to CIA assassination plots in the Eisenhower and Kennedy administrations, developing poison handkerchiefs, poison darts, and various lethal devices, none of which seem to have succeeded in taking out their targets, including Fidel Castro. As if his story weren't already strange enough, in retirement Gottlieb ran a leper colony in India and tended to hospice patients. While some people might say his later devotion to the vulnerable was his way of owning up to earlier misdeeds, Sidney Gottlieb looked at it as part of a continuing struggle for the forces of light against the forces of darkness.

## INNOCENTS ABROAD

Determined to obtain information about LSD as a mind-control agent, Allen Dulles and Sidney Gottlieb found better cover abroad. They created a front organization called the Society for the Investigation of Human Ecology (SIHE). One of the beneficiaries of SIHE grants was a handsome, politically connected Scottish-born psychiatrist at McGill University in Montreal named Ewen Cameron. In the 1950s Cameron used electroshocks and drugs to "depattern" both normal and abnormal behavior, with the goal of creating a temporary amnesia that would lead to recovery without the unwanted behaviors. Cameron also used "psychic driving" to bombard patients with a taped message that was repeated continuously for days. Sensory deprivation was another favorite technique for clearing the mind, often in combination with the looped tapes. There was no scientific basis for these ideas. Later, Cameron's own McGill colleagues concluded that he was at best a fraud and at worst a sadist.

One of Cameron's unfortunate subjects was a young woman named Val Orlikow who in 1956 was diagnosed with a postpartum depression. Under Cameron, her LSD therapy consisted of one to four shots a week mixed with a stimulant or depressant. During these trips she was left alone with a tape recording of excerpts from her previous session with Cameron. Orlikow's recollection of her "terrifying" experience is laced with psychotic imagery:

> You're afraid you've gone off somewhere and can't come back. . . . You become very small. You're going to fall off the step, and God, you're going down into hell because it's so far, and you are so little. Like Alice, where is the pill that makes you big, and you're a squirrel, and you can't get out of the cage, and somebody's going to kill you. . . . Some very weird things happened.

Cameron died in 1967 in full possession of his many academic honors. His "patients" did not forget, however, and in the years following the MKULTRA revelations Val Orlikow was among those who attempted to recover for damages from the U.S. government. She was in a better position to gain attention for her cause than most of Cameron's victims, for her husband was a member of the Canadian parliament in the 1970s. That Orlikow and the other survivors suffered from various mental impairments that may have been caused or aggravated by Cameron's methods was not in dispute. A court battle that was drawn out for years by CIA legal maneuvering finally resulted in an out-of-court settlement in 1988, when the U.S. Attorney's Office agreed to pay the Orlikows $750,000. It was the highest amount allowed under the Justice Department's regulations.

The CIA was not the only agency doing LSD research in Canada. Late in 1998, the Canadian government declassified records showing that its Defense Research Board sponsored LSD experiments at McGill University in Montreal. In 1964 six students and two professional musicians—perhaps because they were thought to be more accustomed to recreational drugs than other people—were recruited to take LSD at McGill. They were then shown ink drawings to test the effects on their visual perception. It was found that rapid eye movements that compensate for the eye's drift occur twice as fast under LSD's influence as they normally do.

A pharmacologist who did some of the animal studies but is critical of the human experiments, Dr. Herbert Madill, recalled that "it was after the Korean War, when mind control and this type of thing was thought to be very important. . . . We researched this family of drugs, and certainly LSD was one." It is unclear whether the Defense Research Board and the CIA consulted each other on their results, but in one respect at least the Canadians were more discriminating: In spite of Ewen Cameron's efforts to obtain funding from his own government's agency, only the CIA supported his work.


## THE BLAUER CASE AND THE
## TWENTY-YEAR COVER-UP

No case better illustrates the unpredictable twists of the cold war medical experiments, and the lengths to which officials at all levels went to keep them secret, than that of Harold Blauer. In 1952 Blauer was 42 years old and had been a ranking professional tennis player for some time. During the winters he taught at the Hudson River Club in Manhattan, in the summer at the Piping Rock Club, and he supplemented his income through the pro shops at both clubs. With his wife and two young daughters, Blauer lived a comfortable life in midcentury America.

Perhaps Blauer was stricken by the "midlife crisis" that in a later decade came to be the hackneyed explanation for every post-40 malaise. By the middle of 1952, Blauer's idyllic life seemed to fall apart. He and his wife divorced and, feeling down, he checked himself into Bellevue Hospital in New York City. There he was diagnosed as suffering from a clinical depression and was transferred to the famous Psychiatric Institute (PI), which specialized in such disorders. The PI was and remains a New York State facility, but it is operated and staffed by Columbia University psychiatrists.

Unbeknownst to Blauer, the PI had a secret contract with the Army Chemical Corps, a result of the Army's interest in the effects of hallucinogens. According to a 1951 internal memorandum, the Army's goal was to obtain data "which will provide a firmer basis for the utilization of psycho-chemical agents both for offensive use as sabotage weapons and for protection against them." Under the contract, the Army would provide chemical derivatives of mescaline to the institute, which would be used in studies with patients. The doctors involved received security clearances.

In fact, some psychiatrists at the time believed that mescaline might prove to be useful in treating mental illness. But the variants of mescaline that were delivered to the institute had never been tried in human beings. Even the animal tests were sorely inadequate. The lethal dose level of the mescaline derivative that was injected into Blauer had only been determined in mice, a test animal that is too distant from a human being to give reliable results on its own. Nevertheless, Dr. Paul Hoch, the institute's research chief, proceeded with the study.

Blauer was admitted to the PI on December 5, 1952, and began a course of psychotherapy, to which he responded well. Exactly what happened next is not entirely clear, but Blauer does seem to have been aware that he was to be given an "experimental" drug. However, he may not have been aware that the drug was not intended to help him, as was clear from the widely varying doses recorded in the medical logs. A court later noted that written consent was not required at the time but that oral consent was required and that a patient had the right to withdraw from a study at any time. Of course, if Blauer was not told the true nature of the experiment, then he could not have given a valid oral consent.

From December 11 to January 8, 1952, Blauer received five different injections of three different mescaline derivatives. The notes taken by the research physician who actually gave the injections, Dr. James Cattell, report that before the first injection Blauer was "very apprehensive" and that "considerable persuasion [was] required" to get him to accept it. His only reactions were a feeling of pressure in his head and a slight tremor in a leg. One week later, just before the second injection, Blauer said he was "apprehensive," but he had no reaction this time.

Before the third injection on December 23 Blauer asked the nurses to make an excuse for him to get him out of the "drug study" by telling the doctors he had a cold. He was injected anyway and experienced tremors throughout his body. Blauer then told his psychotherapist that he did not want any more injections, but he was threatened with a return to Bellevue or Roosevelt hospitals. These were much larger and far less pleasant "asylums" for the mentally ill than the institute. The fourth injection on December 30 caused him to go into violent tremors.

In the days that followed Blauer told his therapist and the nurses that he was very unhappy with the study. Besides his physical reactions he must have been undergoing very disconcerting psychological experiences, hallucinations for which he was wholly unprepared, especially for an individual who had recently been severely depressed. In spite of his protests, around 9:53 in the morning of January 8, Blauer was given a fifth injection. This one was of a derivative that was sixteen times larger than the dose of the same version of mescaline that he had received in the first injection. The drug study notes describe what happened next.

| | |
|---|---|
| 9:53 A M | injection started—legs being moved |
| | "I.V.'s getting me now"—restless movement—protesting injection. |
| 9:55 | injection ended. |
| 9:59 | very restless—has to be restrained by nurse—out of contact |
| | Wild flailing of arms. Sweating profusely |
| 10:01 | patient pulled up in bed—generalized stiffening of body. |

|        | respirations sterterous [*sic*] 32/min. |
|--------|------------------------------------------|

respirations sterterous [*sic*] 32/min.
pulse 120/min
teeth clenched—frothing at mouth.
Rapid oscillation (latent) of eyeballs.

10:04    Neck position suggests opisthotonos
10:05    extremeties held rigidly
         pupils moderately dilated and do not respond to
         light
         corneal reflex intact.
10:09    generalized flushing of face and chest—profuse
         sweating continued
         generalized tremor of lower extremities. Frothing
         at mouth.
         cyanotic
10:10    continued sterterous [*sic*] respirations—28/min
         irregular
         Jaw tightly clenched. rigid.
10:11    generalized rigidity—tonic—neck, arms, legs.
11:05    Some rigidity with restlessness.
         random movements of arms and legs.
         Talking with frequent references to "Murphy";
         mostly incoherent but questionable contact at
         times.
11:12    increasing restlessness.
         Intermittently generalized rigidity.
11:17    No longer talking. Lapsing into coma. Still rest-
         less. . . .
11:30    becoming cyanotic. Respiration rapid and sterter-
         ous [*sic*]. . . .
11:45    Quiet. Deep coma. . . .
Blauer was pronounced dead at 12:15 P.M.

The day after Blauer's death, Cattell's report to the medical examiner omitted the fact that the mescaline was given as part of an experiment, implying that it had a diagnostic purpose. This lie was repeated by Cattell's boss, Dr. Hoch, at every subsequent formal hearing. The next day a representative of the Chemical Corps came to New York and persuaded the medical examiner's office to keep all files confidential. Blauer's psychotherapist was frozen out when he asked for details about the death, and his ex-wife was told that he had suffered an "atypical" reaction to a drug.

What followed was a classic cover-up, in which all parties had enormous motivation. The Army and the state of New York conspired to keep all the embarrassing and potentially expensive facts out of the hands of the Blauers and their lawyers, a goal they could wrap in a cloak of national security. Because the Army wanted to continue its contract research in this area and the institute wanted to keep attracting patients, both feared "adverse publicity." The PI doctors surely had reason to fear for their professional reputations, if the facts were known. U.S. Justice Department lawyers concluded that the case would be worth between $60,000 and $75,000 "in the event the full attendant circumstances were revealed in court." Deciding that the best defense is a good offense, the New York State attorney general's office agreed to pay the family $18,000 but to stress that this was no admission of malpractice. The Army Intelligence Division came up with half the amount and secretly wrote a check to New York State. Even the source of the drug, the Army Chemical Corps, was covered up, and the record made to show that the Army Medical Corps was the supplier.

Blauer's ex-wife moved to Mexico, remarried, and died in 1974, just one year before Army representatives contacted Blauer's daughters and issued a press release disclosing the truth. In 1978 the United States District Court for the Southern District of New York awarded Harold Blauer's estate $702,000 in damages. Of this amount, $500,000 was for the pain and suffering Blauer must have undergone after the fifth injection, trapped "in a sterile, unfriendly atmosphere," where he was given the chemical "against his will."

Blauer was not the only patient to receive an injection that morning. Down the hall a female patient received the same mescaline derivative, but her reaction was so violent it was stopped about one-third of the way through. Later she said, "I've been in hell. Why did they put me in hell?"

## A COMPLEX POLICY PROBLEM

Unlike Olson, Blauer was the victim of behavior that involved physicians and a distinguished medical facility. His death came just as the civilian leadership in the Pentagon was trying to get the Nuremberg Code policy accepted, and only a month before Secretary Wilson signed the order. With such goings-on as the Blauer episode, one can imagine the Pentagon's eagerness to get top-level approval for a policy, any policy, that could get these kinds of projects under some sort of control.

In the postwar period a few people in the national security establishment, including especially Anna Rosenberg and Stephen Jackson, tried to develop and apply a policy on human experiments. But a number of factors foiled these efforts. The issue was scientifically complicated, having to do with difficult scientific questions about the risks of exposing the human body to unfamiliar substances, or in novel ways. When experiments were contemplated, they raised arcane issues of civil liberties and medical ethics. The sensitive nature of the topic prevented it from being subjected to wide public discussion, thus hampering efforts to communicate policies to those who would need to know about them. Fundamentally, the national security establishment felt under enormous pressure to nail down some answers about defenses against atomic, biological, and chemical weapons, and in some cases to evaluate their usefulness in underground activities. A mysterious and implacable foe lurked just over the Aleutian horizon.

Another element was the emergence of a vastly more influential medical scientific establishment, partly as a result of the many successes that researchers enjoyed during the recent world war. Penicillin was, of course, the jewel in the crown of that story. "Our" medical science, along with "our" atomic physics, was the most impressive in the world (especially following the destruction of German society), and the union of political aims and scientific expertise proved to be potent in the defeat of fascism. Surely we were on the right side in that global conflict; surely our science served all that is good and their science served all that is evil.

Finding themselves in yet another confrontation with a totalitarian regime so soon after the war, Americans' confidence in the technical and moral superiority of their science was a natural outgrowth of the nation's recent experience.

As a result, federally funded human experiments pretty much went on with minimal or ad hoc regulation. There were some spectacular consequences to this disorganized situation, which lasted from about the mid-1950s to the mid-1970s. The incident with the bar room chanteuse described in the epigraph to this chapter was one of the more bizarre and humorous examples, and the CIA at that time was responsible for some of the most egregious offenses. But it was by no means acting alone. At least four federal agencies conducted or funded human experiments that even at that very different time could not have been openly described for fear of public reaction.

## THE "ATOMIC SOLDIERS"

About a year before the Armed Forces Medical Policy Council (AFMPC) agreed to endorse Pentagon counsel Stephen Jackson's Nuremberg Code policy in 1952, its then-chairman sounded an alarm about nuclear paranoia among America's fighting men. "Fear of radiation," wrote Dr. Richard Meiling, "is almost universal among the uninitiated and unless it is overcome in the military forces it could present a most serious problem if atomic weapons are used." Meiling favored an active program to demonstrate "that persistent ionizing radiation following air bursts does not occur." The goal would be accomplished by placing a special unit within 12 miles of ground zero, then into the burst area.

If it seems odd that a medical council would propose a potentially hazardous experiment, the AFMPC's important role as a top advisory body to the secretary of defense during a tense period in international relations must be borne in mind. Nor was there a necessary contradiction between this aggressive approach to a problem of military preparedness and the Wilson policy that followed months later, so long as written consent was obtained. In at least some cases this was done. But the question remains whether Meiling's suggestion amounted to a higher-risk study than medical ethics should permit.

In fact, though Meiling's may have been the crucial voice that moved the idea for such studies along, the Pentagon high command was fertile ground for the idea. Army indoctrination pamphlets already urged that fears about lingering radioactivity following a "normal air burst" were groundless. It didn't take long for the Joint Panel on the Medical Aspects of Atomic Warfare (a Pentagon and AEC group), to draft a report on "biomedical participation" in atomic bomb tests. Under Harvard professor Joseph Aub, the joint panel acknowledged that people shouldn't be allowed to just "mill about" in the presence of a detonation. Careful planning was needed to obtain intelligible results.

The program that was at least partly initiated by the Department of Defense's physician advisors finally affected at least two hundred and fifty thousand men and women who worked in some capacity at the atomic test sites in Nevada and in the South Pacific. The several detonations at the Bikini Atoll began in 1946, called Operations Crossroads, and in Nevada in January 1951 before they were halted by the 1963 Nuclear Test Ban Treaty. By then there had been over two hundred tests of atomic and hydrogen bombs in the atmosphere, and dozens more underground.

Two categories of human subjects' research were pursued during the early 1950s' tests: "troop indoctrination at atomic detonations" and "psychological observations on troops at atom bomb tests." A third, experiments on flash blindness, actually started in October 1951 and continued for at least another six years. These categories were considered "human experiments," but at least two other long-term investigations, research on protective clothing and cloud fly-throughs, were not.

The spirit of the indoctrination effort was captured in a 1957 TV program made by the army, called *The Big Picture*. As the sun sets in the desert, a group of GIs nervously await deployment at an atomic bomb test, conveniently accompanied by a reassuring chaplain.

NARRATOR: Chow in the growing dust settling over the flats brings an end to the day. Dusk on the desert is always a reflective time . . . this one, perhaps, a bit more than most. . . . Everything is ready, but in the minds of the men who are about to become part of an awesome experience, fundamental questions remain.

CHAPLAIN: What seems to be the trouble, soldier? You look a little bit worried.

GI #1: Well, I am, Chaplain just a little bit.

CHAPLAIN: Actually, there's no need to be worried, as the army has taken all necessary precautions to see that we're perfectly safe here.

GI #2: Sir, have you ever been at one of these shots before?

CHAPLAIN: Yes, I've had the opportunity to see a number of atomic tests. I feel that as a chaplain it is my responsibility to be with my men.

GI #1: What's it like, Chaplain?

CHAPLAIN: First of all, one sees a very, very bright light, followed by a shock wave. And then you hear the sound of the blasts. And then it seems as though there's a minor earthquake. And then you look up and see the fireball as it ascends up into the heavens. It contains all the rich colors in the rainbow. And then as it rises up into the atmosphere it turns a beautiful pale yellow . . . and then assembles into the mushroom. It's a wonderful sight to behold.

Perhaps the television audience was more enthralled by this account of close proximity to an atomic-bomb blast than the men at Camp Desert Rock. Sheer terror was the dominant recollection of those who came forward as the years went on. Michael Uhl and Tod Ensign of the group Citizen Soldier have been collecting these memories. One who began dying from a muscle-wasting disease twenty years after laying telephone wire under the atomic-bomb site was Jim O'Connor.

I was petrified, with my hands clasped tightly to my eyes and head between my knees; perspiration ran down my cheeks. The sizzling flash stung my body. The bones in my hands glowed through my closed eyelids. Suddenly the rumbling noises turned to a roar. The desert seemed to be rolling. The trench crumbled in its wake, throwing me to the ground. My God! The world is ending!

Another former GI, Stanley Jaffee, remembered that "the explosion itself defied description. After the initial blast, I opened my eyes and saw a fireball which looked like a red sun setting on the desert floor. While I can't be precise about the distance between me and the point of explosion, I don't believe that it was more than two or three thousand yards." Jaffee, who tried to sue the federal government for the breast cancer he contracted twenty-five years later, went on:

We felt an incredibly powerful shock wave, followed by another shock wave moving back toward the bomb site. It was this reverse wave that [created] an enormous mushroom cloud. While this was happening we were ordered . . . to march in the direction of the fireball. I don't know how far we were able to [go], but I do recall that the heat was incredibly fierce and that later a number of the men were ill on the trucks which removed us from the site.

The indoctrination lectures the men received before their deployment seem to have paled before the actual experience of the blast. Anticipating the stress that would likely affect the troops, in 1951 the Army contracted with a group of psychologists to study their psychological and physiological reactions. Some men wore radiation badges for later measurement. The Human Resources Research Organization (HumRRO) administered a questionnaire to soldiers who had witnessed a bomb test after attending a reassuring briefing. The questionnaire included questions such as "if an A-bomb were exploded at 2000 feet, under what conditions would it be safe to move into the spot directly below, *right after* the explosion?" HumRRO listed the "correct" answer as "safe if you wore regular field clothing," but in fact that answer was wrong, because the actual risks depended on the weather, the bomb's yield, and many assumptions about how much exposure is potentially harmful.

The Army was quite skeptical about the scientific validity of the psychological tests, but the feeling was that panic was likely to be the big management problem on the atomic battlefield, so it felt impelled to continue its HumRRO contracts. Yet in a 1952 study the results were even more discouraging than the earlier ones, as it was found that there was no correlation between how much "knowledge" troops had about ionizing radiation and their emotional reactions to the blast. An Army panel determined that the experiment needed to be continued anyway, concluding that "troop participation in tests of atomic weapons is invaluable. As many men as possible ought to be exposed to this experience under safe conditions. Psychological evaluation is difficult and results can be expected to appear superficially trivial, but the matter is of such extreme importance that the research should be persisted in, utilizing every opportunity."

The indoctrination and panic studies took place while the Pentagon was undergoing its internal Nuremberg Code debate and through 1957. They were clearly considered human experiments, as considerable attention was given to scientific design and control groups were included, even though the methodology was flawed. Perhaps the HumRRO studies were one of the reasons that national security officials were moved to include atomic weapons experiments in the subject of the Wilson memo. If so, that policy effort failed, as the HumRRO investigators do not seem to have been told about the Nuremberg Code policy. Nevertheless, in retrospect the project's top psychologist told the president's Advisory Committee on Human Radiation Experiments in 1994 that "no soldier, to our knowledge, went into the test situation with no idea about what to expect. They were adequately informed."

The flash-blindness studies were obviously of special importance to pilots who might have to maneuver in the presence of an atomic detonation. Beginning in 1951, various methods were used to ensure retinal exposure at various distances from the blast site, and at least two subjects sustained temporary damage. What is perhaps most interesting about the flash-blindness studies is that they were handled with relative care, with consent obtained from at least some of the men who participated. To their credit, those in charge of this series appeared to take the issue seriously. Recall that in 1954 an officer with responsibility for the experiment that included the two temporarily blinded soldiers wrote a frustrated memo to superiors complaining about a rumor that the Pentagon had established policy guidance on human experiments but that it had not reached down the line. Complaining that "no serious attempt has been made to disseminate the information to those experimenters who had a definite need-to-know," the author asked that his superiors relax the grip in which the policy was being held.

In spite of the breakdown in communication, retired Air Force Colonel John Pickering recalled signing a consent form for a flash-blindness study in the early 1950s. "When the time came for ophthalmologists to describe what they thought could or could not happen, and we were asked to sign a consent form, just as you do now in the hospital for surgery, I signed one." If so it would be another example of the armed forces' spotty history in using its own in research, sometimes treating military personnel with kid gloves, sometimes being very careless indeed.

How to account for the different attitudes at work in the field tests and the flash-blindness studies? The deployment of tens of thousands of men in battlefield situations is a familiar training situation, while the manipulated environments of the flash-blindness experiments (sometimes including goggles with a shutter that opened just before the blast), arranged and attended by highly skilled ophthalmologists, gave them a more traditional medical air. Even the Advisory Committee on Human Radiation Experiments stated that the primary motive for the troop deployments was training, with the psychological and physiological measurements added at the insistence of a few medical advisors. The differing circumstances—one in a familiar battlefield situation, the other manipulated by doctors—were perhaps enough to generate different sensibilities among those responsible. Similarly, when a soldier's clothing was checked for radioactive particles or when a pilot's radiation badge was examined following a mushroom cloud fly-through, a simple conceptual shift could easily be performed. These activities could be viewed as falling into the traditional category of military experiments with a new kind of weapon, not mainly medical studies.

The president's Advisory Committee on Human Radiation Experiments concluded that the atomic bomb studies were not intended mainly as biological experiments. But the conventional notion that training for the atomic battlefield was the sole motivation for the Nevada test-site exercises meets with skepticism from the atomic soldiers' advocates. One of them, Washington, DC, lawyer Wally Cummins, gave me a one-word response when I recited the prevalent notion that technical questions like fission release or influence of weather patterns were the primary reason for the atomic exercises: "Bullshit!" He elaborated, "they didn't need over 200 blasts to assess fission release or the effect of weather patterns. They were vitally concerned about health effects on humans. They wanted to know how the men's minds and bodies would react, and how to control for that."

Whatever the motivation, one kind of study that could have been undertaken with the men seems never to have been contemplated: long-term epidemiological studies of the effects of exposure to low levels of ionizing radiation. As was candidly stated during the secret Pentagon policy debate, injuries that manifest themselves years after military service are not of particular interest from a combat-readiness viewpoint. Hence record keeping in Nevada ranged from dismal to nonexistent, as it was in Vietnam with regard to Agent Orange exposures, as it was again in the Gulf concerning biological and chemical weapons exposures. One result of this lack of interest in long-term monitoring is an inability to intervene medically as early as possible in a disease process; another is the limitation on veterans' ability to file disability claims for conditions that may have been acquired due to their service, compounding the tragedy.

Where was the Atomic Energy Commission, the agency created to ensure civilian control over the nation's nuclear materials and that pioneered in rule making for medical experiments with radioisotopes? The short answer is that in the early 1950s cold war pressures were such that the AEC beat a slow but sure retreat from trying to reign in the Pentagon. To the dismay of medical advisors like Shields Warren, in 1952 bomb-test planners decided that 7 miles was too far away from a blast and that 4 miles would be the distance for the next test. Warren warned that "deviations from established safety practices would result . . . in larger numbers and more serious casualties the closer the troops were to the point of detonation." But Warren's own AEC chairman, Gordon Dean, gave clearance for the Pentagon to put troops as little as 7,000 yards away.

Misgivings about this deviation from the AEC's standards were apparent even within the Defense Department's reviews of its Desert Rock exercises. Nevertheless, when the AEC let the Pentagon take responsibility for higher exposure levels for troops, it decided to set the limit at 6 roentgens and the limit for officers who volunteered for still higher exposures at 10 roentgens. Though this was far lower than some had proposed, it was still greater than the AEC's level of 0.9 roentgen per week. In the atmosphere created by the Korean War, Senator Joseph McCarthy, and the Soviets' hydrogen-bomb tests, the pressures on even civilian agencies were great enough to force these gradual increases in permissible exposure levels.

Today, what the atomic veterans and their families want most to know, of course, is how much greater risk of disease their experiences created for them. Partly because of the history of poor record keeping, expert analyses so far have been inconclusive. For a ballpark figure, President's Clinton's Advisory Committee on Human Radiation Experiments suggested taking the average reading of the radiation film badges worn by some of the men. Combine that figure with an approximate number of participants in at least one bomb test, and then take the lifetime risk of fatal cancer due to a certain amount of radiation exposure as stated in a standard radiation science textbook. That calculation would yield about 106 excess cancer deaths among approximately 48,000 that would be expected in this population. While this result would be relatively small (except of course for each of those 106 individuals), if the calculations were based on those who experienced higher exposures, the rates could be much worse. In fact, a statistically significant excess death rate from leukemia has been observed among those who participated in one particular high-yield test in 1957. In the federal government's 1997 response to the advisory committee's findings, the main emphasis was on the benefits currently available to all veterans, including the Veteran's Administration medical system, and on improving the claims system for veterans' benefits.

## INTO THE CLOUDS

Not only on the ground, but also in the air, radiation exposures took place coincident with national defense operations and training. Like many of the infantry exercises, the Air Force activities around the atomic-bomb blast sites also had a medical angle. Men wore radiation badges and had their bodily fluids checked. But, once again, ambiguity reigned about the reach of rules on human experiments.

One day in 1948, during airborne exercises designed to track information about an atomic cloud and to warn civilian aircraft about its direction, Colonel Paul Fackler inadvertently got too close. These were the early days of atomic weaponry and the whole business was quite mysterious. When Fackler landed there was general amazement that, in his words, "no one keeled over and no one got sick." Before that incident the Air Force relied entirely on drone aircraft to obtain environmental samples, but the drones were clumsy and often failed to obtain the quality of samples required to assess a detonated bomb's fission release. Air Force brass immediately saw the advantages in being able to use aircraft equipped with the "sniffers" piloted by human beings.

The resulting ten-year program of mushroom cloud fly-throughs or "penetrations" is told in an official Air Force history that fairly drips with testosterone. The "History of Air Force Atomic Cloud Sampling" begins by announcing its story as "one of the greatest adventures in the history of aviation," and goes on to describe each series of atomic blasts and attendant aerial assessments in great detail over several hundred pages. The mushroom cloud sampling duty was viewed as a very attractive assignment for a very few flyers.

One aspect of the fly-throughs was the investigation of radiation and air turbulence levels within minutes of detonation. Along with the Fackler incident, drones containing mice, monkeys, and instruments had given the Air Force the impression that any humans on board would be safe if the external gamma radiation dose was minimized. About a dozen test subjects were employed to "learn exactly how much radiation penetrates the human system" during a mushroom cloud fly-through.

The men swallowed film in watertight capsules that were attached to a string held in their mouths, so that it could be pulled up after their flight. For the first experiment, as part of Operation Teapot in 1955, the AEC waived the 3.9 roentgens exposure limit and allowed four Air Force officers to receive up to 15 roentgens. As it turned out, two crew members received more than 17 roentgens over several missions. In 1956, at Operation Redwing, the dosage level was raised to 25 roentgens, and reports had to be filed if it reached 50 roentgens. Once again, several flights exposed the crew members to about 15 roentgens. The notion that "permissible" body burdens can be set for what are largely experimental missions is an odd one, though bureaucratically necessary. Any doubt that these exposures were thought of as experiments is eliminated by the project's final report. There the director, Colonel E.A. Pinson, wrote: "Although a considerable amount of experimentation has been done with small animals which were flown through nuclear clouds, the early cloud-penetration project of Operation Redwing was the first instance in which humans were studied in a similar situation."

What consent procedures were applied to the penetration experiment, and how much did the men appreciate the long-term risks? A passage from the 1963 Air Force history of the project provides a window to the way the fly-throughs were perceived at the time: "The Strategic Air Command pilots picked to fly the

F-84G sampler aircraft were pleased to learn that they were doing something useful . . . not serving as guinea pigs as they seriously believed when first called upon to do the sampling."

No one wants to think of himself as a mere guinea pig, and in fact the maneuvers the pilots had to perform and the information they gathered made them far more than passive test subjects. Also, the scientists themselves were on board the planes, so they were accepting the same radiation hazards as the pilots. In a sense, then, the fly-throughs were a case of self-experimentation. When now-General Pinson was interviewed by the president's Advisory Committee on Human Radiation Experiments in 1995, he expressed the self-experimentation ethic: "The way you convince other people that at least you think it's all right, is do it yourself."

Nevertheless, the tests that began in 1955 were clearly medical experiments. They should have been governed by the secretary of defense's 1953 Nuremberg Code memorandum, which required written consent. In General Pinson's 1995 interview he said he was unaware of the policy at that time, and that, if he had known, he "would have gotten written consent from the people that were involved in this." It was another case of the failed implementation of the Wilson policy.

The results of these experiments allowed the Air Force to conclude that the internal hazards of radiation were insignificant. Pinson's final report recommended "that no action be taken to develop filters for aircraft pressurization systems nor to develop devices to protect flight crews from the inhalation of fission products."

## "THE BUCHENWALD TOUCH"

Besides the many activities that were part of the atomic tests, the Pentagon sought information about external radiation effects from sources other than soldiers in the field. In a project that started in 1950, even before the first atomic-bomb blasts on U.S. soil, hospitalized cancer patients in Houston were studied for their reactions to total-body irradiation (TBI) with Defense Department funding. For over two decades civilian researchers in Houston, Cincinnati, New York City, and Bethesda, Maryland, conducted studies with patients that could not be done with "normal," healthy subjects, studies believed to be justified because the patients might be benefited by the radiation. Not everyone, however, thinks the studies extended only to the point of theoretical benefit, and the physician researchers have even been accused of contributing to the premature death of some of their patients.

The idea of substituting patients for troops in radiation experiments was a direct result of the secret debate in 1949 and 1950 about the nuclear-powered airplane. Robert Stone was pushing the use of human subjects, perhaps prisoners, but an ad hoc Department of Defense committee concluded in 1950 that there was already sufficient evidence from Hiroshima, Nagasaki, and the Manhattan Project that a cumulative exposure of more than 200 roentgens would reduce normal life expectancy. One member of that group was the University of California's Joseph Hamilton, who had been instrumental in evaluating the results of the plutonium injections. Hamilton wrote to Shields Warren that only animals should be used in such research. I have already alluded to Hamilton's phrase, that "if this is to be done in humans, I feel that those concerned in the Atomic Energy Commission would be subject to considerable criticism, as admittedly this would have a little of the Buchenwald touch. The volunteers should be on a freer basis than inmates in a prison."

While the AEC hesitated about human radiation experiments, the Defense Department acted on an alternative. Shortly before Hamilton wrote his letter, the Air Force entered into a contract with the M. D. Anderson Hospital for Cancer Research in Houston. The main goal of the work, involving 263 cancer patients from 1951 to 1956, was to find a "biological dosimeter," a way to measure radiation exposure in human beings. Another effort involved psychomotor tests for skills similar to those needed by aircraft pilots, tests that were administered following a session of total-body irradiation. Researchers did find that symptoms were temporarily relieved by the radiation treatment at the higher levels of exposure. A few years after the M. D. Anderson research started, the Army also funded TBI studies at Baylor College of Medicine in Houston and the Sloan-Kettering Institute for Cancer Research in New York.

AEC officials who voiced reservations about the use of normal subjects, even prisoners, do not appear to have objected when cancer patients were involved. It seemed to be ethical to gather information from people who might be helped by the procedure. In practice matters were more complicated. In the most celebrated TBI case, a distinguished University of Cincinnati radiologist named Eugene Saenger received Pentagon contracts from 1960 to 1971. By the end, Saenger's was the only TBI-effects study being sponsored by the Defense Department. Ever since, his work has been subject to investigations by university bodies, professional groups, courts of law, and even the U.S. Congress.

One problem with Saenger's research is that it seems to have straddled experimentation and therapy. People with "radioresistant" tumors were irradiated if there was thought to be a chance of benefit to them and to learn about how the treatment effected them, especially psychological and psychiatric effects. Aggrieved family members and other critics believe that Saenger would not have done these studies if it were not for the military funding, but Saenger claims that the research was carefully separated from patient care.

Though it is very hard to tell if any of Saenger's patients died sooner because of the TBI treatments, they may well have been made more uncomfortable because of them. This might have been ethically acceptable if benefits were a fair possibility, or if the patients were told that they could become nauseous and vomit due to the radiation. But because the study doctors did not want people to assume they would become sick, it appears they were not told about these risks. This is a serious ethical problem, because comfort is an important consideration, and arguably it is especially important for people who are terminally ill.

Saenger's research team began using written consent forms in 1965 when the university started to require them, but only years later did they start to mention risks like nausea and bone marrow suppression that could be fatal. Why didn't the Pentagon require Saenger to get written consent right away, as the Wilson memo required since 1953? When President Clinton's Advisory Committee on Human Radiation Experiments examined the Saenger case in 1994, it found no evidence that Saenger was ever told about the Defense Department Nuremberg Code directive. Apart from the question of Saenger's own conduct, there is the irony that military-medical research with civilians who were sick was often even more poorly controlled than it was with soldiers who were well. Without realizing the implications of their attitude, even today researchers sometimes tell themselves that, since this person is sick anyway, adding a little more risk for the sake of science is acceptable. And so the case might be, but only if the added risks are very carefully assessed, scientifically justifiable, and agreeable to the subject-patient. Too often in the history of human experiments this has not been the case.

## THE "SCIENCE CLUB"

Although the CIA and Pentagon experiments were revealed in a rush of information in the mid-1970s, other studies remained mostly rumors until the early 1990s. In 1993 the Boston Globe reported on studies with radioactive materials that had been conducted during the 1940s and 1950s at the Fernald School in Waltham, Massachusetts, outside Boston. Fernald was a residential institution for children generally described as "mentally retarded," though that term was used very loosely in those days and could include all kinds of problems relating to psychological or social development. There were also studies at another school with a similar population, called Wrentham.

Working in the schools' archives, a Massachusetts task force set up to investigate the experiments found that studies had been done with residents of the schools on nutrition, thyroid function, and the use of radioactive isotopes for therapy or diagnosis. The research spanned the period 1946 to 1973 and involved radioisotopes supplied by the U.S. Atomic Energy Commission.

A parent of a child residing at Fernald in 1949 might have received the following letter from the superintendent, written on school stationary that bore the impressive seal of the Commonwealth of Massachusetts:

> We are considering the selection of a group of our brighter patients, including, to receive a special diet rich in the above mentioned substances for a period of time. . . . It will be necessary to make some blood tests at stated intervals, similar to those to which our patients are already accustomed, and which will cause no discomfort or change in their physical condition other than possibly improvement. The Massachusetts Institute of Technology plans to reward patients taking part.
>
> Enclosed please find a blank which I request that you sign and return in the enclosed stamped addressed envelope, as soon as possible. The signed and witnessed blank will signify that you have no objection to your son participating in this project as outlined above.
>
> You may rest assured that I personally feel this project will be of great importance and that much valuable information concerning nutrition can be obtained which eventually will be of considerable benefit to mankind. I hope that I can count on your cooperation.

The letter did not mention that minute amounts of radioactive substances would be part of the "special diet." Though the consent form is a nice gesture, it should be remembered that parents of impaired children had few options for institutionalization and were in a poor position to decline a "generous" offer from the superintendent.

In 1953 a similar letter was prepared by Clemens E. Benda, M.D., Fernald's "clinical director." Benda reminded the parents that:

> In previous years we have done some examinations in connection with the nutritional department of the Massachusetts Institute of Technology, with the purpose of helping to

improve the nutrition of our children and to help them in general more efficiently than before.

For the checking up of our children, we occasionally need
to take some blood samples, which are then analyzed. The
blood samples are taken after one test meal which consists of a
special breakfast containing a certain amount of calcium. We
have asked for volunteers to give a sample of blood once a
month for three months, and your son has agreed to volunteer
because the boys who belong to this Science Club have many
additional privileges. They get a quart of milk daily during that
time, and are taken to a baseball game, to the beach, and to
some outside dinners and they enjoy it greatly.

I hope you have no objection that your son is voluntarily
participating in this study. The first study will start Monday,
June 8th, and if you have not expressed any objections we will
assume that your son may participate.

The privileges of "Science Club" membership must indeed
have been attractive to both the boys and their parents, especially under the circumstances of daily life at Fernald. But those
privileges did not include knowing what the studies were really
about.

It looks very much like the AEC's own rules were violated at
Fernald. In 1948 its human investigations committee decided to
allow radiation experiments involving "larger doses for investiga-
tive purposes" with people who were sick, but only with their
consent. Experiments with children and pregnant women were
discouraged.

But the AEC's rules do not seem to have received much cur-
rency in the radiation agency's laboratories or among its contract
scientists. By 1951, personnel at the Argonne National Laboratory
in Chicago seem to have known nothing about a human experiments policy. Some scientists and administrators did think about
the issues involved, showing that guidance from the central office
wasn't needed to recognize some basic ethics. In 1956 the Division
of Biological Medicine stated that radiation should be limited to
low or "trace" doses and should use only informed volunteers,

without even referring to the general manager's 1947 letters. Despite the understanding of at least some people that research volunteers must be informed, regardless of radiation dose, the AEC-sponsored studies at Fernald and Wrentham violated that principle.

These are some of the details of the experimental series that gained the most attention in the 1993 investigation. In a 1946 nutritional study sponsored by the Quaker Oats Company and conducted by researchers from MIT, Fernald residents were fed breakfast cereals with milk that contained radioactive tracers. The researchers were interested in the way the body absorbed minerals like iron and calcium from different cereals. Quaker Oats wanted to prove that the nutrients in their cereal travel throughout the body, so that they could win an advertising coup over their chief rival, Cream of Wheat. The trace levels of radiation would help them identify the rates of absorption and elimination of the nutrients. Interesting results encouraged further testing. From 1950 to 1953 the AEC and Quaker Oats supported MIT and Harvard scientists in studies involving dozens of Fernald residents. These experiments combined tracer-containing breakfast cereals with calcium tracer injections. It was this 1950 to 1953 series that prompted the two letters.

As was normally the case, a number of scientific articles reported the results of these experiments without elaborating on the identity of the subjects or the manner of their recruitment. The Massachusetts investigators identified at least six journal articles that used results from the nutrition studies. The state task force also hired a radiation epidemiologist to assess the health consequences for the boys, in light of the published dosages. He concluded that by 1970 those who did not exhibit leukemia were not likely to have any ill effects.

There were other studies at Fernald and Wrentham, among them experiments on the thyroid gland using radioactive iodine, the use of radioisotopes for diagnosing various medical conditions, and the medical effects of radioactive iodine. That no physical harms can be associated with the experiments at the schools could lead some to dismiss the moral issues. After all, the nation was in urgent need of important information, and these young people were readily available.

But these were not benign environments in which concern for the children's well-being was overriding. The nature of these institutions, the kind of environment they provided their charges, easily led to their exploitation, and the experiments must be seen in that light to be fully and fairly judged. Conditions at institutions like Fernald and Wrentham were grim in those days. As the Massachusetts task force that investigated the allegations about experiments at the schools put it:

> Until the 1970s, the buildings were dirty and in disrepair, staff shortages were constant, brutality was often accepted, and programs were inadequate or nonexistent. There were no human rights committees or institutional review boards. If the Superintendent (in those days required to be a medical doctor) "cooperated" in an experiment and allowed residents to be subjects, few knew and no one protested. If nothing concerning the experiments appeared in the residents' medical records, if "request for consent" letters were less than forthright, or if no consent was obtained there was no one in a position of authority to halt or challenge such procedures.

These schools were not leafy, carefree campuses but asylums in the old-fashioned sense. Abuse of the children was not uncommon, apparently. Doris Manson, the mother of a long-term resident, a mentally retarded girl, told the Massachusetts commission about conditions in one of the buildings.

> On visiting I occasionally got a glimpse of the day room. It was a large, bare room with a cement-like floor. In the middle of the room there was a circular grating where urine and feces were hosed down. Needless to say, the little girls wore no panties. The room had no chairs, the children sat or laid down on the cold flooring. Most of the children laid on the floor because they were given Valium two and three times a day. . . .

I never saw the bedroom until much later. It was a very large, ward-like room with many beds and only inches apart. The only shower I ever saw was on the back porch. The children were taken naked, outside in view of any passerby, to be showered. I am convinced this could not have been a warm shower. . . .

Dorothy [her daughter] was so tranquilized that she could not defend herself. On two separate occasions she had the skin torn off both sides of her face, neck and back. . . .

She was moved upstairs. It was here I saw roaches, red ants and mice darting in and out to pick up a few crumbs left on the floor. My daughter was delighted with the mice. . . .

I saw children in Dorothy's area restrained in straight chairs and left alone in outside halls with all doors closed to them. There were no rules in place regarding restraints. The bathroom was one long row of stalls with no doors. There was no privacy. . . .

It was an experience getting in and out of this building. Dorothy would get very nervous when many of the men would get close to us and would strike out at them. Many a belt she received in turn, before I could intervene.

In the words of Fred Boyce, a former Fernald resident and experimental subject:

I won't tell you now about the severe physical and mental abuse, but I can assure you, it was no Boys' Town. The idea of getting consent for experiments under these conditions was not only cruel but hypocritical. They bribed us by offering us special privileges, knowing that we had so little that we would do practically anything for attention.

Experiments with human beings must take into account not only the fairness of using one group of very vulnerable people rather than those who are harder to manipulate but also the setting from which they are being recruited. A harsh, even brutal asylum is in no position to advocate for the best interests of its residents in research, and there can be no such thing as "ethical" research stemming from such a place. Just as racially "separate but equal" schools cannot be equal, so immoral institutions cannot be settings for ethical research. In the words of the Advisory Committee on Human Radiation Experiments:

> Perhaps the investigators, who were not responsible for the poor conditions at Fernald, believed that the opportunities provided to the members of the Science Club brightened the lives of these children, if only briefly. Reasoning of this sort, however, can all too easily lead to unjustifiable disregard of the equal worth of all people and to unfair treatment.

These are lessons that were brought home only many years after Fernald and Wrentham, too late, sadly, for the children who were so thoughtlessly used there. In 1997 Quaker Oats and MIT announced a $1.85 million settlement with about thirty of the Fernald alumni. As is usual in such deals, neither the institute nor the company admitted guilt. MIT noted that the 1994 Massachusetts task force had found no evidence of physical harm. Without mentioning the competitive advantage it was seeking forty years before, a Quaker Oats spokesman minimized its role, pointing out that the cereal had been donated and that the research grant was a small one. But was the company's moral responsibility for the project directly proportional to the level of funding it provided?

## EXPERIMENTS OF OPPORTUNITY

The young people at Fernald were liable to be used in research because they were conveniently institutionalized. Yet convenience comes in many forms, by way of poverty or employment as well as incarceration. From 1932 to 1972, U.S. Public Health Service officials sponsored the most notorious medical research project in American history, the so-called Tuskegee syphilis study. Over four hundred poor black sharecroppers were observed for the natural course of their disease for decades, including undergoing invasive medical tests, without being told the nature of their condition, and without being offered an effective treatment when it became available: penicillin. The men knew only that they had "bad blood." Some of them died of the effects of the disease, and the precise impact upon the health of their wives and girlfriends will probably never be known. In 1997, President Clinton offered a long-overdue apology to the men who involuntarily participated in the syphilis study.

The affair in Alabama was not secret. Physicians, nurses, and bureaucrats from the national to the local levels knew about it, yet it was continued for decades, apparently without serious protest. Its original purpose, to show that this sexually transmitted disease has a similar course in black men as it does in white men, could even be regarded as a laudable response to medical racism and the popular eugenic philosophy of the day. But as the civil rights movement came into full bloom the moral problem with simply observing the progress of a serious disease without attempting to intervene, especially with a socially and economically distressed population, became too obvious to ignore. Finally, when a journalist published an account of the study, it was brought to a halt in its fortieth year and a national commission was created to investigate how it could have gone so far. Their conclusions led to the current, much-improved (though far-from-perfect) system of research ethics.

The syphilis study represents a failure of medical ethics, but not because the men were deliberately exposed to the disease. They were exposed to tertiary syphilis, which was epidemic among African-American men in that part of Alabama. Such conditions that conveniently presented themselves enabled an "experiment of opportunity" to take place in that the disease could be studied without causing it. The moral failing resulted from physicians standing by and watching the disease take its toll on the victims' bodies, minds, and spirits, and on their families. The justification, to advance medical science, is unassailable on its own terms. But scientific progress cannot be justified at any cost, especially not when judged against the rights of vulnerable people.

Though not nearly as well known as the syphilis study, other observational studies conducted during the 1950s involved even more people and caused hundreds of deaths. Unlike the Tuskegee scandal these were outgrowths of cold war military needs. Marshall Islanders were continually exposed to an unnaturally radioactive environment, including the food they ate, in the decades following the South Pacific atomic tests. The AEC carefully followed their physiological reactions through its doctors, who also provided the islanders with routine medical care. But the doctors were not given the opportunity to explain to their patients that they were research subjects or that their injuries were radiation-related. Similarly, Air Force physicians studied the thyroids of Alaskan natives who had been exposed to fallout in the 1950s and 1960s. The Alaskans, too, were not informed of the reasons for the U.S. military's interest in providing medical care.

Incidents involving people from overseas'cultures or domestic minority cultures who were misguidedly dismissed as "primitive" took place outside the mainstream continental United States. But another, similar study was conducted within our own borders and may have had the worst health consequences of all. In the late 1940s and early 1950s there was a "uranium rush" in the southwestern states of Colorado, New Mexico, Arizona, and Utah. The dangerous work of mining and milling this material so useful in the construction of atomic weapons fell mainly to Navajos, who could not find other work that was nearly as well paid, if they could find any other jobs at all. The profitable mining business was fueled by AEC contracts.

By 1950 there was a great deal of accumulated experience with high levels of lung cancer in uranium mines in both Germany and in what is now the Czech Republic. While the American uranium mines and mills got into full swing, as early as 1949 an AEC sanitary engineer named A. E. Gorman tried to call his superiors' attention to the agency's moral responsibility to write certain safety standards into its contracts. The radiation danger came mainly from radon as well as radium, for which international safety standards already existed. In taking no action, the AEC set the stage for the tragedy to follow.

The Public Health Service (PHS) did have an opportunity to step in where the AEC had failed. In 1949 it started to study both the environment of the mines and the conditions of the miners. A 1950 study of four mines located on the Navajo reservation showed radon levels far higher than what had been expected and recommended "that a control program must be instituted as soon as possible to prevent injury to the workers." In 1951 PHS officials met with mine owners and urged them to have the mines ventilated, a measure that would have added very little to their expenses but could have made an enormous difference in the miners' safety. But the owners evidently did not believe that the government health officials would take action, and they were right. A 1952 PHS study noting the potential danger was "restricted" to state and federal officials and mining companies, thus ensuring that pressures could not be brought to bear from outside the system. But there was one voice that was too independent, some might say too cranky, to be silenced, and he is today an all-but-forgotten hero, a man who inspired Rachel Carson and is the shadowy grandfather of the modern environmental movement: Wilhelm Hueper. The writings of historian Robert Proctor have helped to give Wilhelm Hueper's work its proper place.

Hueper was born in Germany in 1894 and emigrated to the United States in 1923. He had worked as the doctor at a steel mill in the Ruhr Valley and became interested in industrial and environmental hazards. In 1930 he took a position as chief cancer pathologist at the University of Pennsylvania. His lab was funded by the industrialist Irenee du Pont, who arranged a tour of his dye works in Deepwater, New Jersey. On the tour Hueper learned that certain chemicals were used in DuPont's manufacturing process that were known in Germany to cause cancer of the bladder. He warned Mr. du Pont himself and, sure enough, a number of such cases had in fact come to the attention of the company's medical director. Now that the chemicals were implicated, exposure to them could be controlled.

In 1934 Hueper took a job at a new DuPont laboratory in Wilmington, Delaware. However, he found himself fighting a constant war against industrial secrecy. He discovered, for example, that workers handling dynamite were sometimes stricken with heart failure after being poisoned by inhaling nitrites. When some experimental animals were getting sick, he found out that the company had started adding lead to their nylon. At another DuPont facility he found that workers were being exposed to benzidine, which the company made great efforts to conceal, even from him; the material had been implicated in an industrial accident at the plant that had killed and injured hundreds of workers years before. After repeated attempts to publish his findings and to attract Mr. du Pont's attention to these issues, Hueper was fired, allegedly because his services were no longer affordable.

Hueper's sad experience at DuPont was the pattern of much of the rest of his career, in which his practical influence was marginal but his discoveries were important, though often (and in some respects still) controversial. The origins of disease are often difficult to trace, and there could be multiple explanations for many conditions, including genetic factors and nonindustrial toxins, to which workers are exposed. Still, Hueper probably deserves more credit than anyone before the 1960s in calling attention to workplace risks.

In 1942, Hueper published his 900-page classic, *Occupational Tumors and Allied Diseases*, that established him as an authority on the environmental and workplace dangers that were a sad by-product of modern industrial substances and conditions. Rachel Carson called it the "Bible" of environmental cancer. But most of the dangers for human beings, he pointed out, are preventable, including several forms of cancer associated with various manufacturing methods. Often the protections were simple. For instance, the production of thread required a carcinogenic shale oil that led to a high incidence of scrotal cancer among spinners, but when the spindles moved more slowly, less oil was thrown off and the incidence of disease markedly declined.

When the National Cancer Institute (NCI) hired Hueper to found its new Environmental Cancer Section in 1948, one might have thought that he had found a stable job that would permit him to pursue his theories. It was then that he began his study of the uranium miners in Colorado. Unfortunately, NCI publications having to do with radiation had to be cleared by the AEC. Of all people, Shields Warren, who had been such a stalwart on the use of human subjects in clinical radiation research, was a prime instrument in censoring Hueper's attempts to publish his conclusions about the miners' risk. Responding to Warren's demand that he remove from a paper references to the hazards of uranium mining, the stiff-necked Hueper said he did not accept his NCI position to become a "scientific liar."

In various ways, from the early 1950s until his retirement in 1964, Hueper was restricted in his work at the NCI. His only experiments were to be on animals, he could do no more work on cancer epidemiology, and he was essentially prohibited from doing any on-site research in the western United States. Many reviled him, and he was by no means a simple character. Although an accusation by a jealous colleague about Nazi sympathies was withdrawn, historian Robert Proctor has recently revealed that Hueper did attempt to secure a position back in the "new Germany" in 1933. The Nazi regime was investing heavily in cancer population research, an excellent opportunity for a bright, young, German-speaking scientist. Later Hueper was also accused of being a communist. His combative style was sure to attract angry charges, whether factual or not. Yet after his retirement, Hueper did receive many honors for his contributions, including the prestigious National Institutes of Health Director's Award shortly before his death.

None of Hueper's failed efforts resulted in more tragic consequences than the blocked paper on the uranium miners, for his was the last independent, authoritative voice that was raised in protest before decades of neglect. Since PHS officials had no authority to enter the mines without the companies' permission, the continuing epidemiologic study of the miners put the government doctors in a moral dilemma. If they did not cooperate with the owners, they would lose access and their continuing study would be threatened. If they did cooperate, the miners would in effect be used as test subjects without their consent. According to the sworn testimony of a former PHS employee, the doctors and agency officials resolved the dilemma by simply agreeing not to "alarm the miners" by telling them what they faced. After all, the health of a few uranium miners, including many "Indians" no less, paled in comparison to the importance of facing down the Soviets and gaining medical knowledge.

The toll of the PHS's silence built for thirty years. Families came to expect that their fathers would die in their forties, and they associated it with the men's work in the mines, but there were few other jobs available. Finally, in 1979, former Secretary of the Interior Stewart Udall filed a lawsuit on behalf of a group of miners. Four years later, the federal court in Arizona found that the government was motivated by national security in maintaining an uninterrupted flow of uranium. But on several further points the court's reasoning was flawed or simply wrong. The court implied that safety standards would impede mining, but radon levels could have been minimized by a simple and fairly inexpensive ventilation method. The court also commented that the epidemiological information the PHS researchers were gathering would not have been helpful to individual miners, but of course it would have told them something about their individual risk.

For over twenty years the miners underwent medical exams by PHS research physicians. Did they assume that if anything bad was happening to them the doctors would have told them? Perhaps. If the miners during their periodic physicals were warned about the radon danger—and there is disagreement about whether there were any informal warnings—those warnings did not do much good. Of the 4,100 men in the study group, exactly 10 percent had died of lung cancer by 1990, more than five times as many as would have been expected.

In spite of its errors, the court found that the plight of the uranium miners "cries for redress" and is "a tragedy of the nuclear age." The tragedy was compounded, however, by the fact that the miners and their families were not covered by the federal Radiation Exposure Compensation Act (RECA) because they could not demonstrate that their occupational exposure to radon had caused their cancer. Noting that the risk threshold specified in RECA is far higher than that required for other radiation victims, the president's Advisory Committee on Human Radiation Experiments recommended in 1995 that the requirement be adjusted so that those who have worked underground for a certain minimum period would be covered. In 1996 President Clinton announced that his administration had accepted this recommendation. Wilhelm Hueper's eminent but frustrated career was not wholly in vain, though a similar tragedy can only be avoided in the future if more thought is given to the way that national security needs may be brought into harmony with worker safety standards.

## SUBJECTS OF CONVENIENCE

Like the men in the syphilis study, the uranium miners were originally exposed to serious risks to their well-being without external intervention; only later did authorities have the opportunity to lessen the damage, and they decided not to do so. Research involving another group with little power, prison inmates, has often taken place in a much more active manner. Prisoners are especially attractive medical subjects because they can be monitored for a defined period. As we have seen, World War II-era studies relied heavily on prisoners, a fact that came back to haunt the Nuremberg prosecutors. When Robert Stone urged that "long-term prisoners" be used in radiation research on the proposed nuclear-powered aircraft in the late 1940s, there was general agreement that this was a plausible option, even after the Nuremberg Code seemed to cast suspicion on the ethics of prison experiments.

Prison research continued and flourished in the United States through the 1950s and 1960s, much of it financed by private sources. Research contracts awarded by the Army to university researchers often ended up supporting their work with prison inmates. Ethical and legal concerns rarely surfaced because volunteers were plentiful and encouraged by much better money (especially for Army-sponsored studies) than could be earned in other prison occupations and the prospect of "good time" that would count toward parole. Sometimes prison officials were asked to certify their approval of the research. Often the inmate subjects signed release forms, which met conventional standards of the day but provided little information about the procedures or risks involved.

Temple University criminologist Alan Hornblum has documented one of the most extensive prison research operations in the country, at Philadelphia's Holmesburg Prison. A distinguished University of Pennsylvania dermatologist, Dr. Albert Kligman, directed the research program at Holmesburg. Kligman was enthusiastic about the prison as a source of subjects, and he conducted many dermatology studies there over the years, vividly described by Hornblum in his book, *Acres of Skin*. The title of the book was taken from Kligman's excited description of the way the prison looked to him as a young researcher, eager for subjects.

Prominent among Kligman's projects were skin-hardening experiments conducted during the mid-1960s for the Army, which was apparently interested in developing a natural body armor for soldiers to protect against irritants encountered in the field. Kligman tried a variety of agents and processes, although to obtain results, significant inflammation and crusting of the subjects' skin was required. Many inmates that Hornblum interviewed had considerable scarring from wounds they claimed to have suffered in the skin-hardening research.

Though expert in his own field, Kligman seems not to have been qualified to direct the chemical weapons research at Holmesburg that his Army sponsors paid him to do. The studies of drugs that produce delirium required subjects who could be followed for longer periods than those available to the Army at Edgewood Arsenal, so Holmesburg's long-term prisoners were preferable. However, reviews of the prison operation by Edgewood officials expressed grave reservations about the competence of Kligman and his staff to conduct the kind of research that they had already been funded to do. Quite apart from any long-term harms to the experimental subjects (harms that are often hard to prove), there is universal agreement that sloppy research with human beings is a basic breach of medical ethics.

Drug studies were also being conducted at Holmesburg by the Chemical Corps. LSD was among the psychoactive substances being tested, a drug for which neither the doctors nor the inmates were well prepared. The researchers at Holmesburg didn't know what to make of LSD's effects, and the inmates were familiar with street drugs but not with hallucinogens. They also couldn't be told much about the drug, including its name, because at the time the research was classified. Hornblum also describes extensive CIA-sponsored research with EA 3167 (3-quinuclidinyl cyclopentyl-phenyglycolate), which was thought to be central to Soviet behavior control efforts. The potent drug was said to cause delirium that could last as long as two weeks. Ex-convicts interviewed by Hornblum said that they had all sorts of psychological problems ever since the psychoactive drug tests, but theirs is not a population likely to evoke much public sympathy.

The AEC was another important source of federal funds for human experiments in the 1960s, and Kligman sought support to conduct research on the way the skin absorbs various materials, using radioactive tracers to keep track of the processes. Kligman had trouble convincing the AEC that the Holmesburg setup was competent to deal with radiopharmaceuticals, but finally his licenses were granted and amended. So Kligman also used the radioactive agents in his skin-hardening experiments at Holmesburg. But compared to his colleagues in the Pacific Northwest, Kligman was a small-time player in the world of prison radiation research.


## THE FAMILY JEWELS

Harold Bibeau was in an Oregon penitentiary back in the 1960s when he was given the opportunity to volunteer for an experiment. Bibeau was instructed to lie on his stomach while his scrotum was put in a plastic box containing warm water so the testes would descend. A calibrated dose of radiation was then emitted from each side. Bibeau was then vasectomized, as he had agreed, in case the radiation caused chromosomal damage, and his testicles were biopsied. He received $25 for submitting to the vasectomy and the same amount per biopsy, far more than the 25 cents a day that was the then-going rate for work in prison industry.

Of all the sensational tales to emerge from the heyday of national security human experiments of the 1950s, none excites more curiosity than the irradiation of prisoners' testicles in Oregon and Washington state penitentiaries from 1963 to 1973. Perhaps because of the delicacy of the subject matter, these were among the few instances in which consent forms were filled out, at least sometimes, by some of the men. It was also a rare instance in which clergy were consulted: Catholic prison chaplains objected to the participation by prisoners of their own faith because of the required vasectomy.

Why testicular irradiation? The studies were another example of dual-purpose experiments: the possibility of a new male birth control technique joined with military concerns about the implications of long-term, low level radiation exposure of that part of the body. The AEC provided $1 million in funding to leading endocrinologist Carl G. Heller for the Oregon research, and it also supported his student, C. Alvin Paulsen, for similar studies in Washington State.

The AEC was not the only federal agency to take an interest in the results. Heller's former research assistant recalled that National Aeronautics and Space Administration (NASA) officials and even some astronauts were briefed on the research. NASA scientists wondered if the radiation to which astronauts were exposed could compromise the production of testosterone, thereby reducing muscle function in space. Dr. Heller's prominence in his field was probably sufficient to gain him attention, but he did have connections to federal authorities that extended beyond his professional influence, as his brother was Walter Heller, President Kennedy's principal economic advisor.

The testicular irradiation research was fated to run into changing attitudes toward human subjects' research in general, and prison research in particular—attitudes that were beginning to roll through the country in the early 1970s. Although Heller and Paulsen submitted their proposals to suitable university committees, and although consent forms were signed, in 1973 the Oregon prison director halted the project. The syphilis study scandal had hit the press, and so had the Attica prison riots in upstate New York, in which several dozen prisoners were killed. The public was aroused about the possible exploitation of African-Americans who were poor or incarcerated.

Ironically, prison research in the United States, including the testicular irradiation research, was generally confined to white men. Because participating in prison research was considered a privilege, it was denied to minorities—at least until the civil rights movement succeeded in equalizing social opportunities for African-Americans, including research opportunities.

After Nuremberg, America was the only Western country that maintained an extensive program of prison experiments. By 1974 about three-quarters of all approved drugs in the United States had gone through prison research, and several drug companies built state-of-the-art facilities adjacent to prisons. When the federal government decided the consent issues were too complicated for prisoners and ordered them stopped in the federal prison system, states followed as well. Drug companies resigned themselves to finding other sources of experimental subjects. Only one group threatened legal action: prisoners themselves, who complained that they were being deprived of their right to consent to being experiment volunteers. But the testicular irradiation alumni were not so sanguine about their experiences, and they filed several lawsuits. Nine plaintiffs split $2,215 in damages in 1979 for pain for which they had not been prepared.

In 1970, several years before the testicular irradiation studies were stopped, the research chief of the Department of Institutions in Washington State, Dr. Audrey Holliday, wrote a letter to her boss that proved to be a bellwether of the changes in social attitudes about human experiments soon to sweep the country. The national security establishment would not be immune from these changes. And though the subject was prison research, one can sense in this letter other attitudes that sound very contemporary, decades later. Dr. Holliday wrote:

> . . . There is no question but what the Federal Government has made a considerable investment in this project. The Federal Government, however, as a reading of any newspaper will show, has supported a number of projects over which there have been many moral-ethical questions (both large and small) raised, e.g., nerve gases, toxins, etc. . . .

... There is no doubt but what the prison setting is an ideal setting for this type of research. ... I suppose concentration camps provided ideal settings for the research conducted in them.

By 1970 a scientist and government official could draw an analogy between U.S. government-sponsored research and the concentration camp experiments in a note of protest to her superior without being fired. Indeed, shortly thereafter her judgment about the propriety of the prison research became national policy. But no concentration camp analogies were seriously made in 1950 by anyone in Dr. Holliday's position. Of course, Holliday wrote her memo in the midst of the Vietnam era in which trust in government was being undermined, perhaps never to fully recover. Human rights were becoming a major public focus, national security concerns no longer excited automatic allegiance, and military-medical research was soon to be caught in the same tide. Only seventeen years after Harold Blauer's fatal injection with mescaline derivatives, as described earlier, times were changing.

## THE AIR OUT THERE

Experiments that involved normal volunteers and hospitalized patients proved difficult to keep secret. Sometime the subjects would protest alleged ill treatment, and scientists wanted to publish their results. The lines between data that was sensitive and data that was publishable were not always clear, and at some point individual test subjects had to be obtained, further straining secrecy.

But field tests were another matter entirely. Their goal was improving the means for detection of potentially dangerous substances in the environment, especially those that can be airborne. Unlike in clinical experiments, in those environments the presence of human beings was often coincidental. Persons present in the area of a field test might be unwitting bystanders, not targets.

Secrecy is also easier to manage in field tests than in many medical experiments because of the personnel involved. Medical experiments can involve a number of independent-minded doctors. By contrast, products of nuclear fission processes could be released without any individuals being involved other than a small group of workers at the nuclear plant itself. The same was true of biological warfare tests, which became the responsibility of the Biological Weapons Research and Development program in the Office of the Secretary of Defense after World War II. This high-level placement suggested the seriousness with which biological warfare was taken by the Pentagon, which was also trying to digest the implications of the Japanese experiments in Manchuria.

In 1948 the Committee on Chemical and Biological Warfare reported to the secretary of defense that the United States was prone to attack by biological weapons; furthermore, the research and development program the Department of Defense currently had underway was not sufficient to "defend against subversive BW operations." The committee proposed to undertake projects of vulnerability tests on "ventilating systems, subway systems, and water supply systems with innocuous organisms." According to a report to Congress nearly three decades later, "open-air testing of infectious biological agents was considered essential to an ultimate understanding of BW potentialities because of the many unknown factors affecting the degradation of microorganisms in the atmosphere."

Over the next twenty years biological warfare research programs were carried out "in the continental United States, in Hawaii, in the Canal Zone, and in theaters of operation." A high Army official told Congress in 1977 that "most [experiments] were done on government installations, under controlled conditions; however, testing was also conducted off Government installations." The areas in which research was conducted were termed *the chamber, the field, the lab, Conus* (continental United States), and *Oconus* (outside the continental United States). As the details of these field tests have become known, they have been a terrible embarrassment to the biological defense establishment.

Well before the congressional investigation the fact that the Army conducted open-air field testing was by no means classified, though the details were often classified and the risk was underestimated. An Army chief chemical officer, Major General Marshall Stubbs, told the Armed Forces Chemical Association on April 14, 1959, that "the proven effectiveness of biological warfare attack over large areas has also been confirmed by a number of field trials. Test attacks have been made both from ships lying offshore and from planes flying over the continental United States. These tests, in which a harmless tracer material was used, proved that coverage up to several thousand square miles could be achieved, with the population being wholly unaware that the attack had occurred."

During the period 1949 to 1969 more than two hundred open-air tests of U.S. vulnerability to biological warfare attacks took place. Sites for these tests included Panama City, Florida; Washington National Airport, Washington, D.C.; Oahu, Hawaii; Minneapolis, Minnesota; and St. Louis, Missouri. The substances used in these tests were *Bacillus globigii*, *Serratia marcescens*, *Aspergillus fumigatus*, and zinc cadmium sulfide. As Major General Stubbs implied in his 1959 speech, the Army never informed the residents of these areas, nor the local governments, that such tests were taking place. Moreover, the dangers presented by this "harmless tracer material" to some individuals—especially those whose immune systems are depressed by illness—were not recognized.

In one test the city of San Francisco was exposed to a simulated biological warfare attack in which *Serratia marcescens* was sprayed from a boat just offshore. *Serratia* is a soil bacterium that produces rust-colored colonies that are easy to spot, as on shower curtains or on the filter of a freshwater fish tank. Though *Serratia* bacteria are generally thought to be harmless to humans, a professor of microbiology at the State University of New York (SUNY) at Stony Brook, Dr. Stephen Weitzman, told Congress that they can indeed cause disease in a healthy person, and that hospitals "have recurring problems with *Serratia* infections in hospitalized sick patients." Several articles suggesting the dangers of *Serratia* were available in publications available to Army researchers at the time.

Shortly after the offshore spray exercise, eleven patients at the Stanford University Hospital developed *Serratia* infections. One of those patients, Edward Nevin, subsequently died. More than two decades later, his relatives learned of the Army's "simulated attack" and sued for negligence. The Army contended that they had believed, and continued to believe, that the organism used was not normally capable of causing infection. The court hearing the case found that the government properly exercised its discretion to choose both the site for the attack and the bacteria to be used in the attack, and the case was dismissed.

New York City was also the site of biological warfare field testing, in June 1966. Without the knowledge of the local civilians or public health authorities, the Army introduced *Bacillus globigii* into New York City subway tunnels and from mid-Manhattan streets. *Bacillus globigii* is another soil bacterium. It appears as black spots on shower curtains or other such surfaces that have not been cleaned for a while. Like *Serratia*, *Bacillus globigii* is generally regarded as harmless to humans. However, any bacterial organism can infect someone whose immune system is depressed, and that might be what happened to the California patient who died after the *Serratia* release.

As in many field tests, the goal of the New York City subway study was apparently to learn about dispersal patterns, this time in an urban environment with an extensive underground public transportation system. To determine how the material was dispersed, a covert Pentagon team positioned air samplers and took swabs of surfaces of objects and of people. Unsurprisingly, the Army found that "large numbers of people could be exposed to infectious doses" if a similar attack using pathogenic agents were to occur.

Critics of the scientific and ethical basis for conducting this test question the necessity for using actual cities for the open-air tests. "It was unclear to me what additional information was gained by releasing bacteria in the New York City subways . . . that could not be gathered by a similar experiment done in the tunnels of a deserted mine shaft; or why in studying aerosolization patterns unpopulated areas could not be used, instead of populated cities," said SUNY Stony Brook's Weitzman. However, if one is interested in defending a subway shaft from a biological attack, then one needs a populated model. The movements of people create air currents that must be taken into account. There was then and still is reason to be concerned about a subway attack. In 1933 German agents reportedly tested *Serratia marcescens* in ventilation shafts of the Paris Metro and near several French forts, and the Aum cult released sarin gas in the Tokyo subway in 1995, killing twelve people.

Unlike the clinical experiments conducted by physicians, the U.S. field tests were the province of engineers. Though there are now university courses on engineering ethics, traditionally engineers have been trained to think in terms of what can be physically accomplished rather than in terms of what is ethical to try to accomplish. This doesn't mean that people who become engineers are "less ethical" than, say, people who become doctors; both of my maternal uncles were engineers and they were among the most decent and principled people I have ever known. Rather, it means that the engineer's normal ways of operating and professional socialization didn't historically include ethical assessments. What these cases do show is that, once again, the national security establishment failed to factor in ethical considerations that were stated in its policies.

Another of the agents used in some of the Army open-air tests is zinc cadmium sulfide, which has proven to be controversial in the subsequent investigations of those tests. This substance is made up of fluorescent particles that, when released in the air, are an excellent medium to trace dispersal patterns. Rutgers University professor Leonard Cole told Congress that "the Army was literally using the country as an experimental laboratory. In 1957 and 1958, a cargo plane crisscrossed the country releasing tons of zinc cadmium sulfide." Since the tests became public knowledge and questions were asked, the Army has consistently responded that at the time of the tests they thought zinc cadmium sulfide presented no health hazard. Responding to the Army's defense, Cole said,

I have looked at the scientific literature, not all of it, but a good deal. . . . It is true that some would suggest that at very, very low concentration, cadmium might not offer the toxicity suggested by [a 1932] report. But it seems to me that when you are going to be spreading that material around millions of people it would be prudent to err on the side of caution.

Critics of the Army, like Cole, surely have an easy time criticizing these field tests, for they seem very hard to justify in retrospect. The Army's defenders respond that important information was gained and that there is still no concrete evidence of harm, despite the speculation of Cole and others.

Though it is hard to prove that the substances that the Army introduced to the civilian areas were the cause of injury, interesting correlations have been made. In the 1977 congressional inquiry into Army open-air testing, Pennsylvania Senator Richard Schweiker pointed out that in 1952 the Army conducted tests using *Serratia* and *Bacillus globigii* in Fort McClellan, Alabama. The year before the Army tests, the Alabama county in which the tests took place reported 4.6 percent of the statewide total of pneumonia cases. In the year of the tests, that percentage was 12.3 percent, nearly three times as great. The year after the test, 1953, there was a flu epidemic. Nevertheless, the rate dropped to 4 percent, which became the norm for succeeding years.

To be sure, like the radiation experiments, the open-air biological warfare field testing had a legitimate national security justification. But unlike the radiation experiments, that justification may actually be greater now than it was in the 1950s. In 1956 the Soviet Union publicly announced that it would use chemical and biological weapons "for mass destruction in future wars." In response the United States changed its public stance from using biological and chemical weapons only for retaliatory purposes to using them "to enhance military effectiveness" (though that might already have occurred secretly in Korea).

However, most military tacticians have not been enthusiastic about biological weapons, due to their indiscriminate and unpredictable nature. Though the United States destroyed its biological weapons stocks on President Nixon's order in 1971, the problem of defending civilian populations against a terrorist attack has, if anything, become more pressing since the cold war. Unlike the Soviets during the cold war era, terrorist groups might consider disruption of civilian life for its own sake enough of a motivation for a terrorist attack, if they have sufficient hatred for the United States. If the country becomes sufficiently concerned, it might even agree that open-air tests are necessary for national security in the new world order.

As in the case of the radiation experiments, the Pentagon realized it needed review procedures for proposed field tests. As the U.S. biological warfare program grew in size and scope into the 1960s, higher echelons of the Department of Defense became more intimately familiar with and active in the biological weapons projects. The secretary of the Army submitted the proposed test programs to the secretary of defense, who approved only some of the projects, reflecting what the Army called "the extreme care taken to assure the ultimate in safety, the highest level of review and approval, and appropriate government coordination." Moreover, "a national policy directive was issued by the President on 17 April 1963 requiring presidential approval of all tests which might have significant or protracted effects on the physical or biological environment." As we have seen before, however, secret policies are hard to square with the principles of a liberal democracy, especially when they present a potential body burden to every citizen in whose name national security goals are being pursued.

For both field and clinical testing, through the 1950s the Pentagon's human research policies subsisted quietly amid a forest of other military regulations. Considering its long-standing concerns about atmospheric radiation exposure and other aeromedical issues, it is perhaps not surprising that the Air Force's policy for the conduct of clinical research at Air Force medical facilities, known as 80-22, actually preceded Secretary Wilson's memo by nearly a year. It required the review of proposed human experiments by a School of Aviation Medicine research council or, in some cases, by Air Force headquarters. Like those of the other services, the Air Force rules looked good on paper, but their significance in terms of true voluntary and informed consent was poorly understood. In general, the armed forces' rules were erratically disseminated, both within the medical corps and among civilian contractors. Under these conditions the paper requirements were no match for an avalanche of cold war experiments. Nonetheless, there were rules and, with so much human experimentation being conducted both within classified government projects and outside of them, it was perhaps only a matter of time before their implications would have to be faced.

# THE RULES CHANGE

Man, in his personal being, is not ordained to the utility of society;

rather, the community is ordained to the good of man.

*Pope Pius XII, addressing the International Conference on the*
*Histopathology of the Nervous System, 1952*

## HENRY BEECHER'S WAR ON THE NUREMBERG CODE

Though it is too easy to caricature the 1950s as a decade in which Americans preferred not to look too closely at their society's shortcomings, it is nonetheless true that other matters, like the spread of communism, preoccupied the nation. Critical assessments of important institutions, such as the actions of national security agencies and the conduct of medical science, would have to wait.

The first stirrings of renewed public interest in discussions about the ethics of human experiments took place in 1959. That year a Harvard professor of anesthesiology who was also a well-known researcher, Dr. Henry Beecher, published an article in the *Journal of the American Medical Association* called "Experimentation in Man." In his article Beecher agreed that it is of course "unethical and immoral to carry out potentially dangerous experiments without the subject's knowledge and consent," but that didn't suggest an unqualified endorsement of the Nuremberg Code.

Over the next decades Henry Beecher came to be known in medical ethics circles as a hero for his exposure of numerous unethical experiments. Yet the man who went on to become the greatest icon of ethics in human experiments was a severe critic of the code, the greatest document in the field.

Beecher was especially critical of the Nuremberg Code's requirement that people have sufficient knowledge of the proposed experiment before they agree to be subjects, because only a very few people have the expertise to truly understand the hazards of an experiment. Even the scientists themselves may not really comprehend the mysteries involved, especially in advance. Beecher also objected to the code's assertion that human experiments should not be "random." In fact, he noted, many medical breakthroughs had occurred by accident, including the discovery of X-rays and penicillin, as well as anesthetic agents. "It is not my view that many rules can be laid down to govern experimentation in man," Beecher concluded. "In most cases, these are more likely to do harm than good."

Anyone who would advocate "an understanding of the various aspects of the problem" on the part of researchers as the best protection for the people they would use in their experiments, and not the Nuremberg Code, seems an unlikely candidate to be the greatest hero in the history of research ethics and human rights.

Henry Knowles Beecher was a complex person. Born Henry Knowles Unangst in Wichita in 1904, his family lived modestly on his father's income as a night watchman and carpenter. He put himself through the University of Kansas and, in 1928, left for Harvard Medical School, from which he graduated with honors in 1932.

A classically ambitious and hard-working young American, Henry was determined to leave rural Kansas and his unlettered family far behind him, not only physically but also spiritually. To do that he sought more than just a change of venue; he also decided on a change of name. The obscure and provincial "Unangst" did not fit a young man with Henry's plans, and certainly not in blue-blood Boston. Fortunately, through his maternal grandmother he was related to the great Beechers, Henry Ward and Harriet. It was a perfect solution. By becoming a Beecher, Henry could feel he was not only remaining true to his roots but also expressing an identification with his more intellectual ancestors. In addition, he acquired a familiar New England moniker suited to a graduate of Harvard Medical School and one of its most distinguished future professors.

Thus prepared, for the next thirty years Beecher's career was a professional tour de force. He interned at Massachusetts General Hospital, won a Mosely Traveling Fellowship from Harvard, worked for a year in the Copenhagen laboratory of physiology Nobelist August Krogh, was appointed instructor at Harvard and chief anesthetist at Massachusetts General Hospital, founded the world's first anesthesia research institute, and published the dominant text in the field. In 1941 he became the first endowed professor of physiology. During the war Beecher served with distinction in North Africa and Italy, developing innovative approaches to the battlefield administration of morphine, for which he was awarded the Legion of Merit.

Upon his return to Harvard, Beecher threw himself into an enormously productive period of teaching and research. He trained hundreds of anesthesiologists, including fifty who became medical school professors themselves. Among his most important scientific accomplishments were techniques for quantifying subjective states like pain, thirst, and mood, and the recognition of the importance of the placebo effect (the physiological consequences of belief states), leading to new scientific study designs that are now standard for research to be considered sound.

For reasons that are not entirely clear, this giant of his medical discipline gradually became preoccupied with ethical concerns. Beecher's deep Christian faith may have had something do with it—he is said to have read a chapter of the Bible every day—perhaps in combination with some residual guilt over human experiments in which he had a hand. In 1965 Beecher gave a lecture on "Ethics and the Explosion of Human Experimentation" in which he said, "Lest I seem to stand aside from these matters I am obliged to say that in years gone by work in my laboratory could have been criticized." Following this speech, which was purposely prepared for a group of journalists, *The Boston Globe* ran the headline "Are Humans Used as Guinea Pigs Not Told?" The front-page story on March 24, 1965, was next to an article about Martin Luther King's march in Montgomery, Alabama.

Beecher more than lived up to the rabble-rousing name he had adopted. In his own way Beecher was also a campaigner for human rights, though in a much more esoteric field than his abolitionist namesakes. In 1966 he published the most controversial and influential single paper ever written about human experiments, "Ethics and Clinical Research," which was foreshadowed by his speech to the press the year before. In the article, published in the prestigious *New England Journal of Medicine*, Beecher did what in the genteel world of academic medicine was all but unthinkable: He identified twenty-two cases of published research as unethical, an unprecedented act of whistle-blowing that was greeted as scurrilous by many of his erstwhile colleagues.

Yet though Beecher believed in research ethics, he also believed in protecting the independence of the medical researcher, and he shared with his fellow physicians a deep skepticism of rules imposed on doctors' conduct by forces outside the profession. Between his two important articles that shocked so many, and several years before his historic lecture and brief confession, Beecher played an important role in impeding the Army's renewed efforts to impose the orphaned Wilson policy on recalcitrant scientists.

## THE ARMY REGULATIONS

Since 1954 the Army's Office of the Surgeon General had its own version of the Wilson policies. They were intended to apply the Nuremberg Code-based rules to research in Army hospitals and to contracts with civilian researchers. Though it is not known why, starting in 1961 the Army seemed to make a greater effort to insure that the "Principles, Policies, and Rules of the Surgeon General" were inserted into its contracts. Among the major institutions receiving Army contracts was Harvard University. As a member of the medical school's administrative board, and as a researcher who would himself be subject to these rules, Henry Beecher found the Army's version of the Nuremberg Code— Article 16 of its boilerplate contract—no more acceptable than he did in the original.

The medical school board asked Beecher to draft an alternative statement to that of the Army, in the hopes of finding an acceptable understanding that would allow the university to continue to receive Army contract funds but under its own rules. Predictably, Beecher's draft downplayed the likelihood of valid informed consent and elevated as the primary consideration for ethical research "a special relationship of trust between subject or patient and the investigator." Prefiguring his later conclusion in his landmark 1966 article, Beecher argued that only the virtuous investigator can afford protection to humans in research, and not "rigid rules." Beecher proved to be his usual persuasive self. When medical school representatives traveled to the Pentagon to clarify the situation in July 1962, the Army surgeon general agreed that the "principles" in the Harvard contracts were indeed not the "rigid rules" that Beecher and his colleagues feared, but only "guidelines."

By the middle of 1962 attention had been drawn to the Army's policy, not only by Harvard but also by the Army itself. On March 26, 1962, the Army published A.R. (Army Regulation) 70-25, which updated and supplemented the 1953 Wilson memo. The publication was timely. That year the news was full of stories about the Thalidomide tragedy. Tens of thousands of European women had been prescribed the drug Thalidomide to combat nausea during the early months of pregnancy. What resulted from the drug use were severe birth defects. Photographs of children who were perfect except for the flippers where their arms or legs should have been shocked a public more accustomed to heroic tales about miracle drugs like penicillin. In the United States there were few cases, however, because the drug was held up for licensing by a Food and Drug Administration (FDA) officer. The disaster prompted a congressional reassessment of the drug approval process, one that finally gave the FDA vastly expanded powers.

The newly published Army rules did not attract the attention of the general public, however, which did not generally associate human experiments with the armed forces. But A.R. 70-25 did have some important quirks. While the Wilson memo appeared to apply only to atomic, biological, and chemical warfare experiments for defensive purposes, A.R. 70-25 appears to apply to all human experiments, and with all the same requirements for written consent and subject protections. But, importantly, several kinds of research were exempt from the rule. The exemptions covered research that involves "inherent occupational hazards to health or exposure of personnel to potentially hazardous situations encountered as part of training or other normal duties," disclosures to participants that would invalidate experiments having to do with human factors, and "ethical medical and clinical investigations" that might benefit the subject.

None of these exemptions is surprising, and they say a lot about what human experiments the U.S. government was willing to countenance during the cold war. The exemption about "occupational hazards" could have covered the atomic test deployments. The exception to giving full information in research on human factors would permit failing to tell the troops engaged in exercises near atomic detonations precisely what their experience was going to be like. The last exception, "ethical medical and clinical investigations" for the subject's benefit, is essentially the tautology that ethical human research is allowable—as long as it is ethical! In other words, the Army wrote into its new policy what it realized had been going on under the former policy without being explicitly permitted.

Even these exemptions weren't so clear. While A.R. 70-25 can be considered an interpretation of the original Wilson memo, the 1962 regulation itself was subject to subsequent interpretation. In support of its testimony during the 1975 Senate hearings on "Human-Use Experimentation Programs of the Department of Defense and Central Intelligence Agency" (S. 25515), the Department of the Army presented the statement "III.C. Army Projects from Outside the Medical Department." This statement appears to eliminate A.R. 70-25's first exception, that of "hazardous situations encountered as part of training or other normal duties." According to the Army's 1975 statement, the Office of the Surgeon General (OTSG) at that time interpreted A.R. 70-25 broadly. The effect of the OTSG interpretation appeared to *include* the application of rules on the use of the human volunteers to experiments involving "an operational examination of prototype machinery or equipment." In other words, these kinds of experiments would not be considered to fall within the range of a soldier's "normal duties." The original text of A.R. 70-25 seems to be ambiguous on this point.

Elevated to the status of a published regulation, the modified Wilson policy was applied to a number of experiment proposals in the 1960s. The usual procedure was for the secretary of the Army to certify them as satisfying the Army rules under A.R. 70-25. Fifteen of these proposals were sent to the president's Advisory Committee on Human Radiation Experiments, with the earliest dated April 19, 1963. Yet the spirit of A.R. 70-25 was not new. As early as World War II, or even earlier, high-level approval for use of military personnel or civilian employees was generally required. What was new was not the policy, but the evident need to make sure it was on the record and, in the case of Article 16, in the contracts that Harvard and other universities started to receive, so that contractors were held to the same standard. That was a significant step, but it wasn't enough to make substantive change. Instead, a series of public scandals about human experiments outside of the national security arena, and a decade of deterioration in the public's trust in authority, finally paved the way for some modest light to be shed on the history of sensitive research.

## SCANDAL!

Shortly after the Beecher-Army compromise two events in civilian medical research opened the modern era of research ethics scandals. A well-known researcher at New York's Sloan-Kettering Institute for Cancer Research, Dr. Chester M. Southam, had been working on the immune system's ability to fight cancer. In particular, he wondered if people who were debilitated by another disease could reject cancer cells. To answer his question Southam needed human beings on which to do experiments. Some years ago physicians at Sloan-Kettering told me that Southam had proposed doing some of the research there but that he had been rebuffed.

Southam succeeded, however, in convincing the director of the Jewish Chronic Disease Hospital in Brooklyn, Dr. Emmanuel E. Mandel, that he should be permitted to conduct his research there. He also told Mandel that patients did not need to be told they were being injected with live cancer cells, even though it was an experiment and it was not intended to help them with the disease that led to their being in the hospital. It seems some patients were told that they were going to be involved in an experiment, but they were never informed in writing, and the word *cancer* was never used. Southam later defended his conduct by noting that no patient was at risk of developing cancer because of the experiment (the immune system would ultimately reject the foreign cells even though the patients were sick), and he said he did not want to upset the patients. In any case, at least some of the patients were too ill to understand and could not have consented.

Some younger doctors who had patients at the hospital heard about Southam's work and complained to a hospital board member who was also a lawyer, William Hyman. Hyman sued to obtain the records of the experiment and, as it turned out, several doctors who were primarily responsible for the patients had told Southam they did not want their patients in the research, but he used them anyway. It took three years for the case to wend its way through the legal and regulatory bureaucracy. Finally, in 1966, the New York State Board of Regents took the virtually unprecedented step of censuring Southam and Mandel and placing them on a year's probation. Though the punishment may not seem significant in retrospect, at the time it was extraordinary for a public body to find doctors engaged in research guilty of fraud, deceit, and unprofessional conduct.

The Jewish Chronic Disease Hospital case was the first incident since the Nuremberg trials themselves to draw widespread attention to issues of research ethics. It was one of those cases Beecher cited in this landmark 1966 paper. In fact, this case and those that followed were "homegrown" American ethics scandals that really began to change attitudes in the 1960s about the rights of research subjects, and not the Nuremberg Code and the Nazi experiments, which seemed so extreme and foreign to the American experience.

Beecher wasn't the only important scientist who felt the winds of change. Perhaps even more prescient was the director of the National Institutes of Health (NIH) in Bethesda, Maryland, James Shannon. Since the end of World War II the NIH, which had started in the 1930s as a government-sponsored cancer research laboratory called the National Cancer Institute, had blossomed into a mammoth enterprise. It included a number of institutes specializing in research on various diseases, as well as a pioneering research hospital called the Clinical Center. Some NIH work is done by its own scientists, but even more is funded research done by experts throughout the country. Using federal funds, the NIH is able to pursue lines of scientific investigation that are not attractive to private industry because they are too far from potential profits. Much of the basic research done at NIH is then applied by drug and device companies in the development of marketable products.

Shannon was known as a remarkably strong, even visionary, leader. By 1963 he had been at the NIH helm for eight years and was firmly in command. Well aware of the vulnerability that comes with growth for a federal agency (in 1996 the NIH funded $5 *billion* of research that involved human experiments), Shannon was among the first to see that the moral integrity of the NIH was the key to its continuing to receive public support.

He was disturbed by the Jewish Chronic Disease Hospital case. The same year, 1963, a researcher who was partly supported by NIH funds transplanted a chimpanzee kidney into a human being. The patient had given consent, but there was no reason to think the transplant would work, and little basis for believing that it would provide enough new information about animal-to-human transplants to justify the risk to the patient. Worst of all for a responsible government official, even though some of the money came from his agency, Shannon only learned about the experimental surgery from the newspapers. Shannon ordered a review of the problems of doing experiments with people. But the report, written by one of his staff members, largely put responsibility for ethical conduct on the individual scientists themselves, just as Beecher had advised in his 1966 paper, without advocating any further review. Like the failed Nuremberg Code policy thirteen years before, the report was an indication of how hard it was to open up medical experiments to public scrutiny. Shannon was disappointed by the weakness of the report, but he used it as the basis of discussions with the U.S. surgeon general. In 1966, the Public Health Service (PHS), which includes the NIH, ordered that anyone who wanted to do human experiments with its support must meet certain standards, including informed consent and review of the proposed experiment in advance by a committee composed of professional and public members. It was a small start, perhaps, but the 1966 PHS rules started a process of bringing publicly funded human experiments under reasonable rules.

Shannon's conviction that an even stronger response was needed was right on target, but even he could not have foreseen how much damage would be done to the country by yet another scandal, the infamous Tuskegee syphilis study. Public health officials at all levels of the government, from county to federal, knew of the ongoing observational research on the African-American men in Tuskegee, Alabama. Finally, a journalist was provided documentary evidence of the study and it was revealed in 1972. The syphilis study was another blow to the prestige of social institutions at a time that was full of such events, like Vietnam and Watergate. But while warfare and politics have frequently been sullied, this time it was the vaunted human pursuit of medical knowledge.

Coming only a few years after Henry Beecher's articles and the surgeon general's new rules, the syphilis study raised questions that were in some ways even more shocking, because it related to America's historic curse of slavery and its aftermath. It also threw the solution recommended by the critics of the sixties, ultimate reliance on the personal ethics of medical scientists, into grave doubt. After all, the PHS officials who started the syphilis study were good scientists, not venal racists, but the ethical issues at stake escaped them. The problem was not simply a failing in their moral character but the inability to see the flaws of an idea until they are put under a public spotlight. Though the syphilis study was not intentionally secret, neither was it widely announced or even subjected to systematic review by an independent group that could review the science and the ethics.

After the syphilis study came into public view an expert federal commission was appointed to reassess the government's system for protecting human research subjects. The work of the National Commission for the Protection of Human Subjects of Biomedical and Behavioral Research from 1974 to 1978 continues to dominate our current system. As for the study's survivors, the men received financial compensation in 1978, but it took nearly another twenty years for the federal government to apologize for its actions. President Clinton hosted some of the survivors in a dramatic White House ceremony in 1997.

The events in Tuskegee were not military-medical experiments, but their revelation contributed to unprecedented pressure on the record of secret human research in the Pentagon and the CIA. In fact, one of the experiments cited by Beecher in 1966 took place partly with military funding. From the late 1950s a team of infectious disease experts from New York University working under a distinguished researcher, Dr. Saul Krugman, had been doing hepatitis research at the Willowbrook School on Staten Island, New York. Willowbrook was a state facility that housed profoundly impaired children and adolescents, most of whom contracted hepatitis from exposure to one another's bodily fluids. The institution became infamous in the late 1960s when television news cameras recorded the horrific conditions under which the children lived. The local TV reporter who broke the scandal about conditions at Willowbrook became a household name: Geraldo Rivera.

In the context of the Willowbrook scandal the Krugman's team's research, which had already been controversial since Beecher criticized it in 1966, looked far worse. Trying to find a way to protect people from hepatitis, Krugman and his colleagues deliberately infected some of the children with the virus. He did so with the parents' permission, but many claimed that the parents were coerced into agreeing so that their children would gain admission to the facility, as there are very few that can take care of children with severe disorders.

The Willowbrook case is one of the most controversial in the history of medical ethics. Some still defend the research, while others question whether it would have been done had the children not been so impaired. What is not generally appreciated is that Krugman's original funding for his work at Willowbrook came from a source that had long been interested in a vaccine for hepatitis: the Armed Forces Epidemiological Board. Here again, national security concerns played a quiet but profound role in the history of ethics in human experiments.

## THE LSD ARSENAL OF DEMOCRACY

Hard on the heels of the syphilis study revelations, and just a few months after Richard Nixon left the White House in disgrace, the country's confidence in its institutions was further undermined by news stories about clandestine CIA activities within the United States during the 1950s and '60s. A congressional committee under Senator Frank Church of Idaho and a presidential commission under Vice President Nelson Rockefeller were established to investigate the charges. In the summer of 1975 the truth about domestic experiments with psychoactive drugs such as LSD and mescaline began pouring out: Frank Olson's leap from a

Manhattan hotel tower and Harold Blauer's death at the Psychiatric Institute were two of the more spectacular individual tragedies that unfolded. The revelations' ripples went far and wide. Many of the men who came forward after decades of patriotic silence about the World War II mustard gas research were emboldened by the new atmosphere of truth.

Army testing of mustard and lewisite declined at the end of World War II and probably no testing of these substances occurred after 1960. However, military interest in other types of chemical compounds increased, and, correspondingly, so did its human subjects experimentation with those compounds. From 1950 to 1975 the Army conducted research to develop incapacitating agents, "including nerve agents, nerve agent antidotes, psycho chemicals, irritants, and vesicant agents." Approximately six thousand seven hundred human subjects were used by the government in experiments with psychoactive chemicals, most pervasively LSD, but also in private contract research with universities and chemical companies, other agents were used, including morphine, demerol, seconal, mescaline, atropine, psilocybin, and benzedrine. The Army inspector general's report refers to the kind of work done at Holmesburg Prison by the University of Pennsylvania: "An unknown number of other chemical tests and experiments were conducted under contracts with universities, hospitals, and medical research facilities. In some of the tests and experiments, healthy adults, psychiatric patients, and prison inmates were used without their knowledge or consent or their full knowledge of the risks involved." And though the Army and CIA studies of LSD using unwitting human subjects are best known, the Air Force performed similar experiments through contracts at several universities.

One of those used in LSD experiments while he was in the Army, James B. Stanley, was inspired to undertake an historic attempt to get the Supreme Court to recognize the Nuremberg Code as having the force of law in the U.S. armed forces. In February 1958, Master Sergeant Stanley was stationed with his wife and children at Fort Knox, Kentucky. Responding to a posted notice, he volunteered to be a subject in a study advertised as developing and testing measures against chemical weapons. Stanley then became one of thousands of men to be trans- ferred to Edgewood Arsenal in Aberdeen, Maryland for LSD experiments.

But Stanley was never told that the clear liquid he drank for the test contained a psychoactive drug. Nor was he debriefed or mon- itored for the hallucinations that followed, nor did he understand the source of the emotional problems that disrupted his personal life, leading finally to his divorce in 1970. In 1975 Stanley finally learned the truth when he received a letter from the Army asking him to come to the Walter Reed Army Medical Center in Washington for a follow-up study of the LSD subjects.

Another subject, James R. Thornwell, learned about his LSD exposure about the same time as Stanley, but his specific circum- stances underline the wide range of studies and locations where the Army's LSD experiments took place. Thornwell was a private stationed in France in 1961, when he was imprisoned as part of an Army investigation of the theft of some classified documents. During his interrogation Thornwell was confined in an isolation chamber for months, deprived of sleep and toilet facilities, physi- cally abused, showered with racial slurs, and threatened with death. An Army team from Operation Third Chance then arrived to test LSD as a truth serum. The official report stated that the experiment demonstrated the "usefulness of employing as a duress factor the device of inviting the subjects' attention to his (LSD) influenced state and threatening to extend this state indefinitely, even to a permanent condition of insanity or to bring it to an end at the discretion of the interrogators."

Thornwell was one of several veterans who tried to press a case against the government for the suffering the LSD experiments caused them. James Stanley's went the farthest, all the way to the U.S. Supreme Court. But his action finally failed in 1987, in a deeply divided court. By only 5-4, the justices found that, like all other current or former members of the Armed Forces, Stanley was barred from suing the United States for injuries incurred "incident to service," a legal rule known as the Feres doctrine. James Thornwell lost his district court case for the same reason. In his dissent in *Stanley*, Justice William Brennan cited the Nazi doctors' trial and the code that followed.

> The medical trials at Nuremberg in 1947 deeply impressed upon the world that experimentation with unknowing human subjects is morally and legally unacceptable. The United States Military Tribunal established the Nuremberg Code as a standard against which to judge German scientists who experimented with human subjects. . . . [I]n defiance of this principle, military intelligence officials . . . began surreptitiously testing chemical and biological materials, including LSD.

Actually, in spite of Justice Brennan's assertion, the code was not used "as a standard against which to judge German scientists," for it was written after they were convicted. But his claim obviously gave force to his dissent, and the important point is that the code *did* exist when the LSD studies began.

Justice Sandra Day O'Connor added her own dissent.

> No judicially crafted rule should insulate from liability the involuntary and unknowing human experimentation alleged to have occurred in this case. Indeed, as Justice Brennan observes, the United States played an instrumental role in the criminal prosecution of Nazi officials who experimented with human subjects during the Second World War, and the standards that the Nuremberg Military Tribunals developed to judge the behavior of the defendants stated that the "voluntary consent of the human subject is absolutely essential."

The irony of Stanley's defeat is that it shows how toothless the Pentagon's Nuremberg Code-based policy was. The Wilson memo's rules were in effect during his participation in the LSD experiments (conducted by the CIA at Fort Detrick, by the Army at Edgewood). But even following the Army's own study that concluded that the policy was violated, someone victimized by the results of failed implementation could not recover damages in a court of law. Was James Stanley's uninformed and nonvoluntary participation in an LSD experiment truly "incident to his service" in the armed forces, as the Court's majority concluded? If so, what little regulation seemed to apply to military-medical experiments during the 1950s was largely worthless.

## THE ARMY CALLS ITSELF TO ACCOUNT

The Church Committee hearings and Rockefeller investigations were not only productive in themselves, they also stimulated a significant internal Army study of its own conduct concerning hallucinogenic drug testing with soldiers at Fort Detrick, Maryland. Extending from 1953 to 1971, this project (or rather, series of experiments) overlapped the syphilis study. Most importantly, the Army inspector general's investigation forced a confrontation between the intent of Secretary Wilson's Nuremberg Code-based policy and the fact that the Army had failed to act according to the intent of its own rules.

Entitled "Use of Volunteers in Critical Agent Research," the inspector general's report is a fascinating and generally frank assessment of the Army's experimental program. It begins by acknowledging the "inadequacy of the Army's institutional memory" about the experiments, even though they had only taken place a few years before, and that written records had in many cases been destroyed as part of routine destruction schedules. To reconstruct the events surrounding the history of the experiments, the investigators interviewed sixty-five witnesses in thirty-two cities and the District of Columbia, and assembled tens of thousands of pages of documents from several federal depositories and military installations.

The investigation showed that field tests of LSD had been conducted at Fort Bragg, North Carolina; Fort McClellan, Alabama; Fort Benning, Georgia; and Dugway Proving Ground, Utah. These studies were mainly aimed at determining the disruptive effects of the drug for military groups and military operations. They were distinguished from intelligence-oriented experiments for interrogation purposes, which were done at Maryland's

Edgewood Arsenal. Though records were incomplete, it appears that thousands of soldiers were involved, always characterized as volunteers.

The report explained that in the early 1950s the Soviet Union had made large purchases of argot, from which LSD is derived. American officials, who were also concerned about the "brainwashing" rumors that circulated during the Korean War, recognized that the United States was largely unprepared for chemical and biological warfare. In 1958 the Army Chemical Corps leadership drew public attention to what appeared to be a growing gap between the communist bloc and the United States and its allies in the area of chemical and biological warfare. (At around this time, the launching by the Soviets of Sputnik, the first artificial satellite, created a generalized anxiety about America's military preparedness in all fields.) In 1959 a House committee issued a series of recommendations about chemical, biological, and radiological (CBR) warfare, which included the statement that the Pentagon should at least triple its budget for these weapons programs. President Kennedy took office in 1961, having campaigned partly on what proved to be groundless charges of a "missile gap" with the Soviets. His administration was more than prepared to support innovation in developing and defending against novel weaponry, contributing to an atmosphere in which the secret research already being conducted could enjoy marked growth. The House committee also observed that disarmament efforts should not be permitted to obscure "the great potential of CBR [chemical and biological weapons research] and the ease of evading detection of CBR activities." This was a lesson the United States learned in Iraq nearly forty years later.

The inspector general's report included a number of insights about the reception of the Wilson memo within the Army and the Chemical Corps itself. After the memo was signed but before the Army had prepared its implementing directive, top corps officials and advisors met at Edgewood Arsenal in March 1953 to interpret the policy. Among other things, the group agreed that only hazardous experiments fell within the policy, that "blanket type approval" could be obtained rather than submitting individual experiment proposals for review, that "line of duty" projects

involving nonhazardous materials were not covered, that voluntary consent involved such factors as the volunteer's age and mental capacity, and that no coercion is permissible. These interpretations were reasonable and sound. Altogether, the Chemical Corps'
official approach to the use of human subjects was, with few exceptions, light-years ahead of practices in the civilian world.

Again, though, official policy and actual practice did not mesh.
For example, in 1955 a Defense Department Ad Hoc Study Group
on Psychochemical Issues recommended that any subjects being
administered LSD be given a training lecture to prepare them for
its effects. However, in January 1956 an assistant chief chemical
officer who was helping design an LSD experiment with a group
of soldiers commented, in response to the recommendation: "in
view of the fact that a great many of the effects observed in the
group may be the result of suggestion (placebo effect) it would
appear desirable to have one control group which has neither been
given a training lecture on LSD-25, nor any information as to the
symptoms of the drug being administered."

The officer who wanted to avoid influencing the results of the
experiment with advance knowledge that the subjects might have
that could skew the results was engaged in sound scientific design
but vacuous research ethics. The point of the Nuremberg Code
and the Pentagon rules that were based on it was precisely that a
desire for greater knowledge could not simply trump the subject's
rights.

In other cases the evasion of consent requirements was more
subtle, demonstrating the difficulties involved in simply transmitting a complex policy through routine bureaucratic means. A former Chemical Corps officer told the inspector general that he had
volunteered for an LSD experiment, knew he was to receive the
drug, but did not know when. Some time after volunteering he
went to Fort Bragg to observe some tests being conducted with an
airborne artillery corps:

> I was there to observe what was going on and also to brief the
> CG [commanding general], XVIII Airborne Corps. I went to
> the site with CWL [Chemical Warfare Liaison?] project officer

and a major; it was early and it was cold. I was asked if I wanted some hot coffee, which I did. I was given the coffee and
apparently it had the LSD in it; they told me later, it had a dose
of 200 micrograms of LSD.

In this instance the officer was properly briefed but did not
know when the experiment would begin. Can that be called
informed voluntary consent? Or was it, as the inspector general
suggested, "an overly broad interpretation" of the requirement?

A carefully drawn policy framework was no match for the quest
for information with eminently available human subjects. As the
inspector general's report commented, with as much neutrality as
it could muster, "in spite of clear guidelines concerning the necessity for 'informed consent,' there was a willingness to dilute and in
some cases negate the intent of the policy." Indeed, the report
continued, "this attitude of selective compliance was more the
norm than the exception."

When the content of Army policy was not ignored, the chain
of command was. In one instance, the inspector general found that
a series of experiments for intelligence purposes at Edgewood
were not vetted through the hierarchy, in spite of longstanding
policy that predated the Wilson memo. The studies included lie
detector tests, memory impairment examinations, motor reaction
experiments, exercises under isolation and other stressful conditions such as a hostile interrogation, all under the influence of
LSD. Though the experiments may have been approved by the
Intelligence Center command (and even this point was unclear),
there was no evidence that regular Chemical Corps channels or
the surgeon general's office reviewed or approved of the plan.

When James Stanley received his letter the Army's investigation had revealed the full scale of the LSD experiment, leading the
Army's inspector general to some very sobering conclusions about
the effectiveness of the policy for research volunteers. The inspector general concluded that the "volunteers were not fully
informed, as required, prior to their participation; and the methods of procuring their services, in many cases, appeared not to
have been in accord with the intent of Department of the Army

policies governing use of volunteers in research." In other words, the men were lured into the experiment under false pretenses and never told what was planned or what they might face. They were not informed, nor did they have the opportunity to give signed, witnessed consent, all the provisions that Anna Rosenberg and Stephen Jackson had insisted upon.

## OPERATION WHITECOAT

In the 1940s and 1950s, there were sometimes careful policies and cautious handling of soldiers and others in experiments, but there were also serious lapses and abuses. In other cases the record is just too vague to make a precise judgment. For example, under a 1954 approval from the secretary of the Army, Fort Detrick contracted with Ohio State University to test tularemia in human volunteers. Tularemia has been described as "an acute infectious disease, often bizarre in its manifestations. . . . The symptoms begin abruptly with fever (between 101° and 105° F), severe headache, sharp chill, nausea, vomiting and extreme prostration. Drenching sweats, aching pains in the back and extremities, and weakness are likely to be present. . . . The typhoid and ingestion types [of symptoms] are severe, and convulsions, coma and death may come quickly." The volunteers were drawn from the Ohio State Penitentiary. The tests were challenge studies in which some subjects were vaccinated against the disease while others were not; "exposure of subjects began in 1956 and ended in 1958." This project was reviewed and approved by the secretary of the Army, and six publications in medical journals described the study. Additional research involving testing tularemia, Q fever, Rift Valley fever, and "other disease producing agents" was conducted under contract with the University of Maryland using prisoners from the Maryland House of Corrections, from July 1956 to 1975.

The biological warfare prison studies began around the same time as the LSD experiments. Although the latter became a prime example of abuse of human subjects, the prison studies are harder to evaluate. Illustrating how diverse the treatment of human subjects was in those days, another Army program began at that time and became a paradigm of research ethics. Starting in 1954 and for nearly twenty years, a special arrangement between the Army and the heads of the Seventh-Day Adventist Church allowed soldiers who were church members to volunteer for medical research under Operation Whitecoat. Seventh-Day Adventists believe in community service but not in combat. The conscientious objectors among them were sent to Fort Sam Houston where they were recruited for voluntary assignment as potential human subjects in biological experiments at Fort Detrick. As many as two hundred Seventh-Day Adventists took part each year, for a total of 2,300 volunteers in about one hundred fifty experiments.

The first study involving Whitecoat volunteers exposed them and some prisoners to Q fever, a flulike condition. Thirty-eight Whitecoat participants became symptomatic and all responded to antibiotics that were administered eight to ten days following exposure, thus establishing the correct schedule for therapy. This favorable result appears to have been characteristic of Whitecoat. Through all the years of the project there were no deaths and only one documented complaint of "undue suffering" in a study.

But at least two Whitecoat alumni have said that they suffered permanent injuries from experiments. Glenn A. Meekma of Newfolden, Minnesota, was in a 1964 study of the disabling respiratory disease tularemia. "I've got a severe case of asthma, and I'm sitting on the edge of going into emphysema." Another veteran, Bob Kline from Burtonsville, Maryland, was discharged in 1956 after he had been part of a Q fever study. Kline's liver was inflamed, a possible effect of Q fever. His claim was denied. Out of hundreds of men in their fifties, some are not going to be well, and it is hard to trace the causes. Fort Detrick does not do follow-ups on the soldiers, but it does keep all records open and responds to all inquiries.

What no one seems to dispute is that the Whitecoat soldiers were truly volunteers. Washington, D.C., businessman W. Jay Nixon served from 1969 to 1971, near the end of the project. "If they were pulling the wool over anybody's eyes, I don't think it was in the Whitecoat program, because there were too many civilians involved who had no allegiance to the Army." Robert F. Cooke, an accountant from Silver Spring, Maryland, was recruited for Whitecoat in 1968, at the height of the Vietnam War. "By the time I got out of the Army, I lost four friends—three of them from my hometown—in Vietnam. If I came down with something 35 years later, that's still 35 more years I had than they did." The sense of public service was high in Whitecoat. "To a man, we didn't want to be there but we owed allegiance to our country," says Nixon.

Early correspondence about the project illustrates its high-level endorsement in the church, and also shows a commitment to service that today may seem old-fashioned. In 1954, the head of the church's medical department wrote of his gratitude to the Army surgeon general for the opportunity that was being presented.

> The type of voluntary service which is being offered to our boys in this research problem [*sic*] offers an excellent opportunity for these young men to render a service which will be of value not only to military medicine but to public health generally. I believe I speak not only the sentiments of our administrative group in this office, but also of our Adventist young men in the services in observing that it should be regarded as a privilege to be identified with this significant advanced step in clinical research.

There was intense interest in Whitecoat at the highest levels of the military-medical establishment and great solicitousness of the continued support of Adventist leaders. In October 1955 the Army surgeon general wrote a church official:

> It is good to share with the admiration we feel for the service rendered by the Adventist young men who participated voluntarily, with courage and devotion, in the medical research program . . . All concerned in this important work, and a wide audience of people of our country, will be pleased to know of these services and accomplishments.

The surgeon general's letter was quoted in a church publication, the *Review and Herald*, in a November 3, 1955, article celebrating the program. Entitled "Beyond the Call of Duty," the piece quoted the exchange of letters with the Army and described the recruitment process. "Each made his own personal decision whether or not to volunteer for the project. All that was promised to them was an opportunity to save the lives of others, and to add to the knowledge of medical science, by their own participation and probably suffering."

The attention paid to Whitecoat at these command levels, and the publicity it received from the very beginning, helps to explain the careful arrangements that seemed always to characterize the program, in contrast to the LSD studies. A 1969 fact sheet described the process for particular studies:

When a research study in volunteers is to be conducted, the required number of WHITECOAT personnel are given a comprehensive briefing by the Commanding Officer as to the purpose and nature of the project, the risk involved, and exactly what is expected of each participant. After answering any questions that might arise, each subject is interviewed individually, given an additional opportunity to ask questions, and then indicates his desires as to participation in that particular study. If he volunteers he is required to sign the standard consent form. When an individual indicates that he would prefer not to participate in a particular study it usually is for personal reasons such as his wife is having a baby, he is to be the best man at his sister's wedding, or some similar reason.

One objection to the Whitecoat system is that the church leaders' enthusiasm in a close-knit faith community made it hard for them to turn it down. Yet some did not volunteer, and those who did had elected to be part of the church community, with all its values. The men also had the advantage of mutual support and group solidarity, which could help them to resist being in a dubious experiment. This is something that few potential human subjects have today. The group aspect of Whitecoat survives in a modern project at Fort Detrick, the Medical Research Volunteer Subjects Program, that I will describe in the last chapter.

In 1998, 200 Whitecoat alumni held a reunion in an Adventist church near Fort Detrick. Not only an occasion for nostalgia, it was also an opportunity for Army doctors to examine the men for long-term health effects. In this group, at least, even those who believed their health problems were attributable to their service expressed no regrets. Said 60-year-old Thomas Ford of Nashville, "By helping the Army out like that, they probably found maybe a cure for something or helped other servicemen who came in the Army after me."

## REIGNING IN THE HUMAN EXPERIMENTS

Years before Senator Church's hearings and James Stanley's unsuccessful lawsuit about the LSD experiments, before names and faces were attached to allegations of human experiment abuses in national security research, criticism of biological and chemical warfare research intensified. The site of Operation Whitecoat, Fort Detrick in Frederick, Maryland, had long been a favorite object of peace demonstrators. Beginning in 1943, out of concern that German "buzz bombs" could be outfitted with biological agents, the airfield was transformed into a scientific center. Its intellectual credentials were impressive from the very start. Drug company founder George Merck advised President Roosevelt on the development of a first-rate technical staff. The concept of a world-class biological warfare think-tank came in 1941 from the president of the National Academy of Sciences, Frank Jewett, not from the military. Shortly after the war ended, it was Fort Detrick investigators who were sent to Japan to study the nature and extent of Unit 731 and Ishii's horrific experiments.

As in the radiological labs, the first challenges at Detrick had to do with ensuring worker safety, lessons that would prove important for more general protections from pathogens later on. All sorts of decontamination and sterilization procedures were studied. Much early research involved protection of crops from chemical herbicides that could jeopardize wartime food supplies. One herbicide tested at Fort Detrick was a defoliant that came into wide use during the Vietnam War to clear vegetation around Viet Cong supply routes, the infamous Agent Orange.

In 1969, Senator Eugene McCarthy charged that there had been thousands of accidents in Fort Detrick's biological weapons program, and he began a highly effective campaign to have the Nixon administration review the nation's entire biological and chemical warfare agenda. At the same time, the National Security Council was investigating the chemical warfare program at Edgewood Arsenal, also in Maryland. The complexity of the technical issues, the superheated political atmosphere of the day, and the lack of public information about these activities led to considerable confusion. Demonstrators supporting Maryland Senator Charles McC. Mathias' call for a suspension of chemical warfare nerve gas experiments showed up at Fort Detrick to protest, though the chemical warfare center was Edgewood.

During the 1969 Thanksgiving holiday President Nixon scored a political coup when he announced that he would ask the Senate to ratify the 1925 Geneva Accord. Long resisted by the United States, the agreement prohibited the offensive "first use" of biological and chemical weapons. Over the next several years the Army programs were significantly curtailed and converted to defensive research. By 1974 biological and chemical weapons research had been greatly marginalized. The Fort Detrick brain trust was especially hard hit, having lost a number of world-class scientists. In 1969 a far smaller operation was organized into the U.S. Army Medical Research Institute of Infectious Diseases (USAMRIID).

It was a demoralized Fort Detrick that a young Army doctor, Art Anderson, first encountered when he arrived at USAMRIID in 1974. Anderson had come under the spell of the moral philosophers as an undergraduate at Wagner College on Staten Island, New York, and he brought with him idealism about finding ways to treat or prevent the suffering that could be caused by biological agents. Anderson grew up less than two miles from the Willowbrook State School and recalls his shock upon hearing about the children's living conditions from adults who worked there. Anderson made it clear to his superiors when he accepted the Fort Detrick assignment that he would not participate in research for offensive purposes. Such was Anderson's zeal for human protections that he was quickly made the chair of the base's new Human Use Committee, a position he has held ever since. Nearly two decades later, Anderson was outspoken in debates about the ethical use of drugs during Operation Desert Storm that might be protective against Saddam Hussein's biological and chemical weapons.

From the time of Anderson's arrival at Fort Detrick, policymakers and military planners were caught in a paradox, one that finally started to catch up to them, and the nation, during the Gulf War. Offensive biological and chemical weapons research was not permitted, and even defensive research on these agents was highly sensitive in post-Vietnam, post-Watergate America. From the mid-1970s through the late 1980s human subjects research came under the watchful eye of a new generation of Army administrators and scientists like Anderson, determined not to repeat the mistakes of their predecessors and adhering carefully to new and more refined regulations.

The changes at Detrick were set in motion in 1969, when President Nixon banned all offensive biological weapons. The Army claims that since then it "has confined its BW technical program to demilitarization and to defensive development involving physical protection and medical procedures." As a result, Art Anderson arrived at Detrick just as Army research involving human subjects was undergoing among the most significant changes in its history. At the Senate's 1977 hearings on the biological testing program, an Army assistant surgeon general said that "all existing protocols for human subjects in chemical and antidote research" have been revoked and that "written notification" would be required for any further human research to be conducted. All prisoner research was also terminated.

The new vigilance about medical ethics in the military was accompanied by a vastly greater public awareness among civilians. In 1978, six years after the syphilis study came to light, the

National Commission for the Protection of Human Subjects of Biomedical and Behavioral Research published a report setting out the ethical principles that should govern the use of human beings in experiments. The new ethics of research requires scientists and government agencies that pay for research to show respect for experimental subjects, to try to do as much good for them as possible, and to be fair by recruiting people from various groups and not only those who are convenient. These principles are still the touchstone for human research ethics in the United States, including that which is conducted by national security agencies.

The idea that both the burdens and the benefits of research should be distributed throughout society, without taking advantage of the poor or vulnerable, was a new and powerful concept. In retrospect, if the principle of justice in human experiments had been widely recognized during World War II and in the early days of the cold war, many convenient groups, including some servicemen, would not have so readily been recruited in research. With the new emphasis on justice, widespread use of American prisoners in research ended in the 1970s, and protections for children and other vulnerable subjects were written into federal law in 1981. In this atmosphere, some might say, the military had no choice but vigilance. In addition, research on nuclear, chemical, and biological weapons was controlled by new treaties through the 1970s and '80s.

These social changes did not leave out the military establishment itself, of course, which had been shocked into deep self-reflection by the Vietnam experience. Art Anderson's insistent idealism about protecting the soldier in research would not have allowed him a seat at the Pentagon's table in 1950, yet thirty-five years later he was given a critical role in policing biological weapons research in the Army. The rules changed, but the American armed forces changed with them. With the passing of another fifteen years and the advent of America's first major armed conflict since Vietnam, some would say the rules changed too much, leaving our troops vulnerable to Saddam Hussein's weapons of mass destruction.

# ONCE MORE INTO THE GULF

"The main thing is that you have to be thoughtfully skeptical that you are doing the right thing. You need to have an awareness of the need to truly ponder the ethics of what you are doing when you are dealing with powerful technology."

*Tara O'Toole, formerly Assistant Secretary of Energy*

## ZERO TOLERANCE

Over the past half century, American attitudes about risks incurred in the line of duty have changed greatly. In the years immediately following World War II the primary concern was how much exposure to radiation or biological or chemical agents human beings could withstand. In practical terms, defense planners worried about the ability of men to function in combat when exposed to these new kinds of weapons, and medical researchers struggled to determine how much exposure was "permissible" in the course of an experiment.

That heroic era seems quite distant from our attitudes today. Not that heroes do not come forward anymore, but no longer is it presumed that heroic national service is an ideal to which all citizens should actively strive. The sea change in public sentiment presents interesting obstacles for defense planners, both in planning for combat operations and for conducting human experiments with national security goals in mind. It is difficult to sustain a role as a dangerous world's only superpower with a risk-aversive attitude. Nevertheless, Pentagon officials and political leaders know that the American public's tolerance for casualties in military interventions approaches zero. They also know that there is virtually zero tolerance for risky human experiments without offsetting benefit, especially if they involve military personnel.

Today's military leaders are members of a generation that grew up during the Vietnam tragedy. Partly as a result of that bitter memory, they resolved to conduct the Gulf War while risking as little as possible. Out of nearly 700,000 men and women who served in Desert Shield and Desert Storm, there were 148 combat deaths. Almost as many people died of diseases or accidents unrelated to warfare while serving in the Gulf. This amazingly low death rate and the few injuries recorded (497) reflected the high priority given by the military leadership to minimizing casualties in this action.

Unfortunately, on their return from the Gulf many veterans began to report debilitating illnesses, including fatigue, muscle and joint pain, headaches, and memory loss. Of the many theories that have surfaced to explain some of these conditions, there is one that is especially ironic: Drugs that were developed to protect our soldiers from several nefarious weapons are suspected by some to have ended up causing long-term damage. Worse, because the drugs were not approved or tested for battlefield conditions, their use appears to some at best reckless though well intended and at worst a loose and poorly considered experiment.

Whether or not there was physical damage done by this experience, the suspicion that Gulf War soldiers were used as guinea pigs has clearly damaged morale in some units. In March 1999 Airman First Class Jeffrey A. Bettendorf was discharged "under other than honorable conditions" when he refused to accept an anthrax vaccine injection. In the Navy, twenty-three sailors were punished for the same reason. In an online chat one of the sailors said, "for you to believe the military would never do anything to hurt me, then I suggest you talk to the many sick Americans that returned from the Persian Gulf. I love this country and I am willing to die, but only in war. Not because they are experimenting on me."

## WAIVING INFORMED CONSENT

As the Pentagon made its preparations for the invasion of Kuwait in the fall of 1990, alarming intelligence reports about Saddam Hussein's chemical and biological warfare capacity prompted inquiries about protections that medical science might offer the troops. Although many different agents were threats, it was possible that some medications might help with several potential chemical or biological weapons. One concern was nerve gas, which in higher doses can cause convulsions, respiratory paralysis, and death within a few minutes. Another was anthrax bacteria, normally found in cattle and sheep, which is hard to diagnose because it begins with flulike symptoms but can lead to death in a matter of days, if untreated. Still another biological agent that Saddam Hussein might have weaponized is botulinum toxin, which is fermented from proteins and causes respiratory paralysis and death in hours or days.

Each of these agents can in theory be countered with protective medications. Pyridostigmine bromide (PB) has been used for many years for persons with myasthenia gravis with no long-term health problems reported. PB may enhance nerve gas antidotes like atropine if taken before exposure. All the troops were given PB pills during the Gulf War, but only about 250,000 elected to take them. Vaccines for both anthrax and botulinum toxin have been used to protect industrial workers against infection. Around 150,000 Desert Storm troops received at least one anthrax vaccination, and 8,000 at least one dose of BT vaccine.

Unlike the anthrax vaccine, the botulism toxin vaccine is considered to be "investigational" by the FDA, and it has never approved PB for use in the military against chemical weapons. The relative lack of experience with these medicines under battlefield conditions, and the fact that the Department of Defense received special permission from the FDA to use these "unapproved drugs" without getting informed consent, made it appear that the soldiers were being used as guinea pigs. But if that were so, then there would have been good record keeping of who took the drugs and what their reactions were. Beyond the rough sense of how many took the drugs, few records were kept, which nullified an opportunity to learn something from the experience. Worse, when veterans started having medical problems it turned out that there were no records of who actually took the drugs and under what conditions.

How did it happen that the FDA gave special permission to use drugs with the Desert Storm troops without informed consent, drugs that were not tested for combat conditions? There was reliable intelligence that Saddam's regime controlled large stores of the chemical weapon Soman, as well as biological weapons, and that it was capable of delivering the agents in combat. During the buildup of forces known as Desert Shield, the Pentagon approached the new Food and Drug commissioner, Dr. David Kessler, for a waiver of the FDA's normal informed-consent requirement for "investigational" drugs. The request was based on the need to protect combat troops with methods thought to provide a reasonable prospect of defense against these threats, an extreme measure demanded by the circumstances. The "therapeutic" purpose of the request was a critical element in the Pentagon's petition.

In response, the FDA adopted Rule 23(d), which created an exception to its regulations, allowing the commissioner to waive the consent requirement for those combat situations in which consent is "not feasible." The rule does require the commissioner to consider whatever evidence there is about the safety and effectiveness of the drug, the context in which it is to be used, the type of condition it is intended to treat or prevent, and the nature of the information to be provided the recipients concerning risks and benefits of taking the drugs. In spite of these requirements, the FDA's exception to its normal informed-consent rules did not exist before the Pentagon request. To many, including some in Congress, the civilian agency allowed itself to be intimidated by the Defense Department. For instance, consistent with the regulation, the deal called for all soldiers asked or ordered to take the medications to be given an information sheet about what they were taking, but that information was rarely provided. The agency failed to call the armed forces to account for this breach of the agreement, even after the war.

FDA officials have told Congress that they were in no position to set limits to the Defense Department when combat was imminent and American troops were endangered. In its own defense, the Pentagon notes that it attempted to minimize risks to soldiers that the drugs might have presented. The agent that was most uncertain in its prospective benefits, pyridostigmine bromide (PB) for nerve gas, was administered on a voluntary basis. Though this might have been the intent of military leaders, many troops in the field got a different message. Of those who took PB when a gas attack seemed imminent, 88 percent reported that they were told that it was not optional.

But even if all who took any of the drugs were truly acting voluntarily, it is not at all clear that the compounds met the first condition on the informed-consent waiver, that they were considered to be "safe and effective." Some observers have said that PB can cause neurologic problems when taken under highly stressful conditions. Others suspect that the PB doses may have created a "synergistic effect" with exposure to members of a class of nerve agents called organophosphates. One such agent is the insect repellent diethyltoluamide (DEET), which was used by some of the soldiers in the desert. Department of Agriculture researcher James Moss found that when PB and DEET are administered together they are both several times more toxic than when administered alone. One study of twenty-three Gulf War veterans published in the *Journal of the American Medical Association* concluded that they suffered from delayed neurotoxicity due to exposure to chemicals that inhibit the production of enzymes that function in neural synapses, the connections between nerves. Among the chemicals that can have this effect: organophosphates, nerve agents, pesticides, insect repellents like DEET, and PB.

Though the botulism toxin (BT) vaccine has not been found to be the cause of severe problems for others who have taken it, it can cause some of the symptoms seen in the Gulf War veterans, like fatigue and muscle ache. Even more disconcerting, the vaccine supply that was used was twenty years old and there was concern that it would break down into toxic products. Whether or not this actually occurred, it is also doubtful that the vaccine was effective anyway because it requires a series of four injections over a year, and most troops received only two. At the Army's Infectious Disease Institute at Frederick, Maryland, the committee in charge of reviewing the use of the botulinum toxoid vaccine was unsure of its effectiveness. President Clinton's Advisory Committee on Gulf War Veterans' Illnesses found it "unlikely" that PB or BT were the cause of vets' medical problems, but suspicions remain. Definitive answers are rendered vastly more difficult in the absence of records showing who took what and when.

## INFORMED CONSENT IN COMBAT

One of the reasons given by the Pentagon for not obtaining consent under combat conditions was that it is not feasible in those circumstances. To Fort Detrick's Art Anderson, this viewpoint represents a lack of respect for persons who wear the uniform as well as ignorance of how medical logisticians could make documentation of informed consent feasible. Illustrating his point, Anderson tells the story of a family treasure, a tattered picture of his uncle, Franklin Anderson, who was in the artillery in World War II. Before storming the beaches with the Normandy invasion force on D-day, Franklin Anderson was transferred to North Africa where he faced Rommel's legendary tanks. In the desert, an Associated Press (AP) photographer snapped a picture of him loading a shell marked "100,000" into his cannon. Though a devout Christian, in the picture Anderson is kissing the shell. On the back of the photograph is a red-stamped consent statement from AP, giving his permission to use the image in their publications.

If AP bothered to get a soldier's consent for his picture in the middle of the North Africa campaign, I asked Anderson, why is medical record keeping given such a low priority in the military, so that consent in Desert Storm became such a controversy later? "Because," the colonel answered, "the physicians who are making this decision aren't the ones who do the record keeping. If they had asked the people who keep the records, they would have said, 'Oh yeah, we have a mechanism for that.' In fact when medical logisticians are deployed they're deployed with file cabinets! Of course, it's not 100 percent effective, but nothing is, and you do the best you can. But because it's not 100 percent effective doesn't mean it's not feasible."

Even before Desert Storm, Colonel Anderson warned about the need to inform troops properly about the unlicensed status of the drugs they were taking. In a 1990 memorandum he cited as precedent an event that even the harshest nonmilitary critics of the Army would hesitate to mention: "A 'military' justification for involuntary receipt of investigational products because of strategic, doctrine and discipline concerns resembles all too closely the logic used by Nazi doctors to rationalize using humans in research that had predictably destructive outcomes."

Tolerance for the military's laziness in such matters appears to be wearing thin in the wake of Desert Storm. At a 1997 congressional oversight hearing on government-sponsored research, Representative Christopher Shays, a Connecticut Republican, blasted the FDA for not taking a more forceful position on informed consent in the Gulf. In return for its waiver of informed consent, the Pentagon had promised to take all feasible steps to inform soldiers what compounds they were being asked to take and why. FDA officials argued, not without merit, that in a combat situation when American lives are in imminent danger a civilian agency is in a poor position to tell the Pentagon what to do. I testified before Shays' subcommittee and heard his response that day: Following the war, knowing that the Department of Defense had not kept its promise, the FDA should have held the generals' feet to the fire in public.

In the final analysis, the problem is one of different institutional cultures. There is a wide gulf between the Pentagon's job, defending the country against armed aggressors, and the mission of the FDA, to protect the safety of the food supply and the integrity of medications. What counts as a reasonable gamble in a military context, such as using a potentially risky drug that is expected to avert more casualties than it causes, is an unacceptable trade-off in the drug monitoring process. Ultimately another entity is going to be needed to step in and manage this living example of the tension between national security and medical ethics.

## BEING A RESEARCH SUBJECT

One of the big concerns that medical ethicists have about human experiments is whether there can truly be informed consent. If the subjects are sick, there is always the hope of a cure. This understandable hope can get in the way of appreciating the limits of the new treatment. People may not hear that there is little or no reason to expect benefit, even when they have been told the experiment is designed or intended, not to help them, but to gain knowledge that might help future patients. If the subjects are not sick, but healthy, normal volunteers, there is the problem of coercing them with money or other inducements. And for all human experimental subjects who are not themselves medically trained, there is the question whether they really understand the nature of the experiment.

Perhaps most insidious of all, research subjects usually go through an experiment in some degree of isolation. People with medical problems hoping for a cure from the latest experimental drug are emotionally vulnerable. They often have a hard time distinguishing between the good will and social authority of their doctor and the real chance they will be personally benefitted by the research. Even those closest to the subjects may not fully appreciate what they are going through. Healthy volunteers who come forward because of idealism or money also normally know little about the science involved, and they may not have anyone with whom to share reservations about a study.

Ever since the end of prison research in the 1970s, drug companies have increasingly relied on normal volunteers when they needed the anwers to basic questions about new drugs, such as how fast they are excreted from the body. Not only healthy people are recruited. All of us have seen and heard advertisements in newspapers and on the radio trying to recruit volunteers to be in studies of many ailments. There are many motivations for signing up for such studies, but money is often part of it. In some drug studies a person can earn thousands of dollars in a few weeks, if he or she is willing to put up with a highly regimented schedule for taking care of bodily functions, restricted diets, and, often, residing in the company's clinic.

Where could one find a group of healthy, bright, well-informed, scientifically sophisticated, and uncoerced potential subjects who require very little money to be in an experiment? Many scientists would love to have an answer to that question. It sounds like an ideal group of research subjects. Probably the best answer is the men and women MRVSs (pronounced "mervs," and standing for Medical Research Volunteer Subjects) at Maryland's Fort Detrick. They are a special group of medics (91 Bravo) who come as close to realizing the ethical ideal of true informed consent as any group of research subjects since Walter Reed's Yellow Fever Commission.

## "DON'T CALL US 'GUINEA PIGS'": THE MEN AND WOMEN OF "91 BRAVO"

An organization the size of the U.S. armed forces is sure to contain contradictions. Though decades of experience with the sensitive issue of human experiments seemed not to help avoid the Gulf War controversy, elsewhere the defense establishment has earned a very different assessment. Of all the amazing things I learned in writing this book, nothing surprised me more than that dozens of soldiers of both genders are still used as normal volunteers in biological experiments. What surprised me even more as I investigated this program at Fort Detrick was my reaction to it: that the Army is actually well ahead of civilian medicine in the ethical use of human experimental subjects.

I spent a day in the spring of 1998 interviewing seven young male and female soldiers from medical units assigned to Fort Detrick. All of them had been recruited from Fort Sam Houston in San Antonio. Part of their assignment in Maryland was routine for medical corpsmen, as they were placed in laboratories to assist in various scientific studies. Another part of their assignment was decidedly more dramatic: They understood that occasionally they would be invited to serve as subjects in medical experiments having to do with the Infectious Disease Institute's bioprotection mission.

One of my first interviews was with 20-year-old Lee Rice, a solidly built young man with a soft Southern accent, an engaging manner, and a quick wit. Growing up in Woodbridge, Virginia, Lee had long wanted to be a doctor but knew that it was too expensive for his family. After completing Bible college, Lee decided that the Army could be the route to his dream, as both his father and grandfather had been in the service. For all his grit, Lee wasn't quite prepared to take the Fort Detrick recruiter's offer when he assembled with his fellow troops at Fort Sam Houston. He laughed as he recalled his reaction to the proposal that he be a test subject in Army medical experiments.

As he learned more about the conditions at USAMRIID, including the opportunity to be "stabilized" at one duty station for several years and to work around highly trained medical scientists, the idea began to look attractive. Lee's mother was anxious about the prospect, his father somewhat amused, but after they checked on the institute's work with Pentagon friends, they felt reassured, and Lee was on his way to suburban Maryland.

In fact, today the military's system for the review of research proposals with human beings is far stricter than that in the civilian world. The descendent of the Wilson memo, Army Regulation 70-25, "Use of Volunteers as Subjects of Research," has evolved into a demanding set of rules that are well recognized. Today's A.R. 70-25 requires multiple levels of review, from the local unit's "human use committee" to several other screens up the chain of command. There is one nearly verbatim vestige of the old Nuremberg Code-based rules in A.R. 70-25: "Voluntary consent of the human subject is essential," it says at one point, and goes on to state that soldiers may not be punished for refusing to be human subjects.

In contrast to the several levels of review in the military, in the civilian world a clinical study might only be reviewed by a single committee at the university or research center. Some critics of the system have questioned the independence and objectivity of some of these review panels. Most research studies involving human beings have to be approved by "institutional review boards" (IRBs) at universities, where colleagues of the scientists proposing the research are responsible for the review. Some IRBs have recently been established outside academia so that experiment proposals can be reviewed more quickly than usually happens in the university panels. These free-standing IRBs are perfectly legal, and their conflicts of interest might be no worse than that of the university panels, where professors know that their colleagues grants and careers are on the line if a study does not seem sound enough to pass muster.

By the time I spoke with Lee Rice he was nearly finished with his three-year tour of duty at Fort Detrick and had volunteered for three studies. When not on a study Lee was the company clerk, but his primary mission was to be available for research. Periodically he had been called into the institute auditorium with his fellow MRVSs to hear a presentation of the upcoming studies for which human volunteers were needed. The only obligation the MRVSs have is to attend these sessions, which take place every two or three months.

Some of the studies involve protection against potential biological warfare agents, such as anthrax, while others are designed to improve the medical treatment of diseases that are common in military environments. The anthrax vaccine study only involves getting the vaccine and then having blood drawn regularly over a period of two years to see if it has still been protective. Other projects are not nearly so benign, and they can involve two weeks on the inpatient unit at the institute and considerable discomfort. The MRVSs refer to some of these projects as "shit protocols," a term that pretty much describes the experience.

As it turned out, Lee was one of the more enthusiastic volunteers, for while most of his fellow MRVSs avoided the especially unpleasant studies, Lee participated in some of the toughest ones. Among these was a study involving a germ called campylobacter that especially plagues the Navy. An intestinal bacterium, campylobacter causes severe diarrhea. The Navy is trying to develop a vaccine against it that uses a mutant form of an *E. coli* toxin (the one that causes travelers' diarrhea) to increase the natural immune response, while also giving an oral vaccine. Lee described his role in the campylobacter study as "the most grueling thing I've ever experienced." Though the first day wasn't bad and he began to think he would get through it easily, the next day he had an excruciating headache, couldn't look into any light, and generally felt just awful. But because Lee reached this endpoint so quickly he was also treated right away, and he soon felt much better following the administration of antibiotics.

Why would anyone volunteer for such a noxious task? It was a question I pressed hard during my day at the institute. The most obvious answer is that soldiers can't really volunteer, that at some point they must be concerned about the consequences of resisting, especially considering that they had agreed to be in the MRVS program in the first place. But one of the young men of 91 Bravo I interviewed had nearly completed his assignment and had not been in a single study. Instead, he was taking pre-med courses at the local community college—complements of Uncle Sam—and his schedule just didn't permit him to participate. But as long as he attended the MRVS briefings, he met his obligation to the program.

Other MRVSs I spoke with carefully avoided the "shit protocols," opting instead for studies like that of the anthrax vaccine, which didn't make them sick and for which they were paid $25 for each blood draw. And over the two-year period of the study there are a lot of "bloods," making for a reasonable piece of change to add to their army salary. Could this be the suspicious part of the story of the MRVSs, that they are unethically coerced with money?

I addressed this question to each soldier with whom I spoke. I found their responses consistent and persuasive. First, they pointed out, whereas civilian volunteers from the community can be paid for every day of residence at the study clinic and for every procedure that is done to them, the MRVSs can only be paid for blood. If anyone is subject to undue influence by dint of money, it is the civilians from Frederick, Maryland, and the rest of the surrounding community. And, of course, the civilians usually lack the peer support and scientific training of the MRVSs.

Second, as several MRVSs pointed out to me, you're not going to get rich giving blood at $25 a draw. The extra money is welcome, especially, for those with families or anticipating a three-day pass, but is certainly not enough to overcome the significant downsides of some studies. For example, a male MRVS with small children told me he was interested in the money but couldn't manage being debilitated when he went home to be with his kids.

Finally, the money issue has to be balanced against the need for the work to be done. Few would volunteer without the extra incentive, all the MRVSs I spoke with admitted. Suppose we acknowledge that the world is a dangerous place and that the United States has legitimate interests and good reasons to maintain a system of national defense, including a bioprotection program. Then waiting for wholly altruistic volunteers may be admirable but not morally necessary—so long, of course, as rigorous protections are in place and the MRVSs are truly free to say no.

The more senior MRVSs told me that they frequently discuss the potential side effects with volunteers. An older medic, 29-year-old Rob Colbert from Jonesboro, Arkansas, told me why: "A lot of the challenges [studies designed to provoke a reaction to a particular agent] that we have, I mean, there's a very high risk of getting severe diarrhea, nausea, cramping, headaches, which is basically the extent of any of the complications. . . . Some of them are worse than others as far as the enterics go."

Though they might not be anyone's idea of a good time, the protocols even attract non-MRVSs in other units assigned to Fort Detrick. Nineteen-year-old Alissa Tevels is in an animal care unit, 91 Tango, but she has participated in the anthrax study and in another on shigella vaccine. Though not part of the MRVS meetings, she socializes with many of the participants and hears about studies of interest or sees them posted around the institute.

I found Alissa and the men and women of 91 Bravo to be both proud of their work and somewhat frustrated at the myths that surround it, myths they encounter inside as well as outside the service. One told me of the ribbing she got back in Houston after she decided to join the MRVS, "from the drill sargent on down: 'You guys are going to be guinea pigs, I feel so sorry for you.' After we were here for three years we were just laughing," she told me. "We had it so good here." They all detest being dismissed as "guinea pigs," viewing themselves as playing an honorable role for medicine and science and, considering their level of knowledge and training, as co-investigators in the effort to find better protections for others like them. Like most Americans who came to consciousness in the late twentieth century, they are skeptical about big organizations like the armed forces. Yet they are also more idealistic, and certainly more service-oriented, than is generally thought to be true of "Generation Xers."

William Frank Fowler, a Lafayette, Louisiana, native, is a quiet man with rock-hewn features and a steady gaze. Though he might be someone's stereotype of the muscular "over the hill" marine (which he was before he entered the Army), he is also a very bright and highly trained medical corpsman who is proud of his work at Detrick. "I wish we could educate more people about USAMRIID.

It's actually a real good place to work," he told me. "It's given me a lot of experience that I feel I'll keep forever, that I'll always use." Fowler spoke passionately about the MRVS's role:

> The MRVS program is really needed, and I wish people wouldn't look down on it so much. That's one thing I have to say, because we're not abused, we're not kept in cages, y'know, fed through the bars. Everything's a volunteer program and then even when we are participating in the program we're treated fairly. And if at any time during the protocol you feel that you don't want to do anything, even after you've been inoculated, even if you're sick, you say "That's it, I want to go," then they'll give you medicine and you leave.

Any assumption that the MRVSs are passive "human guinea pigs" is shattered in a short talk with them. Lisa Sheridan-Cuddy and Lancer Cuddy are alumni of 91 Bravo, now training to be investment counselors in Frederick, Maryland. A strikingly attractive couple, they met and married in college at the University of New Mexico, enlisted together, and volunteered for the MRVSs together. Although Lisa was at first unsure, Lancer convinced her that the Detrick assignment was a cushy situation compared to other military posts. Indeed, Lisa turned out to be a leader among the MRVSs. She was made the MRVS representative on the Human Use Committee chaired by Art Anderson, and in that capacity she was able to revise consent forms for accuracy and readability and even to stop any study she found objectionable.

Lisa's role on the Human Use Committee was yet another respect in which the MRVSs are arguably the least exploited human experimental subjects in the country, if not the world. Sick patients rarely if ever have a representative on research review boards to make sure consent forms are written in a way that others in their position can understand, let alone have the ability to call a halt to proposed research. Even healthy, normal subjects like the local civilians who volunteer for experiments at Fort Detrick couldn't be represented as a coherent, self-conscious group like the MRVSs.

## OPENNESS IN RESEARCH

The openness that made my visit to Fort Detrick possible will be key to ensuring that the future of human experiments for national security purposes will be based on the model of the Army's Infectious Disease Institute, rather than a repetition of the many sad mistakes I have recounted. The young MRVSs didn't know how hard won were the enlightened policies that framed their experience. Theirs is the self-assurance of those who have never had reason to doubt that, even as members of the armed forces, they retain an ultimate measure of control over their lives. Such was not the case for earlier generations of research subjects.

But the MRVSs' self-assurance would be illusory if it were not supported by a system that makes them co-investigators with the research scientists themselves. For that to be the case, they must have access to relevant information about the purposes, risks, and potential benefits of the study. In a sense, the MRVS program is the Army's payment on the promise made in 1953 when Secretary of Defense Wilson signed his Nuremberg Code memo. If the Gulf War experience was a failure of informed consent in military-medical research, at least there are some models of success.

A persistent danger to ethical national security research, how-ever, is presented by the argument that some experiments need to be conducted in tight secrecy. Under such circumstances not only is the public deprived of the right it normally has in a democracy to judge whether the research is justified under the circumstances, the subjects of the research may be deprived of their specific right to give informed consent. The end of the cold war has lessened the threat of cataclysmic conflict, but the simmering resentments of small groups around the world has left Americans feeling as exposed, or perhaps even more exposed, than they were when the world was neatly divided into two principle camps. The need to keep secrets from terrorist organizations can easily substitute for the need to keep secrets from the Soviets (even though their security apparatus knew far more about what the American armed forces were doing than did American voters). Confronted with several small-scale hot wars, the environment of national security research could easily slide again into the mentality demonstrated during much of the cold war.

In its response to the 1995 recommendations of the president's Advisory Committee on Human Radiation Experiments, the Clinton administration took two important steps that should help to avoid both the temptation to future secrecy and the subsequent undermining of informed consent in national security-related experiments. First, the president directed all federal agencies to permanently retain records related to classified human experiments. Records retention will make it possible to reconstruct what experiments have actually been done far more easily than was the case when MKULTRA and the other secret experiments were revealed in the 1970s. Because so many records have been destroyed, either deliberately or accidentally, the information that made this book possible took another twenty years and enormous effort by many people to piece together. So that the record will never be so obscure again, it will be important to ensure that future presidential administrations do not abandon this directive.

Also in response to the Advisory Committee on Human Radiation Experiments' recommendations, the Clinton administration agreed that all classified research must meet informed-consent requirements. It was also agreed that potential research subjects should be told what agency is sponsoring the research (some people might prefer not to be part of research for the CIA, for example) and if the project involves classified research. Just as important, the administration proposed that all ethics review panels for secret projects include one nongovernmental member with the appropriate security clearance. The administration also suggested that an appeals process be established so that any ethics review panel member who disagrees with the panel's decision can go to the head of the agency or the president's science advisor. The seventeen federal agencies that do human subjects research are now developing an amendment to the regulations that govern human experiments. This new Section 125 would pertain to the review of classified research according to the system outlined in the president's response to the radiation experiments report.

## EBOLA ESTATES

I have said much in this book about American medical ethics and
national security because much material is readily available on
that subject. Not necessarily so with overseas' countries. Unlike
the captured records from defeated enemies like Germany,
Japan, and Iraq, and some recently declassified Canadian and
Australian materials, precious little is known about the Soviet
state's activities in fields involving human experiments during the
cold war. Even after the fall of the Soviet Union, a culture of
secrecy still more formidable than that of the West obscures the
historic reality.

Probably no one in the United States is in a better position to
know about the Soviet Union's capacity during the cold war, and
the threat its remnants represent today, than Ben Garrett.
Possessing a Ph.D. in chemistry from Emory University, Garrett
for twenty years has been the Battelle Memorial Institute's expert
on the production and control of biological and chemical
weapons. Most recently he has worked with the federal government as a liaison to the surviving Russian biological and chemical
weapons development complex, helping to convert Siberian factories and laboratories to peaceful uses. Equally important, Garrett
has advised on ways to keep former Soviet biological warfare and
chemical warfare scientists, some facing destitution due to Russia's
economic decline, from selling their wares to countries unfriendly
to America. The importance of this mission was brought home at
the end of 1998, when *The New York Times* reported that Iran had
aggressively courted former Soviet biological warfare scientists
and succeeded in recruiting at least five of them.

When I interviewed Garrett in October 1998, he had just
returned from Harbin, Manchuria, where he was one of only a few
Westerners to attend a conference on the continued failure of
Japan to acknowledge, let alone apologize for, its World War II
experiments. With an ailing Japanese capitalist economy eyeing
Chinese markets hungrily, there is finally a somewhat greater
chance that progress can be made on this issue than has been the
case at any other time since the war.

My main purpose in interviewing Garrett was to get his sense of the extent of human experiments in the later stages of the Soviet Union. It has long been known that the KGB, the Soviet police, plucked people off the streets in earlier decades, particularly under its feared chief, Lavrenti Pavlovich Beria, during the Stalinist period. They were taken to the dreaded Moscow compound known as Lubyanka Prison, where KGB headquarters were located. Many of these unfortunate individuals were women who were used sexually, forced to undergo experiments, and killed. When they disappeared, Garrett said, their families knew what had happened to them.

The worst offenses by the KGB seem to have occurred in the 1930s and 1940s, but military experimentation with biological warfare agents continued into the 1970s. The true nature of the production facility in Sverdlovsk was known to only a few dozen people. In a recent article in the Russian journal *Sovershenno Secretno* ("Top Secret"), interviews with Sverdlovsk physicians confirm the deaths of dozens of civilians from an accidental release of anthrax in April 1979. The authors also report that "experimentation with military strains on so-called 'donors' (meaning people) was conducted at Sverdlovsk-19 until the mid-1970s. Working stiffs from the storage facilities or construction workers agreed to be injected with every sort of disease in exchange for money. The statistical death rate of such 'donors' is not known."

Even in the supposedly reformist era of the 1980s, when hostile intentions were allegedly giving way, Soviet biological and chemical weapons development was in fact ratcheted up. Garrett and his colleagues determined conclusively, for example, that scientists in Siberia were preparing to weaponize smallpox on a large scale by the end of the Soviet era. I asked Garrett if he thought the Soviets continued to do human experiments up to the very end. "I have no doubt in my own mind, but I have no proof," he replied.

And what about chemical and biological warfare programs today in Russia? Could they be continued in the chaos and deprivation of the post-Soviet era? Garrett's response:

In my dealings with Russian scientists today, I keep getting the refrain that "this is what we're doing today, we're not doing anything that's at all harmful to humankind, and we want to continue doing things that are benefiting mankind." I find their comments believable, but I also find them to be typically Russian. What I mean by that is that during former times they were willing to do whatever they were told to do in a very accepting manner, and that I think they would revert to that fairly willingly. I also know, because we keep trying to find it and we keep getting rebuffed in our efforts to find it, that Russia has some kind of biological weapons program that the military controls. The scope of that program is unknown, the nature of that program is unknown. But what we do know about it comes as a result of such things as, one day the Russians declared that their facility in Siberia, Novosibrisk, which we refer to as "Vektor," was the repository of the smallpox cultures. And that's not where it was supposed to be, it was supposed to be in Moscow. They had moved it without informing anybody, without asking permission, probably in 1992, and they informed people in 1994.

I asked Garrett why they would have moved it. "You know, that's really hard to understand," he said. "I have never gotten a good answer, but they say things like, well, we always intended to have it here. I have no way to confirm or deny that."

Much of what is known about Soviet activities in the 1970s and 1980s has been learned from Ken Alibeck, a native of Kazakhstan, who defected to the United States from Russia in 1992, and who is Garrett's close colleague. Alibeck's account of the Soviet weapons development system has been highly publicized in the American media. In 1998 Alibeck broke his silence and, in an interview with *The New York Times*, expressed his belief that Russia continues to conduct biological weapons research and to keep their production capabilities intact. If that is the case, then human experiments must also be continuing. Where would they take place?

Within a half mile of Vektor, site of Russia's most secure biological laboratories and the largest biological weapons laboratory on the planet, is an incomplete shell of a building that was described to Garrett in 1998 as a "rest home." Who in the world would want to wander over to a rest home and take a rest next door to the largest biological weapons lab on earth, Garrett wondered. Apparently that was to be the rest home for the smallpox workers who would be highly stressed by their daily activities, handling and maintaining such lethal microbes. Garrett subsequently dubbed the projected home "Ebola Estates."

Also within the Vektor complex is Building 19, a "biolevel 4" hospital designed to contain the most virulent and deadly organisms, such as Ebola, where people who are suspected of exposure can be transported and observed under extreme biosafety conditions. Building 19 can hold about forty patients, at least ten times more than the hospital for the Army's Infectious Diseases Institute at Fort Detrick. One of Building 19's two wings is set aside for "active" HIV-positive patients, apparently those judged to be more highly infectious.

Otherwise, there has been only one recorded patient in Building 19, Nikolai Ustinov, a victim of a laboratory accident who was exposed to Marburg virus while injecting guinea pigs. As in Ebola, the internal organs of the victims of Marburg turn into liquid, resulting in fatal bleeding from every orifice. Ustinov's infection was an "experiment of opportunity" on the natural course of the virus. With his cooperation, his horrible death was observed by his colleagues and his story was widely publicized in the Western press. He died on April 30, 1988, and he was buried in a sealed, specially constructed steel coffin.

As far as is known, Marburg has never been collected from a human source. A colony of virus obtained from a human being would make a horrible and highly fatal weapon against other humans. Garrett was shown a collection of Ustinov's tissues that was retained, supposedly under conditions that destroyed the virus. Nonetheless, based on his experience with the system Alibeck believes that another team may well have collected the virus itself in order to turn it into a weapon, and that there is more to the story than is known. According to Garrett, however, the chances that a country would attempt to weaponize the Marburg virus are small because it is so fragile and indiscriminate. Its value would be to provoke sheer terror, but it would be uncontrollable.

When Garrett pressed the former hospital director about whether other human subjects had been in Building 19, he got a lengthy and what he construed to be a defensive response. During the conversation the current hospital director appeared and interjected what seemed like a qualifying remark. A conversation between the two continued heatedly in Russian, and trailed off from there. Garrett's summary view of the matter of human experiments in Russia: "I see no evidence of that in my work with Russian scientists today. I see a casual attitude toward what might have taken place in the past."

In December 1998, a few months after I first interviewed Garrett, *The New York Times* reported that Russian scientists in Kazakhstan were conducting animal experiments with Marburg just as the cold war was ending. When I asked Garrett about this report he told me that, if the story was accurate, the strain would have been that collected from the unfortunate Nikolai Ustinov, meaning that Garrett had been lied to in Russia. He also noted that the story could be pure conjecture, or that (unknown to the Russian scientists he spoke with), some other intelligence or military group gained access to Ustinov's remains, harvested his tissues, and disappeared. Some administration officials and members of Congress seem to have adopted the most suspicious of these theories. They believe that Russia continues its biological warfare program and, partly for that reason, have reduced U.S. spending on cooperative exchanges with Russian biological weapons development scientists.

A related concern is that samples of smallpox virus—a long-feared killer that has been eradicated around the world—may have found their way to North Korea from Russia's Vektor program, a charge that Vektor's director has vehemently denied. Worries that rogue states or terrorist groups may have secured smallpox samples formed part of the background for a presidential decision in April 1999 to reverse a promise to destroy the last American stock of the virus. Retaining samples for study, it is argued, could help in the response to a natural outbreak, however unlikely, as well as an attack. Russia has long opposed destruction of their remaining smallpox samples. Thus we may not have heard the last about the virus that a former White House science advisor has called the "most formidable" potential bioterror weapon.

## A BRIDGE TO THE FUTURE?

In the next century, as in the past, military-medical research involving human subjects will be dictated by the limits of information available from other sources. Because a new generation of weapons is being developed that are intended to incapacitate rather than kill an enemy, computer simulations and animal models can only go so far. Among the next generation of weapons is one that may involve a different sort of radiation than that emitted by atomic fission: microwaves. Electromagnetic waves may be used to disrupt an enemy soldier's central nervous system, to cause epileptic seizures, or to warm their body fluids as though they were inside a microwave oven. Low-frequency electromagnetic radiation has been shown to put animals into a stupor by signaling the brain to release natural substances that act like opiates (opioids). Other devices using lasers may cause temporary blindness (lasers designed to cause permanent blindness are outlawed by treaty).

Advances in genetics present stunning possibilities for the design of a manageable biological weapon that will not reinfect the forces that released it, sometimes called the "return" effect. Postcold war exposés of Soviet biological warfare efforts suggest that one genetically based approach has already been pursued. In 1972 the Central Committee authorized work on "Problem F," to develop a lethal virus and, at the same time, a vaccine that acts like a secret genetic key to the virus. Only Soviet military physicians would have that key, so that stricken enemy forces could not infect Red Army personnel if weather conditions suddenly changed and microbes were carried back to their source on a breeze. The operational structure was called the "Orgakov system," after the general at its head.

Prospective biological weapons that would mark still greater departures from previous ones could be developed from genetic technologies made possible by the Human Genome Project. This international effort to "map" the 3 billion pairs of proteins that make up human deoxyribonucleic acid (DNA) is to be completed by the year 2003. Though usually undertaken with the best of scientific intentions, scientific breakthroughs have always been assessed later on for their military applications. Just as genetics is blurring the lines between the sciences of biology and chemistry, the advent of genetic warfare, or "GW," would effectively unify biological and chemical weapons in a single category.

Several classes of weapons could result, among them microbes genetically engineered to target certain human populations based on a virus's ability to "recognize" the DNA variations in specific subgroups. Implanted in the host's cells, such agents could be designed to be either fast or slow acting. The effects of a slow-acting virus might not arouse suspicion until much damage was already done, as in the case of an infection that interfered with the early stages of embryonic development, increasing the rate of spontaneous abortions and over decades causing a significant reduction in the birth rate. These kinds of assaults would initially be "subacute," not noticeable, and their origins would be difficult to identify and trace. The assaults planned on South African blacks during the Apartheid regime, mentioned in Chapter 1, may have been of this variety.

Mechanisms present in people from particular ethnic groups or of certain geographic origins have long been noted to be associated with sensitivities to particular foods or drugs. For example, people of African and Middle Eastern origin often get sick when they eat fava beans. The ancient Greeks and Egyptians noted this reaction. After World War II it was found that people in this region are also often sensitive to antimalarial drugs. The cause of these reactions is a deficiency of the enzyme glucose6phosphate dehydrogenase (G6PD). Biological weapons could seek to capitalize on genetic alterations characteristic of certain groups.

Or consider the possibilities raised by comparison of the human genome with those of lower animals on the evolutionary spectrum. Humans share 98.4 percent of their DNA with chimpanzees, and pound for pound our simian cousins are far stronger than we are. What if the critical gene that controls for upper-body development in chimps could be introduced into human muscle tissue using, say, a virus as vector? That way, when muscle was broken down in exercise it would be rebuilt under the influence of the chimpanzee DNA. Musclebound rocket commanders probably won't make much difference in future armies, but they might be very valuable in simmering civil conflicts that call for small-scale, low-intensity police operations. These genetically engineered operatives injected with primate DNA would give some late-night TV hosts an easy one-liner about "gorilla warfare."

Would such a genetic intervention succeed? There would of course be substantial obstacles, such as the problem of switching on the new genetic material in its human host, and that of controlling the virus so that it does not invade and damage all the rest of the host's tissues. My point is not that it can be done but only that, if at all plausible and potentially useful, it will be attempted. And such attempts must finally involve human experiments.

There are scattered public indications that defense planners are preparing for conditions in which biotechnological warfare is a realistic threat and biotechnological defenses a strategic necessity. Some published statements are much in the spirit of my primate DNA speculations. For instance, in September 1996 an official of the Defense Advanced Research Projects Agency (DARPA was the agency that pioneered the Internet), announced an objective that would provide the ultimate defense against biological warfare. The aim would be to genetically engineer the immune system so that it could "recognize anything—even if it's never seen it before—even if it's a genetically altered mechanism—and be able to neutralize it within the body."

This unidentified official went on to tell *U.S. Medicine*, a government magazine for physicians, that DARPA is funding $30 million in projects on "pathogen countermeasures." And this is not the end of the biotech wish list. By 2005 "at least 50 per cent of programs at DARPA will have some biology aspect to them," the official told the magazine. "We're going to have almost superhuman beings whose own body will be able to defend itself." The ethical problems concerning the human experiments that will be

needed to develop such far-out capacities were not mentioned in
the article.

Comments about genetic superbeings make it seem that
DARPA officials have themselves been engaging in some psy-
chedelic experiences, but more sober explorations of future biological applications are also taking place in the national security
arena. At a 1996 biotechnology workshop sponsored by the
Army War College, several scenarios of conflicts in the world of
2020 were played out. Following one of them, a team's summary
of the impact that biotechnology would have on society and the
military included this remark: "It was postulated that international treaties may be weakened by 2020, with implications for
the US as adversaries explore the potential for 'biotechnology
warfare.'" The report went on to suggest that, given current
treaties and prohibitions that limit offense preparedness for biological warfare, "the US needs to concentrate on dual-use technologies that can be developed in the civilian sector while having
military utility."

When the group was briefed on applications that "would be of
the greatest utility to both the civilian and military sectors," a
question was asked "about controlling the tempo of genetically
targeted attacks (that is, organisms that detect and attach DNA
sequences in a highly specific manner)." The report went on:

> Participants considered how to detect if such an attack, which
> might take place over several years, or even a generation, was
> underway. It was suggested that an enemy might be able to
> control the speed of a genetic attack, although it was not clear
> how. Detection would require keeping detailed records of the
> genetic traits of the populace. If radical or unnatural shifts were
> noticed across a broad spectrum, that would be an indication
> that a genetic-based attack might be occurring.

In a remarkable understatement, the report noted that that if
"detailed records of the genetic traits of the populace were necessary
as a matter of national security," that would raise "many privacy and
other ethical issues," the report noted. In fact, a "genetic library" of

the U.S. population would represent the largest, most invasive, and most potentially divisive biological field test in history.

No province of potential scientific breakthrough seems beyond the realm of speculation in its consequences for national security, and no speculation can be dismissed as too far out. Besides genetics and the interest it might provoke in new areas of military-medical research, dramatic advances are being made in knowledge about the brain. Gathered under the heading of "neuroscience," understanding of electrochemical systems and neuroanatomy are being joined in countless studies throughout the world. Among the areas of greatest interest is the ability to image cerebral processes: As certain regions of the brain and systems of neurons "light up," their activation may be associated with specific mental activities. Someday it may even be possible to achieve a "translation" of neurologic states to thoughts and ideas, thus literally enabling people to read one another's' minds. At-a-distance mind reading would thus also be technically possible.

No less an authority than the chairman of the French National Bioethics Commission, Jean-Pierre Changeux, announced precisely such a concern at the committee's annual meeting in 1998. Changeux, a neuroscientist at the Pasteur Institute in Paris, worried that equipment now being developed could someday become commonplace and used at a distance, opening the door to massive invasions of privacy that would present "a serious risk to society." A researcher at the French Atomic Energy Commission also told the committee that imaging techniques have reached the point where "we can almost read people's thoughts."

Again, human experimentation will be an unavoidable part of efforts to achieve these dubious breakthroughs. Even as society decides whether technologies of these kinds are acceptable, many individual human subjects will be needed to "perfect" the instruments for neuroimaging and the interpretation of the images into thoughts and ideas. The military possibilities of such capabilities are evident, and the potential for human experiments under highly classified national security conditions are too obvious to require much comment.

## AN AVENUE TO JUSTICE

If there is a single lesson to be gleaned from the story of military-medical human experiments, it is that we can expect them to continue in the future. Short of a miraculous and fundamental change in the human personality, nations and political movements will always be interested in novel weapons that might gain them at least a temporary strategic advantage over their adversaries. Accordingly, how those weapons can be rendered most effective and how they can be defended against will be important questions that can only be answered with human subjects.

Nor will such research only be done by countries or leaders we might find of dubious moral standing. We have seen that the United States continues this work, albeit for defensive purposes. Yet much that is learned about defense can also be turned to offensive capacities. Even the esteemed Nelson Mandela, when he learned about the South African biological weapons development program, is alleged not to have ordered its dissolution. Why should viruses or bacteria that can target ethnic groups only be of interest to a white regime? Strategic value knows no race.

If it is true that human experiments on these weapons will always be attractive to some nations, I believe it is also true that these experiments can be done ethically. The Army's infectious disease institute could provide a model of such experiments. Its critical elements will be fair recruitment practices, fully informed consent with an educated group of potential subjects, peer support, no more than modest compensation, and careful review and minimization of risk factors. In principle, at least, the research should also be confined to defensive rather than offensive purposes, in spite of the admitted limitations of these categories.

It is past time for the world to have some mechanism to identify *unethical* experiments and to sanction or at least censure governments that support them. There should also be a system for identifying key individuals in positions of responsibility, and referring their cases to the International Court of Justice. These responsible individuals would include medical scientists as well as political leaders.

The need for an open and procedurally fair legal process at the international level is partly a matter of morality, partly of practicality. The moral argument is that we live in an international community, especially as the conditions of warfare are concerned. Therefore a mechanism that formulates, interprets and applies remedies must also be international and have legitimacy across borders.

Moreover, differential legal jurisdictions and sets of rules in matters of medical ethics have the unsupportable implication that certain basic ethical principles are variable with culture. Rather, certain well-recognized principles of medical ethics know no cultural or national boundaries: Respect for the persons who are to be research participants, minimizing harm and maximizing benefit to them, and ensuring that the benefits and burdens of research are justly distributed are not unique to a single culture. Just as there are international guidelines governing experiments with human subjects in general there should be international understandings of the bounds of national security experiments. To be sure, the interpretation of these principles will be somewhat dependent on cultural circumstances, but the international nature of hostilities demands an international interpretation of the rules that govern, say, field experiments with biological weapons.

The same argument applies to "civil" conflicts in which a politically dominant ethnic group tries out novel weapons in regions populated by a different and subservient ethnic group, as has been alleged in Iraq and South Africa. In cases of that sort the domestic legal system cannot be expected to sort out the equities involved, and because the weapons have implications for international relations they cannot plausibly be characterized as merely "internal" incidents.

Also from a practical standpoint, as the Nuremberg judges appreciated, the values governing military-medical experiments must be international. By definition the issues reach across the boundaries of nation-states, and unless there is widespread understanding of a common set of rules military and political leaders will seek advantages through alleged loopholes. This was one of the problems that the Nuremberg prosecutors faced, as the defense was able to argue that all state-sponsored experiments were essentially alike, even though the conditions under which the Nazi experiments took place were patently inhuman.

There is yet another reason for a recognized international tribunal to interpret and apply ethical standards in national security experiments. Throughout this book, individuals have been identified whose actions have been cited by responsible authorities as morally culpable. To some, the list of names will be disappointingly small. Yet as I learned while working for the president's radiation advisory committee, there is good reason for the sometimes maddening complexities of the legal process: Facts may be in dispute, actions may have multiple meanings and purposes, and judgments must be finely grained. Again, the Nuremberg Nazi doctors' trial provides a salutary example of a circumstance in which justice was delivered to individuals in a satisfactory, if imperfect, fashion. Yet, lawyer-ethicist George Annas and physician-ethicist Michael Grodin of Boston University have pointed out that the lack of an effective enforcement mechanism was one of the defects of the Nuremberg Code.

Throughout the story of medical-military human experiments, we have seen how failures of interpretation and communication have foiled the good intentions of the Nuremberg judges, as well as those many individuals who have tried in good faith to identify and apply ethical standards in human experiments. The international community should take steps toward creating a research ethics court that can implement the universal values that have been repeated time and again, and apply the hard lessons learned through so many failures from World War II to the Gulf War.

A side benefit of an international research ethics court is that it would also help keep tabs on the research that is being done. "Transparency" in the development of novel weapons is one way to sustain a global balance of power and, admittedly, terror. In the future, openness in the conduct of human experiments could do more than help assure that they meet ethical standards against exposing human subjects to undue risks. It might also discourage some so inclined from taking the personal and professional risks of such work and—most importantly—could also help ensure that the weapons themselves are kept at bay.

Yet as long as there are scientists who can be bought or can justify participation in preparation for mass murder, defensive capabilities will be important. A single attempted terrorist attack on the United States, even if unsuccessful, could generate a powerful reaction in a country that has never experienced a modern incursion on its shores. Human experiments, such as those performed at Fort Detrick with truly informed men and women, will be vital to improving our protection, and to reassuring Americans that there are alternatives to lashing out in blind anger. Even field tests with airborne particles to test dispersal under realistic conditions may prove acceptable to the public, so long as there is an ethical review process that earns the public's trust. In a dangerous world, let those who would protect us not add to the sources of undue risk.

# AFTERWORD

The first publication of *Undue Risk* was followed by a flurry of new reports of events involving human experiments. With this afterword I am fortunate to have the opportunity to integrate these new reports into the historical framework I have assembled, a history that could be written because of the sacrifices of many people. These included individuals who were harmed or wronged by secret experiments, their loved ones, and the many advocates, journalists, historians, and conscientious government officials who dedicated themselves to the truth.

As well, that this story could be told is a tribute to the American system and a real victory for the American people. Other countries have proven far less interested in reviewing their cold war activities, and their political systems are far less sensitive to the demands of their citizens who feel aggrieved about their government's actions. To say this is not to settle into uncritical jingoism, to deny that wrong and harms were committed, or to claim that continued vigilance is not needed. My point is rather that *Undue Risk* owes its existence to many courageous people and to the country whose continuing improvement it seeks. Indeed, one of our unifying traits as Americans is a healthy skepticism about the power of government. From New England to the South to the Pacific Northwest, a stubborn individualism manifests itself, albeit expressed in many different ways. This skeptical attitude has served our democracy well for over two hundred years.

Skepticism has its price, however. On many occasions during public lectures or interviews about the book I have had to confess my inability to show that unethical secret experiments are not still being done by our government. It is always easy to formulate "what if's" and "could be's," and negatives are notoriously hard to prove. But this much I do know to be true: No country has been more open about these matters than the United States. Colleagues in other countries, including some of our closest allies, have had to admit to me that a government inquiry like that undertaken by the President's Advisory Committee on Human Radiation Experiments would be all but impossible to get off the ground in their political culture. Let's pause for a moment to rejoice that we do have a constitution and a bill of rights.

Therefore, just as a truly free nation can never tolerate an iconic state with its own life and entitlements at the people's expense, so also we should guard against unreasoning paranoia. In particular, we should resist a tendency to overestimate government as some sort of monolith with the ability to make all its many parts act in lockstep. Of course there is still a great deal of secrecy about some government operations—far too much of which is not justifiable, I believe—but much of the story of *Undue Risk* illustrates how lumbering and clumsy our sizable federal establishment can be. Consider for example the failure of the Pentagon to achieve internal acceptance and understanding of its own Nuremberg Code–based human experiments policy during the early cold war. That failure is one for which the defense establishment is still paying dues in a lack of trust by the American public and by its own troops.

## ANTHRAX WARS

There are now important general protections from forced experiments involving people in uniform. These protections create exceptions to the usual requirement for military personnel to accept medical care that will enable them to return to their post or to accept medical treatment that will protect their ability to execute their duties. For example, following the Uniform Code of Military Justice (UCMJ), United States Army Command Policy (AR 60-200) states that "A soldier on active duty or active duty for training will usually be required to submit to medical care considered necessary to preserve his or her life, alleviate undue suffering, or protect or maintain the health of others."

As I noted in my account of the atomic veterans in Chapter 7, an important issue is whether research participation can ever be considered "medical care" and therefore required. Military person-

nel are protected from coercion or threat of UCMJ punishment by
AR 70-25, which states that "Moral, ethical and legal concepts on
the use of human subjects will be followed as outlined in this regulation. Voluntary consent of the human subject is essential.
Military personnel are not subject to punishment under the
Uniform Code of Military Justice for choosing not to take part as
human subjects. Further, no administrative sanctions will be taken
against military or civilian personnel for choosing not to participate as human subjects." This regulation is the descendent of
Defense Secretary Charles Wilson's Nuremberg Code–based memorandum of 1953.

The most recent version of AR 70-25 was published in 1990.
Unlike earlier versions, this army rule contains no exclusions for
tests or training that involves risk situations or nuclear, chemical,
or biological field exercises. Therefore training activities that
involve unconventional weapons are considered to be protected
under AR 70-25, including informed consent and oversight of
the experiments for their risks. Even classified research, by presidential memorandum, is subject to the twin protections of
informed consent and prior review, and both the experiment subjects and reviewers must have the necessary security clearances in
order to take part.

In spite of these important formal protections, when I put the
finishing touches on the previous edition I suspected that the public reaction to the distrust sown by the Pentagon from decades of
misdeeds and errors concerning human experiments was due a
substantial harvest with the anthrax vaccination program. Citing
concerns about biological weapons caches controlled by countries
such as Iraq and North Korea, the Defense Department initiated
an effort for the mandatory vaccination of all 2.4 million active
and reserve troops against anthrax, long regarded as the agent most
likely to be used in biowarfare. But a small but vocal rebellion
against the vaccination program emerged from the grass roots of
servicemen and women. What followed was one of the gravest
threats to military morale since the end of the Vietnam war.

Anthrax is a bacterial infection that stems from contact with
contaminated animals or animal products. If the bacterium,

*Bacillus anthracis,* enters through the skin—as it can for those who handle contaminated animal hides—it is usually curable. But inhaled or ingested anthrax is almost always fatal. Because it is so deadly, and because its spores can remain dormant for decades in soil, anthrax has long been theorized to be a potent biological weapon. The vaccine that the Pentagon is using in its attempt to immunize the troops has been approved by the Food and Drug Administration for people who are at risk of exposure to the spores. Unfortunately, the vaccine has to be given five times over an eighteen-month period, with annual boosters after that, and it has been tested for protection from inhalational anthrax only in monkeys. The complexity of its administration schedule and the uncertainty of its success in humans as protection against airborne anthrax (the most likely form of delivery in combat) have been part of the criticisms leveled at the Pentagon vaccination program.

In early 1999 only a few dozen servicemen and women had declined to be vaccinated, but a year later there were hundreds. They risked punishments ranging from court-martial to discharge with complete loss of benefits after years of service. The dissenters noted that the vaccine had not been tested for combat conditions, particularly airborne use, and hundreds of adverse reactions had been reported. The laboratory that prepared the vaccine had difficulties getting approval from federal officials for continued operation. Then experienced ex-officers began to weigh in against the program in the media, and a congressional committee published a scathing attack on the Pentagon program. Some of the critics regarded the vaccination program as a PR effort that backfired. "It looked early on that this might actually be a solution [to the anthrax threat posed by potential adversaries]," said Rep. Mark E. Souder (R-IN) who was quoted in the *New York Times* on February 18, 2000. "But the more you dig into this, the more you realize this is more of a political solution than a substantive medical solution to the question of chemical and biological technology."

Testimony like that of Roberta K. Groll, Technical Sergeant assigned to the 110th Logistics Squadron, Battle Creek, Michigan, apparently moved many members of Congress. Sgt. Groll received her first injection of the anthrax series on September 18, 1998, when she was preparing for a possible deployment to Qatar. In a written statement to a House of Representatives committee on April 29, 1999, Sgt. Groll said:

> Prior to volunteering for the deployment I had no knowledge of the anthrax vaccine pro or con. I acted on blind faith in the Department of Defense, my superiors and trusted in the individuals I felt were qualified to administer the vaccine. I considered this vaccine as safe as all other vaccines that I have received in the line of duty. Following the first two shots of the series I noticed that I was extremely fatigued and nauseous. However, during the same period of time I was working numerous hours of overtime in preparation of an upcoming operation readiness inspection. I attributed these symptoms to the extra hours and stress, not to the vaccine.

But Sgt. Groll's health problems continued, and since March 1999 she used nearly four hundred hours of leave due to illness. She reports that she suffers from chronic fatigue, shortness of breath, weight loss, mood swings, abdominal pain, and nausea and diarrhea. "Since I have been receiving the anthrax vaccinations my system is rebelling against something and I have become seriously ill," she said.

Through these withering attacks the Pentagon stood firm, restating the safety of the vaccine and its military importance. They pointed out that 400,000 servicemen and women had been vaccinated without incident, and argued that the troops deserve protection against an agent that can cause death within days. The vaccine, Pentagon medical officials contend, is safe and a risk-benefit analysis compels its use.

Is there a basis for complaints about the vaccine's effects? Verifying that ailments were caused by the inoculations is likely to be frustratingly hard to achieve. Like the long-term effects of the radiation experiments or the bioweapons studies at Fort Detrick in the 1950s, tying actual vaccination effects to later reports of illness is notoriously difficult. It appears that doctors have not been able to tie more than a few illnesses to the vaccinations. Recall, again, the uncertainties about the medical effects among the atomic veterans. Rational evidence may not be the underlying problem, however.

Not all news reports have identified what I believe to be the underlying problem facing the vaccination program. If the anthrax vaccine itself was an isolated issue, the Pentagon might well be able to rely on rational persuasion. It might be able to show Congress and men and women in uniform that few if any adverse reactions can be tied to the vaccine, and it might be able to argue that an invisible and deadly weapon like anthrax requires the kind of ready defense that might be provided by the vaccine. If I am right, though, the problem goes deeper. Decades of mistrust have accumulated around the vaccine issue, as memories of Agent Orange (the defoliant used in Vietnam many believe to have left some veterans with health problems after years of Pentagon denial), and the frank use of soldiers, sailors, and airmen in human experiments. Some of today's troops are the sons and daughters of Vietnam veterans, others had uncles in the Korean era, perhaps deployed at atomic test sites, and some may have had a grandfather in the Navy during the mustard gas tests. An accretion of regrettable events is the underlying geology of the anthrax vaccine debate. No wonder we are left with the result that so many soldiers suspect that they are de facto experimental subjects.

For all its difficulties, the anthrax vaccination program was not per se a medical experiment, contrary to the suspicions of some. Rather, it was a judgment call by defense leaders based on arguable assumptions about the threat, and motivated partly by concerns about what will be said if there is a use of anthrax in combat and it turns out precautions were not taken. Anthrax exposure results in a nearly certain and awful death, but there are other ways to counter it than a questionable vaccine. Some have urged that masks and other filtering technology be made more available, especially for combat units most likely to be at risk. The problem with this solution is that by the time one has been exposed to anthrax defensive measures may be too late. In the end the technical issues may be secondary if the Pentagon concludes that undermining morale with a vaccine of uncertain usefulness and necessity is simply not worth the price of continuing to stoke the fires of a legacy of mistrust.

## THE ATOMIC VETERANS

Even as the anthrax vaccine controversy unfolded, more was learned about one of the decades-old sources of mistrust: allegations about health effects on the "atomic veterans," the men who had been ordered to participate in military exercises during atomic bomb tests. For decades many of these men and their families have argued that the government lied to them about the health risks associated with their deployment at the blasts, or at least should compensate them for their illnesses suffered because of that experience. The problem has been determining whether they really did suffer from more illness than others of their age as they got older.

The Institute of Medicine of the National Academy of Sciences in Washington, D.C., concluded an intensive study of the health effects of atomic tests on 70,000 veterans who were present in exercises at the blast sites in Nevada or the South Pacific. The Institute of Medicine compared this group of atomic veterans to another 65,000 soldiers, sailors, and airmen who served at the same time but were not at the atomic explosions. The institute found a 14 percent higher leukemia death rate. However, that number was not statistically significant and so could have occurred by chance. The report also noted an unexpectedly high death rate among the vets from prostate and nasal cancer, but again the results are inconclusive because there is so little previous data on these cancers in relation to radiation exposure.

A crucial bit of information that would have gone far to helping the Institute of Medicine reach more conclusive findings was data about the size of radiation dose received by each veteran. I have explained how difficult dose reconstruction is, especially when reliable records are lacking. The results of the study of atomic vets are obviously frustrating, especially for individuals and their families. For someone who actually has cancer thirty or forty years after being in the armed forces, there is no comfort in being told that one would probably have gotten it even if one had not been deployed miles from an atomic bomb blast. The feelings of betrayal are greater still when one suspects that these deployments were part of a massive experiment. What, then, are we to say to the relatives of people who were stricken with a vicious form of cancer, and believe their loved ones were being used as experimental subjects without their knowledge or consent?

## A TRIAL IN BOSTON

In spring 1999 I received a telephone call from attorneys representing the relatives of people who had died of glioblastoma decades before. Few diseases are more terrible than glioblastoma, a brain cancer for which, my medical colleagues tell me, effective treatment is still being sought. According to trial documents, from the early 1950s to the early 1960s Dr. William Sweet and his colleagues at the Massachusetts General Hospital tried to treat glioblastoma by exposing their patients' cancer-ridden brains to a neutron beam, hoping to destroy the cancer cells. Nuclear reactors at Brookhaven Laboratory on Long Island and at the Massachusetts Institute of Technology in Cambridge were used in this treatment. The treatment also consisted of attempts to introduce agents into the brain that would attract the neutrons to the cancerous brain cells, hence the term "neutron capture therapy."

Sweet, a distinguished physician who was a codeveloper of the PET scan, was for much of his career on the cutting edge of attempts to take advantage of radiation technology for medical treatment. Unfortunately, neutron capture therapy does not seem to have yielded desired results, though it was tried in dozens of patients. Sadly, the evidence indicated that at least nine patients died as a result of the therapy and not of the tumor. After the Advisory Committee on Human Radiation Experiments helped release the 1947 letters on informed consent from the Atomic Energy Commission, relatives of several of the patients filed a lawsuit. Their loved ones' experience in the neutron capture treatment did not seem to square with the letters' requirements for informed consent and potentially beneficial treatment. This fact perplexed them because the Atomic Energy Commission had provided some of the equipment that was used in the treatment. My role as an expert in the case was partly to explain the historical context of the AEC letters. The statute of limitations was deemed to have run until the families knew or should have known that the experiments were conducted without any therapeutic potential. That date could not have been earlier than 1995 when some of the ACHRE documents were first released and some families got suspicious and began, through their lawyers, a more complete investigation.

It was my first experience in federal court and with a jury. The trial was held in the impressive federal courthouse in Boston. As I walked through the halls it struck me that the majesty and power of the legal system was reflected in the floor-to-ceiling views of the harbor. The painstaking legal process also reminded me of the inevitability of the tides outside the courthouse.

In my report for the plaintiffs' attorneys I assembled the available information, which I believe revealed that the neutron capture therapy was really an experiment and that it did not follow the rules of informed consent and potential benefit that the AEC stated in its 1947 letters. Of course we cannot know how the information affected the jury, though it did award the families $8 million in damages against Massachusetts General Hospital and Dr. Sweet. The case is currently under appeal, but if the decision stands then the case of *Heinrich v. Sweet* will be an important one in the history of the law and the ethics of human experiments.

## PROTECTING PERSONS WITH MENTAL DISORDERS

During the darkest days of the experiments with hallucinogens secretly undertaken by federal agencies, New York tennis pro Harold Blauer was one of the tragic victims. Blauer was hospitalized for depression at New York's Psychiatric Institute in 1953, a case I describe at length in Chapter 7. Although many rules and procedures are now on the books to provide special protections to groups like soldiers and prisoners, it is surprising that there are no special rules to protect persons with mental disorders who might not be able to give valid informed consent to be in research.

In 1998 I had the opportunity to work as a consultant to the National Bioethics Advisory Commission on the issue of research involving persons with mental disorders. The issue had gained increased notoriety in the 1990s as the promise of new medication for these tragic diseases clashed with ethical worries about the ways these drugs were often tested. For example, a common method of testing a new medication for the symptoms of schizophrenia involves removing a person with the disorder from his or her current treatment in order to "wash out" the system so that the effect of the new drug can be seen more clearly. Critics noted that there may be significant risks to individuals who are placed on drug holidays, that the research may do the subjects themselves no good, and that many of them may have diminished capacity to give informed consent to be in a study.

My feelings about research involving people with mental disorders involve my personal experience. My father was the well-known psychiatrist, J. L. Moreno, who pioneered the fields of group psychotherapy and psychodrama. I grew up on the grounds of his small, European-style sanitarium in the Hudson Valley. He was a famous and original anti-Freudian whose reputation as one who truly loved his patients has been confirmed to me by his younger students and colleagues since his death in 1974.

After my father died I perused his memoirs, in which he recalled his work as a second-year medical student at the University of Vienna. He was accepted for work in the clinic of Julius Wagner von Jauregg, an important figure in the history of psychiatric research whom I will revisit shortly. The year was probably 1915, and the place was Vienna, Austria, but the culture of academic medicine sounds familiar.

There was no salary for being a research assistant at the clinic, just a tremendous amount of prestige in being there, a wonderful opportunity to meet and to work with some of the top psychiatrists, both research and clinical, in the world, and, in my case, to have my name on publications, still an important factor in a young scientist's career. I was involved in a few other research projects there, but the only one I remember is a study of iodine metabolism. We went to the Tyrol and injected rats full of Iodine. . . . After experimenting on rats we experimented on inmates at the psychiatric hospital connected with the Von Jauregg clinic, Steinhoff hospital. . . . I have always been appalled at the idea of experimenting on helpless mental patients. I remember projects—I was not involved with them— in which patients were injected with TB bacilli and another in which injections of alcohol were administered.

Shortly after the incidents my father recalled, in his graduation year 1917, his mentor Wagner von Jauregg experimented with the induction of fevers as a cure for general paresis, a condition that occurs during the tertiary phase of syphillis and can cause insanity, paralysis, and death. He injected nine paralyzed patients with malaria, which was subsequently cured with quinine. The malaria-induced fevers were claimed to cure 85 percent of the patients. For his discovery Wagner von Jauregg was awarded the Nobel Prize for Medicine or Physiology in 1927, though malaria therapy for general paresis has of course been superceded by penicillin.

Important as it was, Wagner von Jauregg's work was clouded by his questionable use of patients as research subjects, a practice that was apparently common in Austrian psychiatry and neurology at the time, and one that my father seems to have encountered. Interestingly, Wagner von Jauregg himself was an ardent campaigner for laws to protect the insane from persecution and discrimination.

Throughout the twentieth century the rights of persons with mental disorders continued to be ambiguous. The team that investigated the Nazi crimes did take note of the abuse of the mentally ill in the context of the "T-4" or "euthanasia" program that led to the extermination of many psychiatric patients and was in effect a rehearsal for the mass murders in the concentration camps. In Chapter 3 I described how the chief medical advisor to the

Nuremberg judges, Leo Alexander, unraveled the horrific story of the camp experiments from the records of SS chief Heinrich Himmler, and made the Nuremberg prosecutions possible. Near the end of the trial Alexander wrote a memorandum to the judges, portions of which were incorporated into the famous Nuremberg Code.

In his memorandum Alexander singled out the mentally ill as a population that should be given special protections. The judges deleted this reference in their final draft. A likely explanation is that the judges did not wish to seem to be interfering in legitimate medical judgments about innovative treatment, but only to rule out nonbeneficial and highly risky experiments with easily coerced populations of healthy subjects like prisoners. Even so, much confusion about the judges' intentions has been caused by the code's celebrated first line, "The voluntary consent of the human subject is abolutely essential," a formulation that seems to rule out much research with mental patients as well as children, who also may not be able to give voluntary consent.

In December 1998 the National Bioethics Advisory Commission issued a series of recommendations on persons with mental disorders in research. I served as a consultant on their report. These rules would have blocked the notorious psychiatric experiments that took place in the 1950s, such as the mescaline experiment that led to Harold Blauer's death. For example, the commission recommended that people who might not have the capacity to give an informed consent should not be asked to participate in an experiment if others are available. They also urged that any expression of a desire not to continue in an experiment be respected. Blauer himself tried to leave the study but was not permitted to do so.

As I write this afterword the commission's recommendations have not been made into new regulations. However, the psychiatric community has certainly taken notice of the controversy and I perceive a far greater sensitivity to this issue than was the case in the mid-1990s. Many of the institutions that were conducting drug-free research, for example, have reconsidered the necessity and value of testing new drugs this way. Sometimes heightened

ethical concerns can encourage scientists to rethink the ways they
are doing things and to improve them.

## THE TESTICULAR IRRADIATION EXPERIMENTS

Our sympathies naturally and appropriately extend to soldiers
who, prepared to defend their country, think of themselves as
unwitting or unwilling test subjects. We are also rightly concerned
about people who are seriously ill and vulnerable to hoped-for but
sometimes unrealistic remedies. Along with their families, we look
to doctors and hospitals to help protect people who are not fully
able to speak for themselves. Although many of us may be less
inclined to worry about risks to those in prison, once the decision
is made that society's offenders are less worthy of ethical protections than others we are on a perilous and slippery slope.

In Chapter 7 I described the testicular irradiation experiments in
Oregon and Washington State penitentiaries. The Washington State
research was conducted by a University of Washington scientist. In
fall 1999 sixty-three former prison inmates in Washington State
received financial compensation and an official apology from the
state and the university, though both denied liability. The men
claimed they suffered continuing health problems, including infertility, and the settlement involved cash payments to those still living
or to their estates.

The former inmates in the Oregon case are continuing their
lawsuit. One of them, Harold Bibeau, contacted me shortly after
*Undue Risk* came out. We had met briefly six years before, when he
gave testimony to the president's Advisory Committee on Human
Radiation Experiments, for which I was then a staffer. A building
designer, Hal expressed his desire to be open-minded. He read the
book and we had a series of cordial exchanges in spite of some continuing honest differences in emphasis and interpretation about
the full significance of the experiments.

In our conversations Hal recalled the naive 22-year-old kid he
was when he agreed to submit to testicular irradiation. The whole
experience, he said ruefully, "made me realize what a fool I'd been

for getting into the research in the first place. . . . I was more interested in five bucks a month in my pocket than being rendered sterile from the experiment. . . . I was too young to make that decision
and it was under the wrong circumstances."

But his history as a human subject hasn't soured Bibeau to
medical research. "There's good research going on now and one of
the things that makes it good research is the amount of information that people get." He advises caution, however. "There are too
many doctors trying to sway people to get into research and saying
things like this won't hurt you." These days when Hal goes to his
doctor for routine medical care he takes a special interest in the
details of his treatment. Often he offers his own views about the
risks and benefits of various treatments, and sometimes his opinions are not in line with his doctor's. Hal adds, in an ironic tone
considering what he has been through, that he rarely gets his physician to change his mind.


## THE URANIUM WORKERS

In January 2000 it was disclosed that workers at the Paducah,
Kentucky, uranium processing plant participated in experiments
during the early 1950s. Some agreed to drink a radioactive liquid,
others inhaled gas to see how quickly uranium would be excreted.
The case was part of a much larger set of revelations about cancer
risks for workers at atomic bomb plants across the country. During
the cold war around 600,000 men and women were involved
in producing 70,000 nuclear weapons at dozens of facilities.
Although only a few were in medical experiments, many of these
people have reported being exposed to high levels of radiation and
dangerous chemicals.

In April 2000 the Clinton administration announced an
unprecedented national compensation plan, one that accepted the
federal government's burden for the workers' risks. This approach
reversed a traditional government approach to compensation
claims in which the burden of proof for harms suffered was placed
on the worker. By contrast, under the administration's plan

nuclear workers who believe they suffer from job-related illnesses would receive the benefit of the doubt and expedited claims from the Department of Energy. People with certain cancers will receive $100,000 in benefits. In the words of Energy Secretary Bill Richardson, as quoted by the *Washington Post*, "The government is done fighting workers and now we're going to help them."

When the atomic bomb workers' story first broke most of the concern stemmed from dangerous working conditions for plant employees and environmental hazards associated with air, ground, and water pollution. The experiments added a distinct dimension. For those who followed the plutonium injection cases there was a sense of déjà vu about Kentucky revelations. Those injections of hospitalized patients during World War II were apparently intended primarily to gain information about plutonium excretion rates, motivated by concerns about the safety of the young Manhattan Project laboratory workers. But in the case of the Kentucky workers they were themselves the subjects of the experiment, presumably for their own sake but not necessarily with full knowledge of the risks. As in so many of the other cases I have surveyed the records are not always clear, but it appears that at least fourteen workers "volunteered" in the early 1950s, and there seem to have been previous tests for which no records have been found. Workers were surely aware of radiation hazards in a general sense, but at that time the dangers of uranium dust and byproducts were underestimated. Although they constitute a fraction of the nuclear workers who stand to be compensated, the experimental subjects embody the paradox of being exposed to still more risks in order to manage those that were part of their workplace.

This case, again, appears to have been a violation of the Atomic Energy Commission's rules as expressed in its 1947 letters, which I describe in Chapter 5. Written by the general manager of the AEC, Carroll Wilson, those letters required potential benefit to the experiment subjects. There could have been no direct benefits to the Paducah workers from their deliberate uranium exposure. Only a few years after the letters were written the rules it stated were evidently either forgotten, ignored, or drastically misunderstood.

When the Department of Energy was confronted with the

uranium workers' cases in 1999, they reacted to reports of ethically questionable and sloppy practices quite differently from their predecessors, issuing a tough attack on their own agency's management of the plants and of the workers' health issues. Had it not been for the precedent of openness established a few years before, the uranium workers' grievances might not have been so readily confronted. Even though the uranium workers case was not limited to human experiments, the issues that came out of the radiation studies controversy concerning government responsibility were similar.

The lesson is that the rights and interests of people in medical experiments are related to those of all of us. The government cannot operate with impunity when it puts people at risk, even in matters related to national security.

## MORE ON UNIT 731

When I wrote *Undue Risk* I could not estimate the full scope of the human tragedy in China that resulted from the Japanese biological and chemical warfare experiments before and during World War II. As described in Chapter 4, the most notorious of the Japanese army units that conducted massive experiments in Manchuria was numbered 731, under the command of Dr. Ishii. They exposed thousands of ill-fated local inhabitants to mutilating and terminal experiments in a huge facility near Harbin called the Water Purification Bureau, language that nicely anticipated the "Newspeak" of George Orwell's *1984*. These victims were only those directly victimized, however, and one could only speculate on the tens of thousands injured indirectly through field experiments with biological agents.

Late in 1999 a group of Chinese and Japanese experts concluded that more than 270,000 Chinese civilians were killed in the field experiments. The total may even exceed the number killed in the notorious Nanjing Massacre of 1937. Diseases that were spread included typhoid, cholera, anthrax, lockjaw, and gangrene. Mostly they were exploded from various bacteria bombs that the Japanese army was striving to perfect. A couple of months before the report was issued a Japanese court rejected a compensation claim by Chinese war victims against the Japanese government. Eight of the ten plaintiffs were relatives of victims of Unit 731 experiments. As new information continues to emerge it seems unlikely that this issue in Sino-Japanese relations will soon be forgotten.

And in more backwash from the infamous career of Unit 731, the former lead scientist in the Soviet Union's biowarfare program said that the Soviets gained a trove of information from the Japanese scientists they captured. Ken Alibek, now in the United States and author of his own book on his work for the Soviet Union, claims that the program received an enormous boost by both captured Japanese documents and interrogations of the scientists captured in Manchuria. As I have described, the scientists were tried in 1949 and later released. Alibek has said that Stalin took a particular interest in the Japanese data and ordered his secret police chief to initiate a program that would surpass any in the world.

Alibek's claims raise new questions about the information gained by the United States as well. Recall the allegations that the United States used some of the Japanese data to launch biological attacks on the North Koreans and Communist Chinese during the Korean War. If Alibek is right then the information the United States gained might also have been more useful than has previously been believed. However, the former head of the American biowarfare program, Bill Patrick, who debriefed Alibek when he first defected from Russia in 1992, told *Kyodo News* that he doubts the assessment. Patrick's view is that the Japanese procedures were simply too crude and unquantifiable for either side to obtain useful information.

## FOR INFORMED CONSENT

Though government has too often been the source of doubts about the ethics of human experiments, it may also be the only party that can restore trust in the system. One outrageous limitation of the current system of protections is that, strictly speaking, the requirement for informed consent only applies to federally sponsored research or if it takes place at an institution that receives federal funding. There is no law on the books that mandates informed consent for every human experiment regardless of the source of funding for the research and whether or not the research is classified.

In practice, of course, a researcher would be a fool to impose an experiment on an unwitting person. The courts would recognize the need for consent based on the laws of battery and negligence. But only a federal law can guarantee in advance the right of every human being who is in an experiment, including national security experiments, the twin protections of informed consent and prior review by a qualified group of the risks and benefits of the experiment. Several bills have been introduced into Congress but they have languished.

It is high time that informed consent becomes the law of the land. A complete solution must involve not only privately funded research but also classified human experiments undertaken by national security agencies. Currently only a presidential memorandum requires informed consent and review by an ethics panel before the experiment takes place. A new federal rule is now working its way through the bureaucracy, but both a regulation and legislation from Congress must join with severe penalties for those who violate these standards.

## JUSTICE DELAYED

In Chapter 7 I chronicled some of the outrageous activities of the national security agencies during the 1950s. Perhaps the most famous single case of CIA "mind control" experiments was that of Frank Olson, the scientist who has long been said to have committed suicide by jumping out of a New York City hotel room window after being given LSD without his knowledge. That, at least, is the story that the public has come to know and that is recounted in this book.

However, in the fall of 1999 the A&E cable television network aired a program called "Mind Control Murder" that reiterated previously broadcast doubts about the official story and also offered the most comprehensive alternative theory yet presented. The program noted that the New York City district attorney's office has reopened the 1953 case as a homicide investigation. A January 2000 article in *Gentleman's Quarterly* reported that, although the DA's investigation is continuing, there are indications that he will find Frank Olson's death to have been a probable homicide.

In making the unusual decision to reopen a case after forty years, the New York district attorney was partly influenced by the findings of a forensic pathologist from George Washington University who examined Olson's remains and concluded that Olson suffered a blow on the head with a blunt object prior to his fall. Just as important, the pathologist did not find the facial lacerations that had been recorded by the coroner in 1953 (though the skin was intact upon exhumation of the remains), yet cuts would have been expected from a violent thrust through glass. Others interviewed on the program disputed the likelihood of suicide from a closed window with the shade drawn, and in fact Olson had spoken calmly to his wife on the telephone a few hours before. But why would a quiet scientist like Frank Olson be murdered?

In the spring of 2000 Eric Olson, Frank Olson's son, called me in my office at the University of Virginia. We talked about the standard account of his father's death and he shared with me his theory, one that will be tested by the New York district attorney. According to Eric Olson, his father was eliminated because he posed a threat to the agency's top secret drug experiments, including some that may have been conducted abroad. Frank Olson, it seems, was not only an experimental subject but also engaged as a researcher in the Army's Special Operations Division, which was closely tied to the CIA. As a researcher Olson himself used animals in experiments and perhaps witnessed the use of humans as well. Whatever he saw, perhaps in U. S.-occupied West Germany, seems to have greatly disturbed him. As it happens, Eric Olson told me, the CIA's declassified assassination manual for 1953 specifies a faked suicidal jump as a preferred means of elimination.

I asked Eric Olson for the image that came to his mind after nearly five decades of life with one of the greatest burdens a person can have, the unsolved mystery of his father's death. "I have long thought that accounts of my father's death are very like H. C. Andersen's story 'The Emperor's New Clothes'," Olson said. "After the perceptual cloud is punctured and the emperor is seen to be stark naked one wonders how the illusion of fine garb could have been sustained so long." Olson continued:

> Neither version of the story of my father's "suicide"—neither the one from 1953 in which he "fell or jumped" out a hotel room window for no reason, nor the 1975 version in which he dives through a closed window in a nine-day-delayed LSD flashback while his hapless CIA escort either looks on in dismay or is suddenly awakened by the sound of crashing glass (both versions were peddled)—made any sense. On the other hand both versions deflected attention from the most troubling issue inherent in the conduct of the kind of BW and mind-control research in which my father and his colleagues were engaged.
>
> The moral of my father's murder is that a post-Nuremberg world places the experimenters as well as the research subjects (my father was both simultaneously) at risk in a new way, particularly in countries that claim the moral high ground. Maintenance of absolute secrecy in the new ethical context implies that potential whistle-blowers can neither be automatically discredited nor brought to trial for treason. Nor can casualties arising from experiments with unacknowledged weapons be publicly displayed. The only remaining option is some form of "disposal." This places the architects of such experiments in a position more like that of Mafia dons than traditional administrators of military research. The only organizational exit is a horizontal one. In the face of this implication the CIA enforcers of the early 1950s did not flinch, though historians along with the general public have continued to see the state decked out in all its finery.

My conversations with Eric Olson were one of two experiences that brought his father's case and the CIA's decades-old experiments home to me after *Undue Risk* was first published. A history devoted specifically to American biological weapons programs,

*The Biology of Doom,* also appeared for the first time in 1999. Its author, Ed Regis, is like me a former philosophy professor. Reading Regis's book I learned that Sidney Gottlieb, the CIA spymaster responsible for their chemical warfare program, including the LSD experiments, died at the University of Virginia Hospital. His death occurred while I was putting the finishing touches on *Undue Risk,* and his deathbed was steps from my office in the medical school.

Later a second irony occurred to me. Gottlieb's privacy was scrupulously protected by my physician colleagues, his doctors, as it should have been. They afforded him the moral consideration and human dignity that he seems not to have granted those who were unfortunate enough to be unwitting participants in his experiments. Yet I am more hopeful than ever that efforts to quash the truth about some of the most closely held secrets of cold war experiments, including the circumstances surrounding Frank Olson's death, will ultimately fail. The only way to be sure is to demand that federal officials open the files on biological and chemical experiments, just as they did on radiation experiments. The New York district attorney's handling of the Olson case can light the way for the rest of government, but only if all of us refuse to forget the victims of undue risk.

# NOTES

## PREFACE

xii ...and magazine clippings: "In Kennedy Files, KGB Defector Tells of 1959 Oswald Suicide Attempt," *The Washington Post*, July 26, 1998.

xiv ...would help them overcome fatigue: Lawrence Altman, *Who Goes First? The Story of Self-Experimentation in Medicine* (Berkeley: University of California Press, 1998), p. 67.

xiv ...thousands of soldiers died of the disease: Ibid., p. 124.

xv ...as well as to their defense: Andrew G. Robertson and Laura J. Robertson, "From Asps to Allegations: Biological Warfare in History," *Military Medicine* 160:8 (369–373), 1995.

## CHAPTER ONE

2 ...as one of the U.N. inspectors delicately explained: "Iraq's Deadliest Arms: Puzzles Breed Fears," *The New York Times*, February 26, 1998.

2 ...is that it probably has to do with unsavory activities—unethical experimentation": "Iraq Arms Crisis Linked to Germ War Data," *The New York Times*, November 15, 1997.

3 ...time to clean up surviving evidence: "Rebuking Ex-Arms Inspector, Albright Defends U.S. Role," *The New York Times*, September 10, 1998.

3 ...and ceased all cooperation with us: Scott Ritter, "Saddam's Trap," *The New Republic*, December 21, 1998, p. 18.

3 ...Iraqi criminals and Kurds were used: "Saddam Tested Anthrax on Human Guinea Pigs," *Sunday Times (London)*, January 18, 1998.

3 ...Iraq's first generation of chemical weapons: Peter W. Galbraith, "A New Line in the Sand," *Washington Post*, August 9, 1998.

4        . . . as compared to only three in 1979: "Germ Defense Plan in Peril as Its Flaws Are Revealed," *The New York Times*, August 7, 1998.

5        Though human experiments for military purposes . . . : In this book I will use terms like "military medical experiments" and "national security experiments." In some contexts their scope and content are rather different, as national security can refer to non-military concerns such as economic stability. For the purposes of this book, however, both terms refer to medical experiments involving human subjects conducted or sponsored by federal agencies, experiments that may have national security implications. These experiments may be conducted or sponsored by national security agencies, including military authorities, or by civilian ones such as the Central Intelligence Agency (CIA). The specific cases I describe, and the context of the discussion, will make it clear whether I am referring in that instance to a military or a civilian agency, or both.

6        . . . funded by the Dutch government: "Questions About the Involvement of the South African Apartheid Regime and Its Secret Services in External Operations Like Hit Squads, Chemical and Biological Warfare," Submission to the Research Department of the Truth and Reconciliation Commission by the Netherlands Institute for Southern Africa, November 1997.

7        . . . of the troops occurred: Ibid.

7        . . . that it found the dehydration theory "unlikely": Truth and Reconciliation Commission, "South Africa's Chemical and Biological Warfare Programme, *Final Report*, Volume 2, Chapter 6, October 29, 1998.

7        . . . human rights' violations were committed under this programme": "Questions About the Involvement of the South African Apartheid Regime and Its Secret Services in External Operations Like Hit Squads, Chemical and Biological Warfare," op. cit., November 1997.

8        . . . was a particularly cynical and chilling one": Truth and Reconciliation Commission, op. cit., October 29, 1998.

8        . . . particularly the Iraqi people": "Israel Denies Anti-Arab Bio-Weaponry," *The London Times*, November 15, 1998.

8        . . . should be denied": Ibid.

9        . . . warn the general public about the milk it was drinking": "U.S.
         Alerted Photo Film Makers, Not Public, About Bomb Fallout," *The
         New York Times,* September 30, 1997.

10       . . . might lead to higher rates of head and neck cancer: "Pentagon
         Cites Radium Risk for Up to 20,0000 Ex-Troops," *The New York
         Times,* August 28, 1997.

10       partly supported by the Pentagon: "Gov't Settles Radiation Suit,"
         Associated Press, April 3, 1999.

10       . . . of the alumni of Fernald's "Science Club": "Settlement in
         Lawsuit Over Radioactive Oatmeal," *The New York Times,* January 1,
         1998.

## CHAPTER TWO

13       . . . Nathan Leopold, federal prisoner: Nathan Leopold, *Life Plus
         Ninety-Nine Years* (New York: Doubleday, 1958), pp. 306–307.

13       . . . John William Allen, U.S. navy veteran: Quoted in Committee
         on Veterans' Affairs, U.S. Senate, "Is Military Research Hazardous
         to Veterans' Health? Lessons Spanning Half a Century."
         (Washington, DC: U.S. Government Printing Office, 1994), p. 19.

14       . . . were "under criminal indictment in the District of Columbia":
         Vannevar Bush, *Pieces of the Action* (New York: William Morrow,
         1970), p. 43.

15       . . . to hear a damned thing more about it": Bush. Ibid., p. 44.

15       . . . astronomical sum of $25 million: United States, Office of
         Scientific Research and Development, *Advances in Military Medicine
         made by American investigators working under the sponsorship of the
         Committee on Medical Research,* E. C. Andrus et al., eds. (Boston:
         Little, Brown & Company, 1948), pp. xliii–xliv.

15       . . . would have produced considerable protest": David Rothman,
         *Strangers at the Bedside* (New York: Free Press, 1992), p. 32.

16       . . . given permission for the experiment and three died: Lawrence
         K. Altman, *Who Goes First? The Story of Self-Experimentation in
         Medicine* (Berkeley: University of California Press, 1998), p. 136.

17    It would be murder!: Paul de Kruif, *Microbe Hunters* (New York Harcourt, Brace and Co., 1926), pp. 316–317.

17    . . . high military authorities to start it": Ibid., p. 317.

18    . . . Johns Hopkins Medical School: Altman, op. cit., p. 139.

18    . . . agreed to subject themselves to the experiment: Ibid., p. 321.

18    . . . stamps in her honor: J. Samson, "A Nurse Who Gave Her Life So That Others Could Live: Clara Maass," *Imprint* 37: 81–82, 84, 87 et passim, 1990.

19    . . . Jesse Lazear Army Medical Center: Ibid., pp. 30–31.

19    . . . not to spend the money": De Kruif, op. cit, p. 322.

19    . . . if they contracted the disease: William B. Bean, "Walter Reed and the Ordeal of Human Experiments," *Bulletin of the History of Medicine* 51(1): 75–92, 1977.

19    . . . declined the offer out of patriotism: De Kruif, op. cit., p. 323.

20    . . . reported to Walter Reed for his work in Cuba: George J. Annas and Michael A. Grodin, *The Nazi Doctors and the Nuremberg Code* (New York: Oxford University Press, 1992), pp. 127–128.

20    . . . the voluntary nature of the yellow-fever studies: Susan E. Lederer, *Subjected to Science: Human Experimentation in America Before the Second World War* (Baltimore: The Johns Hopkins University Press, 1995), pp. 22–23.

22    . . . every precaution be taken to prevent accidents": Ibid., p. 54. Although referred to in the advisory committee report, the quotation is from the original document, Charles W. Shilling, Medical Corps, USN, Retired, undated paper ("History of the Research Division, Bureau of Medicine and Surgery, USN"). See fn. 44 in the advisory committee report.

22    . . . receive his approval before they can begin: Advisory Committee, op. cit., pp. 53–54.

22    . . . a more fitting term for these men": Stanhope Bayne-Jones to G. D. Fairbairn, February 16, 1945, "Folder: Commission on Viral and Rickettsial Diseases: Jaundice Publications," National Archives, Record Group 112, Entry 31, Decimal 331, Box 676.

23     . . . by all who knew him": Bush, op. cit., p. 47.

24     . . . greatest medical students in his hands: A. N. Richards' Papers, University of Pennsylvania. Box 8, Folders 4 and 5.

24     . . . more thoroughly than that," he said: Bush, op. cit., p. 47.

25     . . . the CMR's medical administrator: Ibid., p. 49.

26     . . . laboratory for a period of one year": Andrus, op. cit., p. 474.

26     . . . tested on a series of volunteers: Ibid., p. 591.

27     . . . never learned the "secret": Ben Garrett, personal communication, December 30, 1998.

28     . . . the first bold chemotherapy experiments: Institute of Medicine, National Academy of Sciences, *Veterans at Risk: The Health Effects of Mustard Gas and Lewisite,* Constance M. Pechura and David P. Rall, eds. (Washington, DC: National Academy Press, 1993), pp. 44–45.

28     . . . as indeed it was: Andrus, op. cit., p. 47.

29     . . . were lost to gonorrhea: Rothman, op. cit., p. 43.

29     . . . no further explanation: Andrus, op. cit., p. 49.

29     . . . human experimentation is desirable: Advisory Committee on Human Radiation Experiments, *The Human Radiation Experiments* (New York: Oxford University Press, 1996), p. 54.

30     . . . risks involved were described: Ibid., p. 54.

30     . . . by any other means: Cited in Jon M. Harkness, "Research Behind Bars: A History of Nontherapeutic Research on American Prisoners," unpublished doctoral dissertation (University of Wisconsin, 1996), p. 90.

30     . . . satisfy the experimental requirements: Ibid., pp. 90–92.31

31     . . . the use of human volunteers: Rothman, op. cit, pp. 42–47.

31     . . . test experimental preventive measures: Harkness, op. cit., pp. 96–99.

33     . . . is particularly laudable: Andrus. op. cit., p. 1.

34     . . . for a change: Leopold, op. cit, p. 307.

35    ...treatment of infectious diseases: Committee on Medical Research minutes from August 7, 1941, pp. 30–31, A. N. Richards' papers, University of Pennsylvania. Box 12, Folder 22.

35    ...new research in antimalarials: Ibid., pp. 35–36.

35    ...effect of nutrients on fatigue: Committee on Medical Research minutes from September 11, 1941, pp. 1–2, A. N. Richards' papers, University of Pennsylvania. Box 12, Folder 28.

35    ...led to the Norfolk inmate's death),...: Committee on Medical Research minutes from February 12, 1942, letter from Army surgeon general appended to minutes, A. N. Richards' papers, University of Pennsylvania. Box 12, Folder 30.

35    ...being performed in men: Committee on Medical Research minutes from May 1, 1942, p.2, A. N. Richards' papers, University of Pennsylvania. Box 12, Folder 30.

35    ...in Latin America: Letter from A. N. Richards to F. C. Bishopp, October 7, 1942, A. N. Richards' papers, University of Pennsylvania. Box 12, Folder 7.

35    ...objectors in medical experiments: Committee on Medical Research minutes from January 21, 1943, p.2, A. N. Richards' papers, University of Pennsylvania. Box 12, Folder 37.

35    ...in the *Life* magazine story: Committee on Medical Research minutes from May 18, 1944, p. 10, A. N. Richards' papers, University of Pennsylvania. Box 12, Folder 45.

36    ...consented to the research: Cited in Rothman, op. cit, p. 35.

37    ...before passing out: Committee on Veterans' Affairs, op. cit., pp. 16–17.

37    ...severe blistering injuries: Ibid., p. 17.

37    ...its chemical relative: Institute of Medicine, op. cit., p. 1.

37    ...and the most feared. Richard Rhodes, *The Making of the Atomic Bomb* (New York Touchstone/Simon & Schuster, 1986), p. 94.

37    ...nearly 400,000 casualties: Institute of Medicine, op. cit., p. 9.

38    ...investigations into gas masks: Leo P. Brophy, Wyndham D. Miles, and Rexmond C. Cochrane, *U.S. Army in World War II: The*

*Chemical Warfare Service: From Laboratory to Field* (Washington, DC: Office of the Chief of Military History, Department of the Army, 1959), p. 4.

38   . . . to the battlefront: Ibid., p. 9.

39   . . . than in actual use": This account can be found in American University Archives, Bender Library. The story is in "Secret, Deadly Research: Camp AU Scene of World War Training Trenches, Drill Field," *The Eagle* (American University), Friday, January 15, 1965, p.6.

39   . . . had been working with: Ibid.

39   . . . apparently to no avail: Martin K Gordon et al., "Chemical Testing in the Great War: The American University Experiment Station," *Washington History* 35 (Spring/Summer 1994) (citing *Washington Post,* August 4, 1918; *Washington Times,* August 4, 1918).

40   . . . a part of the Army: Ibid., p. 13.

40   . . . treat human injuries: Ibid., p. 10.

40   . . . subjects in gas testing: Richards to Henry Stimson, April 7, 1942, A. N. Richards' Papers, University of Pennsylvania. Box 12, Folder 6.

40   . . . contaminated areas of land: Ibid., p. 31.

40   . . . to four hours: Institute of Medicine, op. cit., p. 36.

40   . . . to intense erythema: Ibid., p. 39.

41   . . . my hometown newspaper: Committee on Veterans' Affairs, op. cit., p. 16.

41   . . . as they approached: Armed Forces Chemical Association (published under earlier name: Chemical Corps Association), *The Chemical Warfare Service in World War II: A Report of Accomplishments* (New York: Reinhold Publishing, 1948), p. 38.

42   . . . among the occupying troops: Ibid., p. 39.

42   . . . all over the world: Locations include Maryland, Utah, and Florida; San José Island, Canal Zone; Finschhafen, New Guinea; and Innisfail, Australia.

42   . . . following the bombing": Institute of Medicine, op. cit., p. 41.

42      . . . with acute conjunctivitis: Ibid.

42      . . . severity of chemical burns: Ibid., p. 31.

43      . . . the contaminated area at once: Armed Forces Chemical Association, op. cit., p. 58.

43      . . . the long-term effects": Ibid., p. 29.

43      . . . the human experimentation": Ibid., p. 21.

43      . . . fifty years later: Ibid., p. 5.

43      . . . making classified material public: *Biological Testing Involving Human Subjects by the Department of Defense, 1977: Hearings on Examination of Serious Deficiencies in the Defense Department's Efforts to Protect the Human Subjects of Drug Research Before the Subcommittee on Health and Scientific Research of the Senate Committee on Human Resources,* 95th Cong. 5 (1977) (statement of Edward A. Miller, Assistant Secretary of the Army for Research and Development) (hearing hereafter referred to as *Biological Testing Hearings*), p. 21.

43      . . . nuclear weapons programs: "Because the Pentagon has surrounded chemical and biological weapons with greater secrecy than it has imposed on nuclear weapons, Congress and the American public have been unaware of this policy change [referring to Congress's call for Nixon to resubmit the 1925 Geneva Convention for ratification]. The Pentagon has spent a minimum of $2 billion on those weapons since 1961 with virtually no congressional review *until this year.*" *Chemical-Biological Warfare: U.S. Policies and International Effects: Hearings Before the Subcommittee on National Security Policy and Scientific Developments of the House Committee on Foreign Affairs,* 91st Cong. 2–3 (1969) (statement of Rep. Fraser) (hereinafter *Chemical-Biological Warfare Hearings*).

43      . . . stunned his constituency: *Cold War Era Hearings,* p. 8.

44      . . . cause of death": Cochrane, *Biological Warfare Research in the United States: History of the Special Projects Division, Chemical Warfare Service* (1947) (page numbers are not marked).

44      . . . was indeed feasible: Leo P. Brophy et al., op. cit., p. 104.

44      . . . only in retaliation: *Biological Testing Hearings* at 28 (report submitted for the record by the US Army, titled "US Army Activity in the US Biological Warfare Programs" (1977)).

45    . . . enemy resort to BW: Leo P. Brophy et al., op. cit., p. 105.

45    . . . called Fort Detrick: Ibid., pp. 106–108.

45    . . . Granite Peak, Utah: Cochrane, *Biological Warfare Research in the United States History of the Special Projects Division, Chemical Warfare Service* (1947) (page numbers are not marked).

45    . . . for the technical program": Leo P. Brophy et al., op. cit., p. 110.

45    . . . numbered almost 3,900": Armed Forces Chemical Association, op. cit., p. 63.

46    . . . could not be confirmed: Cochrane, op. cit.

46    . . . to the test cloud": Ibid.

46    . . . and Serratia marcescens, . . . : Ibid., chapter titled "Defense Against Biological Agents."

46    . . . thought to be inert and harmless to the men: Sheldon Harris, "Japanese Biological Warfare Research on Humans: A Case Study of Microbiology and Ethics," in *The Microbiologist and Biological Defense Research: Ethics, Politics, and International Security* 14 (Raymond A. Zilinskas, ed., 1992), p. 54.

47    . . . lies and half-truths": Institute of Medicine, op. cit., p. vii.

48    . . . enter the gas chamber": Ibid., pp. 346–347.

48    . . . with American GIs: Ibid. p. 39.

49    . . . Atabrine was effective, in 1944: "Troops and Refugees Given Malaria," *Sydney Morning Herald,* April 19, 1999.

49    . . . on account of certain physical disabilities": "The Soldiers of Misfortune," *Sydney Morning Herald,* April 19, 1999.

49    . . . one leg or one eye missing . . . were used.": Ibid.

49    . . . before therapy was commenced": "Sweaty Shivers," *Sydney Morning Herald,* April 19, 1999.

50    . . . never told us anything.": Ibid.

50    . . . and that is why I went.": "Painful Service Was Rewarded with Official Indifference," *Sydney Morning Herald,* April 19, 1999.

50    . . . I recovered, but it took months.": Ibid.

## CHAPTER THREE

53    . . . They were incumbent upon me": Final Statement of
Defendant Karl Brandt, July 19, 1947, in Hugh Gregory Leonard, *By
Trust Betrayed: Patients, Physicians, and the License to Kill in the Third
Reich* (New York: Henry Holt, 1990), p. 303.

57    . . . this is no mere murder trial": "Statement by Telford Taylor,"
reprinted in Alexander Mitscherlich, ed., *Doctors of Infamy: The Story
of the Nazi Medical Crimes* (New York: Henry Schuman, 1949), p. xix.

57    . . . the Nuremberg investigation team: Robert E. Conot, *Justice at
Nuremberg* (New York: Harper & Row, 1983), p. 291.

58    . . . a maximum of 24 chairs: Anecdote related by Jack Robbins,
member of the medical case prosecution team, Tuesday, 9
December 1997, Holocaust Memorial Museum, Washington, DC.

58    . . . than any other profession: Robert Proctor, *Racial Hygiene*
(Cambridge, MA Harvard University Press, 1988), 59

59    . . . these cooling methods": Complete Transcripts of the
Nuremberg Medical Trial, National Archives Microfilm, Exhibit
No. 92, Roll 16, p. 76. In some instances the succeeding notes on
the doctors' trial refer to the complete transcripts, including prosecution and defense exhibits, which are stored on microfilm reels on
deposit at the National Archives and Records Administration
(NARA) in Washington, DC. They are also available in the archives
of the United States Holocaust Memorial Museum in Washington.
The NARA record group number is 30.001M.

60    . . . to serve their fatherland:" Conot, op. cit., p. 286.

61    . . . personal connections to Himmler: Tom Bower, *The Paperclip
Conspiracy* (Boston: Little, Brown & Co., 1987), p. 223.

61    . . . having kidnapped babies: Michael H. Kater, *Doctors Under
Hitler* (Chapel Hill, NC: University of North Carolina Press, 1989),
pp. 125–126.

62    . . . commuted to 15 years in prison: Mitscherlich, op. cit., pp.
33–41.

62    . . . this new possibility arose: *Trials of War Criminals Before
the Nuremberg Military Tribunals Under Control Council Law* 10,
Vol. I, Washington, D.C.: Superintendent of Documents, U.S.

Government Printing Office, 1950). Military Tribunal, Case 1, *United States of America v. Karl Brandt et al.,* October 1946–April 1949, Book 4, p. 88. All page references are to English original text or translations. This volume and another published by the U.S. government in 1950 are abridged versions of the trial proceedings. They do not include much of the important testimony discussed in this chapter.

63      ...emphasis in the original]: Complete Transcripts of the Nuremberg Medical Trial, Reel 37, 14 July 1947, p. 15.

64      ...on precisely this formula: Ibid., p. 9.

65      ...organizations monitoring health law in the 1930s: Michael A. Grodin, "Historical Origins of the Nuremberg Code," in George J. Annas and Michael A. Grodin, eds., *The Nazi Doctors and the Nuremberg Code* (New York: Oxford University Press, 1992), pp. 129–131.

66      ...today's media medical expert: Jon M. Harkness, "Andrew Conway Ivy," in *American National Biography* (New York: Oxford University Press, 1999).

66      ...doctor's strange obsession: Warren R. Young, "Whatever Happened to Dr. Ivy?," *Life* (October 9, 1964), pp. 110–124.

67      ...Illinois State Penitentiary: "Prison Malaria," *Life Magazine* 18(23), June 4, 1945, pp. 43–46.

67      ...perfectly healthy children": From Headquarters Military Government North Rhine Region to Oberprasident, North Rhine Province, 22 June 1946. Defense documents for Karl Brandt, document no. 93.

67      ...decided to employ him": R. A. McCance, "Medical Problems in Mineral Deficiency," *The Lancet,* November 4, 1936, p. 823.

68      ...outgrowths of biological thinking": Complete Transcripts of the Nuremberg Medical Trial, Reel 3, 27 January 1947, pp. 1995–1996.

69      ...historian of medicine, Jon Harkness: Jon M. Harkness, "Research Behind Bars: A History of Nontherapeutic Research on American Prisoners" (Ann Arbor, MI: Dissertation Services, 1996).

70      . . . Ivy: "I doubt that": Complete Transcripts of the Nuremberg Medical Trial, Reel 9, 14 June 1947, p. 9218.

72      . . . important results themselves: *United States v. Karl Brandt et al.,* Book 3, p. 130.72

72      . . . under [the] circumstances": Ibid., Book 2, p. 49.

72      . . . especially in wartime": Ibid., Book 2, p. 47.

72      . . . be taken by the state": Ibid., p. 2567; also Complete Transcripts of the Nuremberg Medical Trial, National Archives Microfilm, Reel 11, 17 June 1947, p. 10735.

72      . . . leaders of the regime: Final defense statement for Brandt, Reel 37, 14 July 1947, p. 4.

74      . . . reflect on his actions: Complete Transcripts of the Nuremberg Medical Trial, final prosecution statement, Reel 36, 14 July 1947, p. 71.

74      . . . was morally unjustified": *United States v. Karl Brandt,* transcript, Reel 7, 14 June 1947, p. 9229.

74      . . . existence of the people": Final defense statement for Brandt, Reel 37, 14 July 1947, p. 9.

75      . . . subjects in medical experiments": *United States v. Karl Brandt et al.,* "The Medical Case, Trials of War Criminals before the Nuremberg Military Tribunal under Control Council Law No. 10," vol. 2, p. 83.

76      . . . matter of common practice": Complete Transcripts of the Nuremberg Medical Trial, Reel 9, 13 June 1947, pp. 9168–9170.

77      . . . in the medical experiments": Complete Transcripts of the Nuremberg Medical Trial, Reel 9, 13 June 1947, pp. 9125–9129.

77      . . . to our [American] experience": Complete Transcripts of the Nuremberg Medical Trial, Reel 10, 16 June 1947, p. 9242.

78      . . . in my own mind": Complete Transcripts of the Nuremberg Medical Trial, Reel 9, 14 June 1947, pp. 9212–9213.

78      . . . this committee and this trial": Complete Transcripts of the Nuremberg Medical Trial, Reel 9, 14 June 1947, p. 9220.

78      . . . a method for doing good": Complete Transcripts of the
        Nuremberg Medical Trial, Reel 9, 14 June 1947, pp. 9220–9221.

79      . . . as those of the committee: Harkness, op. cit., pp. 149–150.

79      . . . its nature and hazards": Complete Transcripts of the
        Nuremberg Medical Trial, Reel 37, 14 July 1947, pp. 10718–10796.

80      . . . ethical and legal concept": *United States v. Karl Brandt et al.*, Vol.
        II, pp. 181–185.

80      . . . for ordinary physicians": Jay Katz, quoted in *Advisory Committee
        on Human Radiation Experiments, Final Report*, reprinted in *The Human
        Radiation Experiments* (New York: Oxford University Press, 1996), p.
        86.

81      . . . after the operations: Complete Transcripts of the Nuremberg
        Medical Trial, Reel 3, 10 January 1947, pp. 1448–1451.

81      . . . still injustice in the world": Leonard, op. cit., p. 303.

82      . . . kill debilitated persons: Gitta Sereny, *Albert Speer: His Battle
        with Truth* (New York: Alfred A. Knopf, 1995), p. 198.

83      . . . conversations with Gebhardt: Robert E. Conot, *Justice at
        Nuremberg* (New York: Carroll and Graff Publishers, 1984), p. 292.

83      . . . power and authority": Complete Transcripts of the Nuremberg
        Medical Trial, Reel 36, 16 June 1947, p. 10.

83      . . . political or moral nature": Complete Transcripts of the
        Nuremberg Medical Trial, Reel 37, 14 July 1947, p. 14.

84      . . . interests of humanity": Philippe Aziz, *Doctors of Death*, Vol. 1,
        trans. Edouard Bijub and Philip Haentzler (Geneva, Switzerland:
        Fermi Publishers, 1976), p. 250.

84      . . . to carry the sign of Cain": Ibid., p. 252.

## CHAPTER FOUR

88      . . . on the low-temperature results: Linda Hunt, *Secret Agenda: The
        United States Government, Nazi Scientists, and Project Paperclip, 1945 to
        1990* (New York: St. Martin's Press, 1991), pp. 232–233.

89    ... some very embarrassing publicity: Interview with Eli Rosenbaum, Office of Special Investigations, U.S. Department of Justice, 24 June 1997.

91    ... if he had wanted to: Hunt, op, cit., p. 85.

92    ... would serve with distinction: Bower, op. cit., pp. 226–232.94

84    ... was in the Russian occupational zone: Ibid., p. 240.

94    ... as a warning to other prisoners: Ibid., p. 112.

95    ... in 1959 and 1960: Hunt, op. cit., pp. 1–2.

95    ... beating a dead Nazi horse": Ibid., 110.

96    ... are wanted for denazification: Walter J. Rozamus, Deputy Director, JIOA, to Executive, Intelligence Division, GSUSA, 18 November 1947.

96    ... be submitted in advance: Bousqet Wev, Director, JIOA, to Office of the Attorney General, 18 December 1947.

96    ... he was a member of the SS: Hunt, op. cit, p. 226.

97    ... lack of sympathy to Nazism: Hubertus Strughold File, JIOA-FSCS, Record Group #330, National Archives and Records Administration, Washington, DC.

97    ... and western civilization ...: Ibid.

97    ... my life was in danger," he claimed: "Nazi Charges Resurface on Ex-Brooks Scientist," *San Antonio Express News,* October 26, 1993.

98    ... would take them to die: Hunt, op. cit., p. 152.

99    ... released for possible prosecution: Ibid., p. 152.

99    ... that led to horrible deaths: Bower, op. cit., pp. 255–256.

99    ... his war record and postwar activities: *The New York Times,* Sunday, October 7, 1951.

99    ... joined Alexander in the effort: Hunt, op. cit., p. 153.

99    ... the School of Aviation Medicine: *The New York Times,* Sunday, February 10, 1952.

100    ... but (also) of the entire country: Ibid.

100    ... Robert Lovett to investigate: *The New York Times,* February 13, 1952.

100    . . . identify him as her tormentor: *Boston Post,* February 11, 1952.

100    . . . were communist-inspired: *Boston Herald,* February 10, 1952.

100    . . . the same as I served mine: Quoted in Hunt, op. cit, p. 154.

100    . . . friendly to Nazi war criminals: Bower, op. cit., pp. 256–257.

100    . . . medical men of Jewish ancestry Quoted in Hunt, op. cit., p. 154.

110    . . . not carried out in short order: *National Jewish Post,* May 30, 1952.

100    . . . extremely urgent: Bower, op. cit., p. 257.

100    . . . May 22, 1952, . . . : Hunt, op. cit., p. 155.

100    . . . a generous travel allowance: Bower, op. cit., p. 257.

101    . . . is eligible under the project: Ibid., pp. 257–258.

102    . . . including chemical weapons detectors: Hunt, op. cit., p. 189.

103    . . . one especially compelling personality: Sheldon Harris, *Factories of Death* (London: Routledge, 1994).

103    . . . of many young geishas: Ibid., pp. 15–16.

103    . . . laboratory studies of bacteriology: Ibid., p. 16.

104    . . . useful bacteriological information: Ibid., p. 19.

104    . . . to begin his work: Ibid., pp. 20–21.

104    . . . and deadly electrical shocks: Ibid., p. 27.

105    . . . of the infamous Unit 731: Ibid., pp. 33–35.

105    . . . who had been poisoned: Ibid., pp. 48–51.

105    . . . over several days: Ibid., p. 54.

106    . . . and countless other diseases": Ibid., p. 59.

106    . . . and even frostbite studies: Ibid., pp. 70–71.

106    . . . even Shanghai and Singapore: Ibid., p. 66.

106    . . . were felt for many years: Ibid., pp. 77–80.

107    . . . over 120 tons of toxic agents: Ibid., p 67.

107  . . . will turn out to have been: "Chinese WWII Warfare Victims Found," Associated Press, May 20, 1997

107  . . . two more of the men died of malaria: Yuki Tanaka, *Hidden Horrors: Japanese War Crimes of World War II* (Boulder, CO: Westview Press, 1996), pp. 150–153.

108  . . . carrying various pathogens: Ibid., p. 158.

108  . . . nearly 1,700 survived: Harris, op. cit., p. 130.

108  . . . memorandum on the subject: Ibid., p. 170.

109  . . . a force of nearly four thousand: Ibid., p. 155.

109  . . . to the Manhattan Project itself: Ibid., p. 158.

109  . . . medicine and agriculture: Ibid., pp. 157–159.

109  . . . to indict the principal figures: Ibid., pp. 176–189.

110  . . . for later negotiations: Ibid., p. 201.

110  . . . gave the Detrick representatives: Ibid., p. 211.

110  . . . had escaped prosecution: Ibid., p. 221.

111  . . . with such awful impunity: Ibid., p. 222.

111  . . . thereby reduce the likelihood of its use": Quoted in Norman M. Covert, *Cutting Edge: A History of Fort Detrick, Maryland 1943–1993* (Fort Detrick, MD: Public Affairs Office, 1994), p. 19.

113  . . . happened to this woman too": *Materials on the Trial of Former Servicemen of the Japanese Army Charged with Manufacturing and Employing Bacteriological Weapons* (Moscow: Foreign Languages Publishing House, 1950), pp. 257–258.

114  . . . during the Korean War: Stephen Endicott and Edward Hagerman, *The United States and Biological Warfare* (Bloomington: Indiana University Press), 1998.

115  . . . prevention of epidemic disease: Ibid., p. 11.

115  . . . and the number of deaths: Ibid., p. 105.

116  . . . the U.S. biological warfare program: Ibid., pp. 148–150.

116  . . . in the years 1951 to 1953: Ibid., p. 48.

117    . . . has come to pass: Department of Justice Office of Special Investigations, Press Release: "Suspected Japanese War Criminals Placed on 'Watch List' of Excludable Aliens," December 3, 1996.

## CHAPTER FIVE

119    . . . this use of their person: Advisory Committee on Human Radiation Experiments, op. cit., p. 160.

120    . . . on April 10, 1945: The following account of the plutonium injections is drawn from several sources: Advisory Committee on Human Radiation Experiments, op. cit., Chapter 5; William Moss and Roger Eckhardt, "The Human Plutonium Injection Experiments," *Los Alamos Science* 23:176–233, 1995; Eileen Welsome, "The Plutonium Experiment," Special Supplement to *The Albuquerque Tribune*, November 1993.

120    . . . who had been secretly injected: Human Radiation Interagency Working Group, "Building Public Trust: Actions to Respond to the Report of the Advisory Committee on Human Radiation Experiments." (Washington, DC: U.S. Government Printing Office, 1997).

121    . . . rolled off the tongue: Welsome, op. cit., p. 6.

123    . . . 5 microgram, tolerance limit: Moss and Eckhardt, op. cit., pp. 184–185.

125    . . . most interesting scientific weddings in history": William Moss and Roger Eckhardt, "The Human Plutonium Injection Experiments," *Los Alamos Science* 23 (1995), p. 206.

128    . . . the physicians assumed full responsibility: Advisory Committee on Human Radiation Experiments, op. cit., p. 151.

129    . . . mainly to treat disease: Advisory Committee on Human Radiation Experiments, op. cit, p. 157.

129    . . . received this unknown mixture": Ibid., p. 157.

130    . . . in the concentration camps: Tom Bower, op. cit., p. 225.

131    . . . what the thing was for: Rhodes, op. cit, p. 491.

133    ... before the human exposures: Gilbert Whittemore and Miriam Bowling, "Unwitting Draftees in Two Wars: Uranium Injection of Terminal Comatose Patients in America's Wars Against Communism and Cancer in the 1950s," Wellcome Institute for the History of Medicine, London, England, September 3–4, 1998.

133    ... too grateful for words: Quoted in Whittemore and Bowling, op. cit.

133    ... of the investigators and the AEC: Advisory Committee on Human Radiation Experiments, op. cit., p. 163.

134    ... into the plutonium injection series: Welsome, op. cit., Part 1, pp. 5–passim.

135 ... of radioactive substances in California: Ibid., p. 10.

135    ... first chief, Carroll Wilson: Advisory Committee on Human Radiation Experiments, op. cit., p. 47.

135    ... packing a sidearm: Jonathan Weisgall, *Operation Crossroads* (Annapolis, MD.: Naval Institute Press, 1993).

136    ... his willingness to receive treatment: John L. Burling, Deputy General Counsel's Office, AEC to Edwin Huddleson, Deputy General Counsel, AEC, 7 March 1947, ACHRE No. DOE-051094-A-468, 2–3. Whenever possible I have given ACHRE numbers to these documents. These are the identifiers they were given when accessioned by the Advisory Committee on Human Radiation Experiments. However, some of the documents referred to in this chapter were accessioned after I had worked with them. In those cases I give as complete references as possible. All ACHRE documents are in the Record Group # 220, National Archives and Records Administration, Washington, DC.

136    ... one belonged to Stafford Warren: John L. Burling, Deputy General Counsel's Office, AEC to Edwin Huddleson, Deputy General Counsel, AEC, 7 March 1947, ACHRE No. DOE-051094-A-468, 2–3.

136    ... have far-reaching results: Advisory Committee on Human Radiation Experiments, op. cit, p. 52.

137    ... to the acceptance of the treatment": Ibid., p. 47.

137    . . . willingness to receive the treatment": Ibid., p. 47.

137    . . . would help Allen: Ibid., pp. 47–48.

138    . . . to off Project experimental procedures: Advisory Committee on Human Radiation Experiments, op. cit., p. 153.

138    . . . influenced by anyone": Ibid., op. cit., Supp. Vol. 1, p. 72.

138    . . . three doctors signed as witnesses: Welsome, op. cit, Part 1, p. 9.

140    . . . were a road to nowhere: "Tracking of Radiation Exposure in Bomb Work is Questioned," *The New York Times,* November 9, 1997.

141    . . . the course of such treatment": Carroll Wilson to Robert Stone, 5 November 1947, ACHRE No. DOE-052295-A-1.

141    . . . to investigation and publicity: Letter from Carroll Wilson to Robert Stone, 5 November 1947, p.1.

142    . . . guinea pig experimentation": Memorandum addressed to the Advisory Committee on Biology and Medicine, 8 October 1947. ACHRE No. DOE-051094-A-50.

143    . . . had never been made: Advisory Committee on Human Radiation Experiments, op. cit., p. 52.

144    . . . body burden of plutonium: Gilbert Whittemore, "Postwar Establishment of Plutonium Exposure Limits," History of Science Annual Meeting, Kansas City, Missouri, October 1998.

144    . . . for what margin of safety?: Gilbert Whittemore, "A Crystal Ball in the Shadows of Nuremberg and Hiroshima: The Ethical Debate Over Human Experimentation to Develop a Nuclear-Powered Bomber, 1946–1951," in E. Mendelsohn, R. Smith, P. Weingart, eds., *Science, Technology and the Military,* Vol. 12, 1988, pp. 431–462.

145    . . . result of international hostilities: The following account is based on a paper by Robert S. Stone, M.D., "Irradiation of Human Subjects as a Medical Experiment," January 31, 1950, included in the records of the Advisory Committee on Human Radiation Experiments, Record Group #220, National Archives and Records Administration, Washington, DC.

146    ... been declassified in 1994: Excerpts here and below are from the
       transcript of the meeting of the Committee on Medical Sciences of
       the Department of Defense Research and Development Board,
       January 31–February 1, 1950.

148    ... for doing exactly the same thing: Advisory Committee on
       Human Radiation Experiments, op. cit., p. 55.

148    ... to make the information we get valid: Excerpts here and below
       are from the transcript of the Committee on Medical Sciences of
       the Department of Defense Research and Development Board,
       May 23, 1950.

150    ... This is a long-term thing": May 23, 1950. Excerpts from the
       transcript of the Meeting of the Committee on Medical Sciences of
       the Department of Defense Research and Development Board.

150    ... at Hiroshima and Nagasaki": September 8–9, 1950. Minutes
       from the Advisory Committee for Biology and Medicine of the
       Atomic Energy Commission.

150    ... a little of the Buchenwald touch: Advisory Committee on
       Human Radiation Experiments, op. cit., p. 55.

151    ... at the age of 49: Welcome, op. cit., Part II, p. 27.

151    ... way of solving the problem": Atomic Energy Commission,
       Advisory Committee on Biology and Medicine, transcript of meet-
       ing, 10 November 1950, ACHRE No. DOE-012795-C-1, p. 15.
       Warren is in many respects a tragic figure of this period who strug-
       gled deeply with conflicting demands. See Robert N. Proctor,
       *Cancer Wars* (New York: Basic Books, 1995), p. 44.

151    ... both civilian and military problems": June 30, 1951. Annual
       report of the Armed Forces Medical Policy Council to the secretary
       of defense.

152    ... at Hiroshima and Nagasaki: Ibid.

153    ... Fallout Raises Health Alarm": *Washington Post,* October 2, 1997.

153    ... Thyroid Cancer from Atomic Tests": *The New York Times,*
       August 2, 1997.

153    ... Not Public about Bomb Fallout": *The New York Times,*
       September 30, 1997.

153    . . . the Hanford, Washington, nuclear facility: Advisory Committee on Human Radiation Experiments, op. cit., p. 320.

155    . . . Native Americans in our community": Advisory Committee on Human Radiation Experiments, op. cit., p. 331.

155    . . . for my children and my grandchildren": Ibid., p. 334

## CHAPTER SIX

157    . . . I am not sure that this is possible today": John R. Paul, Director, AEB, DOD, to Dr. Joseph Stokes, Jr., Children's Hospital, Philadelphia, Pa., 18 February 1948.

158    . . . hair-trigger thinking": *Time,* September 27, 1943, p. 84.

158    . . . to the highest levels of Washington": Carey Reich, *The Life of Nelson Rockefeller* (New York: Doubleday, 1996), p. 140.

159    . . . than any man in the country": "Anna Rosenberg Hoffman Dead; Consultant and 50's Defense Aide," *The New York Times,* May 10, 1983, p. D25.

160    . . . he warned the Navy commanders: Jonathan Weisgall, op. cit.

161    . . . increase their activities in these areas: Secretary of defense directive, December 21, 1951.

161    . . . experiments involving humans": February 11, 1952. Minutes of a meeting of Department of Defense service representatives.

161    . . . little more than a token effort": April 25, 1952. Memorandum from the assistant secretary for special security programs to the secretary of defense.

163    . . . in five seconds: Lawrence Altman, *Who Goes First? The Story of Self-Experimentation in Medicine* (Berkeley: University of California Press, 1998), pp. 29–30.

163    . . . can be gained thereby": Armed Forces Medical Planning Council, February 1951.

163    . . . participation in future tests": Meiling to LeBaron, February 23, 1951.

164    ... to an acceptable level of sufficiency": Windstorm planning, March 5, 1951.

164    ... but entirely groundless": Meiling to the deputy secretary of defense and others, June 1951

165    ... human subjects are used": June 30, 1951. Annual report of the Armed Forces Medical Policy Council to the secretary of defense.

165    ... and report to the Secretary": February 11, 1952. Minutes of a meeting of Department of Defense service representatives.

166    ... this type of research be approved": September 8, 1952. Minutes of a meeting of the Armed Forces Medical Policy Council.

166    ... guiding principles to be followed": December 24, 1952. Memorandum from M. Casburg, chairman of the Armed Forces Medical Policy Council, to the secretary of defense.

167    ... they only use that which suits them": Letter written by the administrator of the Armed Forces Epidemiological Board on 2 March 1953.

167    ... the conditions be so amended": October 22, 1952. Memorandum from S. Jackson, Assistant General Counsel in the Office of the Secretary of Defense and counsel for the Armed Forces Medical Policy Council, to M. Casberg, Chairman of the Council.

168    ... to the exceptional research worker: November 12, 1952. Memorandum from F. L. Mussells, executive director, Committee on Medical Sciences, to F. Miller, vice chairman of the Research and Development Board.

169    ... on the legal aspects of the subject": Ibid.

169    ... he would not oppose it: November 17, 1952. Memorandum from F. Miller, vice chairman of the Research and Development Board, to the chairman of the Armed Forces Medical Policy Council.

169    ... I'm all in favor of it": November 10, 1952. Excerpts from the transcript of the Meeting of the Committee on Chemical Warfare of the Research and Development Board, p. 128.

170   ... has worked quite well": December 9, 1952. Memorandum from the executive director of the Committee on Chemical Warfare of the Research and Development Board to the assistant secretary for Special Security Programs, dated December 9, 1952.

171   ... recommendation from the 'alumni' ": Note from George V. Underwood, Director of the Executive Office of the Secretary of Defense to Deputy Secretary Foster, dated January 4, 1953.

172   ... as you opened for business": February 5, 1953. Office of the Secretary of Defense, re: "Use of Human Volunteers in Experimental Research."

172   ... "damn tommyrot": E. Bruce Geelhoed, *Charles E. Wilson and Controversy at the Pentagon: 1953 to 1957* (Detroit, MI: Wayne State University Press, 1979), p. 15.

173   ... a result of the Nuremberg trials": January 13, 1953. Memorandum from M. Casberg, chairman of the Armed Forces Medical Policy Council, to the secretary of defense.

173   ... standing for "top secret": February 26, 1953. Memorandum from G. V. Underwood, director of the Executive Memorandum from the secretary of defense Wilson to the secretaries of the Army, Navy, and Air Force.

177   ... have a top secret clearance": February 27, 1953. Excerpts from the transcripts of the Meeting of the Committee on Medical Sciences of the Research and Development Board.

177   ... rationalization of apparent discrepancies": March 12, 1953. Memorandum from the chairman of the Committee on Medical Sciences of the Research and Development Board to the chairman of the board.

178   ... set forth in this directive: June 30, 1953. Memorandum through the secretary of the General Staff of the Army for the chief chemical officer and the surgeon general.

179   ... Department of the Army policies: Inspector General Report, p. 38.

180   ... signed off on the proposal: September 9, 1953. Memorandum from the surgeon general of the Army to the assistant chief of staff of the Department of the Army.

182   ... in which this document is now held: March 3, 1954. Memorandum from the acting chief of staff of the Air Force to the assistant secretary of defense, dated "3–5–54" and attached memorandum for the record of the same date "re: discovery of T/S [top secret] memorandum from the Secretary of Defense."

182   ... and laboratory: August 20, 1956. Supplementary agreement between the Kelly Air Force Base and Tulane University.

182   ... to the original 1953 policy: September 12, 1958. Memorandum from the Deputy Commander for Research and Development of the Air Force Research and Development Command.

182   ... the chain of command was informed: March 10, 1953. Memorandum from the Assistant for Atomic Energy of the Air Force to the inspector general of the Air Force.

183   ... radiation treatment for disease: Project specifications for "A Study of Intellectual, Perceptual and Psychomotor Abilities of Patients following Radio-Therapy," for the Air Force School of Aviation Medicine by the M. D. Anderson Cancer Center, p. 1.

184   ... required in basic pilotry": August 29, 1955. Minutes from the Air Force Research Council Meeting, p. 6.

184   ... have participated in these studies: January 14, 1954. Minutes from the Air Force Research Council Meeting, p. 7.

185   ... but highly classified directive": Inspector General Report, p. 38.

185   ... against aerosolized microbes: Report and Recommendations of the Chemical Corps Advisory Council Meeting, 30 June–1 July 1955, Recommendation No. 8–55. Washington National Records Center, Records of the Army Chemical Corps. Record Group 175, Accession # 59A-1403, Box # 6.

185   ... dangerous for human experimentation": Memorandum from Carl H. Brewer to J. F. Escude, "Visit of Dr. A. R T. Denues," 2 May 1956. Washington National Records Center, Records of the Army Chemical Corps. Record Group 175, Accession # 59A-1403, Box #8.

187   ... with U.S. military endeavors": September 3, 1952, letter from secretary of Joint Chiefs of Staff to Joint Chiefs of Staff.

## CHAPTER SEVEN

190   ...but had given up drinking": "Memorandum for the Record; Subject: MKULTRA Subprojects 3, 14, 16, 42, 132, 149 and MKSEARCH 4 [deleted] - Bureau of Narcotics."

190   ...a "human robot" with drugs: Evan Thomas, *The Very Best Men—Four Who Dared: The Early Years of the CIA* (New York: Simon & Schuster, 1995), p. 211.

191   ..."loosening the subject's tongue": John Marks, *The Search for the "Manchurian Candidate": The CIA and Mind Control* (New York: New York Times Books), pp. 3–7.

192   ...$750,000 in compensation: Ibid., pp. 77–85.

192   ...forces of darkness: "Sidney Gottlieb, 80, Dies; Took LSD to C.I.A.," *New York Times,* March 10, 1999, p. C22.

193   ...some very weird things happened": John Marks, op. cit., pp. 139–140.

194   ...Justice Department's regulations: Joseph L. Rauh, Jr., and James C. Turner, "Anatomy of a Public Interest Case Against the CIA," 11 *Hamline Journal of Public Law and Policy* 307, Fall 1980.

194   ...and certainly LSD was one": "Military Funded McGill LSD Trial," *Southam News/Ottawa Citizen,* December 7, 1998.

194   ...that of Harold Blauer: All of the facts in the Blauer case are taken from the trial record: *Barrett v. United States,* 798 F.2d 565 (2nd Cir. 1986); *Barrett v. United States,* 689 F.2d 324 (2nd Cir. 1982), *cert. denied,* 462 U.S. 1131, 77 L. Ed. 2d 1366, 103 S. Ct. 3111 (1983); *Barrett v. United States,* 660 F. Supp. 1291, 1295 n. 2 (S.D.N.Y. 1987).

200   ...does not occur": Advisory Committee on Human Radiation Experiments, op. cit., p. 286.

201   ...to obtain intelligible results: Ibid., p. 287.

202   ...wonderful sight to behold": Quoted in Michael Uhl and Tod Ensign, *GI Guinea Pigs* (Wideview Books, 1980), pp. 3–4.

203   ...The world is ending!: Ibid., p. 5.

203   ...removed us from the site": Ibid., pp. 70–71.

204 ... how much exposure is potentially harmful: Advisory Committee on Human Radiation Experiments, op. cit., p. 288.

204 ... utilizing every opportunity": Ibid., pp. 289–290.

205 ... They were adequately informed": Ibid., p. 290.

205 ... in which the policy was being held: Ibid., p. 292.

205 ... I signed one": Ibid., p. 292.

206 ... and how to control for that": Interview with Wally Cummins, Washington, DC, October 30, 1997.

207 ... as 7,000 yards away: Advisory Committee on Human Radiation Experiments, op. cit., p. 298.

207 ... in permissible exposure levels: Harvey Wasserman and Norman Solomon, *Killing Our Own: The Disaster of America's Experience with Atomic Radiation* (New York: Dell Publishing Co., 1982), p. 69.

208 ... high-yield test in 1957: Advisory Committee on Human Radiation Experiments, op, cit., pp. 301–302.

208 ... the claims system for veterans' benefits: U.S. Government Human Radiation Interagency Working Group, "Building Public Trust: Actions to Respond to the Report of the Advisory Committee on Human Radiation Experiments" (Washington, DC: U.S. Government Printing Office, 1996), pp. 36–39.

209 ... over several hundred pages: Air Force Systems Command, January 1963, "History of Air Force Atomic Cloud Sampling," [AFSC Historical Publication Series 61-142-1], p. 1.

210 ... were studied in a similar situation": Ibid., p. 41.

210 ... to do the sampling: Ibid., p. 66.

210 ... is do it yourself": Advisory Committee on Human Radiation Experiments, op. cit., p. 296.

210 ... of the Wilson policy: Ibid.

210 ... the inhalation of fission products: E. A. Pinson et al., "Operation Redwing—Project 2.66a, Early Cloud Penetrations," p. 51.

211   . . . of some of their patients: Advisory Committee on Human Radiation Experiments, op. cit., pp. 232–247.

214   . . . I can count on your cooperation: Task Force on Human Subject Research, "A Report on the Use of Radioactive Materials in Human Subject Research That Involved Residents of State-Operated Facilities Within the Commonwealth of Massachusetts from 1943 through 1973," April 1974, B-19.

215   . . . that your son may participate: Ibid., B-23.

215   . . . and pregnant women were discouraged: Advisory Committee on Human Radiation Experiments, op. cit, p. 176.

216   . . . at Fernald and Wrentham violated that principle: Ibid., pp. 52–53.

216   . . . prompted the two letters: Task Force on Human Subject Research, op. cit., pp. 14–16.

216   . . . to have any ill effects: Ibid., p. 16.

217   . . . or challenge such procedures: Ibid., p. 33.

218   . . . before I could intervene: Ibid., p. 35.

218   . . . practically anything for attention: Advisory Committee on Human Radiation Experiments, op. cit., p. 212.

219   . . . and to unfair treatment: Ibid., p. 212.

219   . . . the level of funding it provided?: "Settlement in Lawsuit Over Radioactive Oatmeal," *The New York Times,* January 1, 1998.

222   . . . work its proper place: Robert N. Proctor, *Cancer Wars* (New York: Basic Books, 1995).

222   . . . to them could be controlled: Ibid., p. 39.

223   . . . were no longer affordable: Ibid., p. 40.

223   . . . disease markedly declined: Ibid., p. 41.

224   . . . to become a "scientific liar": Ibid., p. 44.

224   . . . in the "new Germany" in 1933: Robert Proctor, *The Nazi War on Cancer* (Princeton, NJ: Princeton University Press, 1999), pp. 13–15.

224    . . . shortly before his death: Ibid., p. 45.

226    . . . would be covered: Advisory Committee on Human Radiation Experiments, op. cit., p. 364.

226    . . . had accepted this recommendation: U.S. Government Human Radiation Interagency Working Group, op. cit.

226    . . . with worker safety standards: Robert Proctor, *The Nazi War on Cancer* (Princeton, NJ: Princeton University Press, 1999). Historian Robert Proctor, the authority on Hueper's career, has recently revealed another dimension of the man. In 1933, the German native, then working at the University of Pennsylvania, applied to the Nazi minister of culture for a scientific appointment in the new Germany, signing his letter with the now familiar "Heil Hitler!" Whether Hueper was at the time a genuine Nazi sympathizer or an ambitious scientist willing to tow the political line isn't clear. As Proctor points out, Nazi Germany was an innovative cancer-fighting political regime with major government support for research, so Hueper would have good reason to want to work there.

227    . . . *Acres of Skin:* Allen M. Hornblum, *Acres of Skin: Human Experiments at Holmesburg Prison* (New York: Routledge, 1998).

231    . . . the research conducted in them: Advisory Committee on Human Radiation Experiments, op. cit., pp. 269–270.

232    . . . after World War II: 1. *Biological Testing Hearing* at 30 (report submitted for the record by the U.S. Army, titled "US Army Activity in the US Biological Warfare Programs" (1977)).

232    . . . with innocuous organisms": *Biological Testing Hearing* at 30 (report submitted for the record by the U.S. Army, titled "US Army Activity in the US Biological Warfare Programs" (1977)).

232    . . . in the atmosphere": *Biological Testing Hearing* at 33 (report submitted for the record by the U.S. Army, titled "US Army Activity in the US Biological Warfare Programs" (1977)).

232    . . . theatres of operation": Leo P. Brophy, Wyndham D. Miles, and Rexmond C. Cochrane, *U.S. Army in World War II, The Chemical Warfare Service: From Laboratory to Field* (Washington, DC: Office of the Chief of Military History, Department of the Army, 1959), p. 110.

232   ... conducted off Government installations": *Biological Testing Hearing* at 10 (statement of assistant secretary of the Army, Edward Miller).

232   ... (outside the continental United States): *Biological Testing Hearing* at 11 (statement of Senator Kennedy).

233   ... that the attack had occurred": Submitted into the Congressional Record by Rep. Sikes, appearing April 28, 1959, appendix page A3520.

233   ... and zinc cadmium sulfide: *Biological Testing Hearing* at 109 (report submitted for the record by the U.S. Army, titled "US Army Activity in the US Biological Warfare Programs" (1977)).

233   ... in hospitalized sick patients": *Biological Testing Hearing* at 265 (statement of Stephen Weitzman, M.D., Department of Microbiology, School of Basic Health Sciences, Health Center, State University of New York, Stony Brook).

234   ... developed Serratia infections: Leonard Cole, *The Eleventh Plague* (New York: W. H. Freeman, 1997), p. 17.

234   ... and sued for negligence: *Nevin v. United States,* 696 F.2d 1229 (1982).

234   ... from mid-Manhattan streets: Jeffrey K. Smart, "History of Chemical and Biological Warfare: An American Perspective," in F. R. Sidell, E. T. Takafuji, and D. R. Franz, eds., *Medical Aspects of Chemical and Biological Warfare* (Washington, DC: TMM Publications, 1997), p. 60.

234   ... was dismissed: *Nevin v. United States,* 696 F.2d 1229 (1982).

234   ... using pathogenic agents were to occur: *Biological Testing Hearing* at 51 (report submitted for the record by the U.S. Army, titled "US Army Activity in the US Biological Warfare Programs" (1977)).

234   ... instead of populated cities": *Biological Testing Hearing* at 266 (statement of Stephen Weitzman, M.D., Department of Microbiology, School of Basic Health Sciences, Health Center, State University of New York, Stony Brook).

235   ... near several French forts: Jeffrey K. Smart, op. cit., p. 32.

235 . . . tons of zinc cadmium sulfide": *Cold War Era Testing Hearings* at 132–133.

236 . . . to err on the side of caution: *Cold War Era Testing Hearings* at 133.

236 . . . the norm for succeeding years: *Biological Testing Hearing* at 18 (statement of Senator Schweiker).

236 . . . for mass destruction in future wars": *Biological Testing Hearing* at 18 (statement of Senator Schweiker).

236 . . . to enhance military effectiveness": *Biological Testing Hearing* at 18 (statement of Senator Schweiker).

237 . . . and appropriate government coordination": *Biological Testing Hearing* at 48 (report submitted for the record by the U.S. Army, titled "US Army Activity in the US Biological Warfare Programs"(1977)).

237 . . . effects on the physical or biological environment": *Biological Testing Hearing* at 108 (report submitted for the record by the U.S. Army, titled "US Army Activity in the US Biological Warfare Programs" (1977)).

## CHAPTER EIGHT

240 . . . "Experimentation in Man": Henry Beecher, "Experimentation in Man," *Journal of the American Medical Association* 169, January 1959, pp. 461–478.

241 . . . graduated with honors in 1932: Jon Harkness, "Henry Knowles Beecher," *American National Biography* (Oxford University Press), 1998.

242 . . . by many of his erstwhile colleagues: Henry Beecher, "Ethics and Clinical Research," *New England Journal of Medicine* 274, June 1996, pp. 1354–1360.

243 . . . than he did the original: Advisory Committee on Human Radiation Experiments, op. cit., pp. 89–92.

243   . . . the 1953 Wilson memo: March 26, 1962. Army Regulation
      70-25, "Use of Volunteers as Subjects of Research," 25 January 1990.

246   . . . he had been rebuffed: Ruth Faden and Tom L. Beauchamp, *A
      History and Theory of Informed Consent* (New York: Oxford University
      Press, 1986), pp. 161–162.

248   . . . under reasonable rules: Ibid., pp. 206–208.

248   . . . the infamous Tuskegee syphilis study: James H. Jones, *Bad
      Blood* (New York: Free Press, 1981).

250   . . . children with severe disorders: Faden and Beauchamp, op. cit.,
      pp. 163–164.

250   . . . the Armed Forces Epidemiological Board: Armed Forces
      Epidemiological Board, minutes of 24 May 1957 meeting (ACHRE
      No. NARA-032495-B).

251   . . . these substances occurred after 1960: Institute of Medicine,
      National Academy of Sciences, *Veterans at Risk: The Health Effects of
      Mustard Gas and Lewisite,* Constance M. Pechura and David P. Rall,
      eds. (Washington, DC: National Academy Press, 1993), p. 45.

251   . . . irritants, and vesicant agents": *Cold War Era Hearings* at 84 (writ-
      ten statement of Michael Parker, Executive Director, U.S. Army
      Chemical and Biological Defense Command, Aberdeen Proving
      Ground).

251   . . . lysergic acid diethylamide (LSD) . . . : Institute of Medicine,
      National Academy of Sciences, op. cit., p. 46.

251   . . . full knowledge of the risks involved": *Cold War Era Hearings* at
      23 (written testimony of Frank Conahan, GAO, submitted for the
      record).

251   . . . contracts at several universities: *Cold War Era Hearings* at 25
      (written testimony of Frank Conahan, GAO, submitted for the
      record).

252   . . . for LSD experiments: *Stanley v. CIA,* 639 F.2d 1146; 31 Fed. R.
      Serv. 2d (Callaghan) 988; *Stanley v. United States,* 574 F. Supp. 474
      (S.D.F. 1983).

252   . . . the discretion of the interrogators": *Thornwell v. United States of America,* 471 F.Supp. 344.

253   . . . including LSD: Advisory Committee on Human Radiation Experiments, op. cit., p. 107.

253   . . . is absolutely essential": Ibid., p. 108.

254   . . . of routine destruction schedules: Ibid., p. 4.

254   . . . several federal depositories and military installation. U.S. Army inspector general, "Use of Volunteers in Critical Agent Research," 1975, p. 1.

255   . . . detection of CBR activities": Ibid., p. 24.

256   . . . no coercion is permissible: Ibid., p. 35.

256   . . . the drug being administered": Ibid., p. 40.

257   . . . 200 micrograms of LSD": Ibid., p. 16.

257   . . . more the norm than the exception": Ibid., p. 40.

257   . . . approved of the plan: Ibid., pp. 137–138.

258   . . . the secretary of the Army . . . : *Biological Testing Hearing* at 240.

258   . . . and death may come quickly": J. H. Rothschild, *Tomorrow's Weapons* (New York: McGraw-Hill, 1964), p. 241.

258   . . . and ended in 1958": *Biological Testing Hearing* at 240.

258   . . . medical journals described the study: *Biological Testing Hearing* at 217 (report submitted for the record by the U.S. Army, titled "US Army Activity in the US Biological Warfare Programs" (1977)).

258   . . . from July 1956 to 1975: *Biological Testing Hearing* at 241.

259   . . . "undue suffering" in a study: U.S. Army Medical Institute of Infectious Diseases, "Project Whitecoat: A History," Section III, p. 7.

259   . . . responds to all inquiries: "Project Whitecoat: Human Testing Done with Care," *Baltimore Sun,* April 3, 1994.

260   . . . says Nixon: Ibid.

260  . . . advanced step in clinical research: T. R Flaiz to Major General George E. Armstrong, October 19, 1954.

260  . . . these services and accomplishments: S. B. Hays to G. W. Chambers, October 27, 1955.

261  . . . and probably suffering": "Beyond the Call of Duty!" *Review and Herald,* November 3, 1955.

261  . . . or some similar reason: Fact Sheet, Project Whitecoat, Department of the Army, U.S. Army Research Institute of Infectious Diseases, Frederick, MD, 28 November 1969, p. 3.

262  . . . who came in the Army after me": "Research Subjects Meet in Maryland," *Washington Post,* September 27, 1998.

264  . . . was also terminated: *Biological Testing Hearing,* p. 248 (report submitted for the record by the U.S. Army, titled "US Army Activity in the US Biological Warfare Programs" (1977)).

## CHAPTER NINE

267  . . . would have been part of the solution": Ben Garrett, personal communication, May 21, 1997.

269  . . . experimenting on me": "Sailors Refuse Anthrax Shots," *The Washington Post,* March 12, 1999.

271  . . . that it was not optional: Claire Alda Miller, "Gulf War Guinea Pigs: Is Informed Consent Optional During War?" *Journal of Contemporary Health Law and Policy* 13:199–232, 1996.

272  . . . than when administered alone: Miller, op. cit.

272  . . . insect repellents like DEET, and PB: Robert W. Haley et al., "Evaluation of Neurologic Function in Gulf War Veterans: A Blinded Case-Control Study," *Journal of the American Medical Association* 277:223–230, January 15, 1997.

272  . . . was unsure of its effectiveness: "Objection to Gulf War Vaccine Was Overridden," *Cleveland Plain Dealer,* December 21, 1997.

273  . . . doesn't mean it's not feasible": Interview with Colonel Arthur Anderson, February 19, 1998.

273    . . . had predictably destructive outcomes": "Objection to Gulf War Vaccine Was Overridden," p. 16-A.

277    . . . for refusing to be human subjects: Army Regulation 70-25, "Use of Volunteers as Subjects of Research," 25 January 1990, pp. 4–5.

280    . . . as far as the entries go": Excerpt from USARIID interview, April 16, 1998.

281    . . . and you leave: Ibid.

283    . . . do not abandon this directive: United States Government Human Radiation Interagency Working Group, *Building Public Trust: Actions to Respond to the Report of the Advisory Committee on Human Radiation Experiments,* March 1997, p. 6.

283    . . . the president's science advisor: Ibid., p. 19.

283    . . . the radiation experiments report: Gary Ellis, Director, Office for Protection from Research Risks, personal communication, October 23, 1998.

284    . . . recruiting at least five of them: "Iranians, Bioweapons in Mind, Lure Needy Ex-Soviet Scientists," *The New York Times,* December 8, 1998.

285    . . . of such 'donors' is not known": Sergei Pluzhnikov and Aleksei Shevdov (Ken Alibek and Jennifer Gurnsey, trans.), "Investigation: Murder From a Test Tube," *Sovershenno Secretno* 4:12–4, 1998.

286    . . . and they informed people in 1994": Excerpt from an interview with Ben Garrett, October 16, 1998.

286    . . . their production capabilities intact: "Soviet Defector Warns of Biological Weapons," *The New York Times,* February 25, 1998.

288    . . . harvested his tissues, and disappeared: Ben Garrett, personal communication, December 30, 1998.

288    . . . exchanges with Russian biological weapons development scientists: "Germ Weapons: In Soviet Past or in the New Russia's Future?," *The New York Times,* December 28, 1998.

289    . . . potential bioterror weapon: "Clinton to Announce That U.S. Will Keep Sample of Lethal Smallpox Virus, Aides Say," *The New York Times,* April 22, 1999.

289   . . . are outlawed by treaty): "Wonder Weapons," *U.S. News & World Report,* July 7, 1997, p. 38–passim.

289   . . . after the general at its head: Sergei Pluzhnikov and Aleksei Shevdov, op. cit.

291   . . . will be able to defend itself: "DARPA Launches Ambitious Program to Halt Pathogens," *U.S. Medicine,* September 1996, p. 1–passim.

292   . . . the potential for 'biotechnology warfare': Science Applications International Corporation, "Biotechnology Workshop 2020," May 29–30, 1996, U.S. Army War College, Carlisle Barracks, PA, Summary Report, August 1996, p.30.

292   . . . a genetic-based attack might be occurring: Ibid., p. 31.

293   . . . read people's thoughts": "Advances in Neuroscience 'May Threaten Human Rights,' " *Nature* 391, January 22, 1998, p. 316.

294   . . . not to have ordered its dissolution: Ben Garrett, personal communication, 26 October 1998.

296   . . . the Nuremberg Code: George Annas and Michael Grodin, "Legacies of Nuremberg," *Journal of the American Medical Association* 1996; 276:1682–1683.

# INDEX